A Forward Glance

A Forward Glance

New Essays on Edith Wharton

Edited by
Clare Colquitt, Susan Goodman,
and Candace Waid

DELAWARE

Newark: University of Delaware Press
London: Associated University Presses

Associated University Presses
440 Forsgate Drive
Cranbury, NJ 08512

Associated University Presses
16 Barter Street
London WC1A 2AH, England

Associated University Presses
P.O. Box 338, Port Credit
Mississauga, Ontario
Canada L5G 4L8

The paper used in this publication meets the requirements of the American National Standard for Permanence of Paper for Printed Library Materials Z39.48-1984.

Library of Congress Cataloging-in-Publication Data

A forward glance : new essays on Edith Wharton / edited by Clare Colquitt, Susan Goodman, and Candace Waid.
    p.   cm.
    Includes index.
    ISBN 0-87413-667-9 (alk. paper)
    1. Wharton, Edith, 1862–1937—Criticism and interpretation.
2. Women and literature—United States—History—20th century.
I. Colquitt, Clare. II. Goodman, Susan, 1951–   . III. Waid,
Candace.
PS3545.H16Z6475 1999
813′.52—dc21

98-42688
CIP

For R. W. B. Lewis

Contents

8 CONTENTS

Acknowledgments

This book owes its existence to the labors of many people. The editors' first thanks must go to all those who participated in the conference to honor R. W. B. Lewis. Support for the conference came from Yale University, San Diego State University, the University of Delaware, and the Edith Wharton Society. For additional funding, we are especially indebted to Mary Richards of the University of Delaware and to the College of Arts and Letters and the Department of English and Comparative Literature at San Diego State University. Special thanks go to David Marshall and the Whitney Humanities Center at Yale for hosting the series of dialogues which gave rise to these essays.

We are grateful to everyone who worked on the manuscript itself. Matthew T. Ison, Jennifer Butler, and Julie Simpson provided needed assistance with research and computer technology. Without the technical expertise and patience of Jim Edwards and Rachel Litonjua-Witt, computing consultants at San Diego State University, this book would still be in production. Windy Counsell of the University of Delaware and Julia Ehrhardt and Jennifer Greeson, both from Yale University, also deserve credit for helping with research and editorial tasks.

Many of the essays in this volume make use of material from the Beinecke Rare Books and Manuscript Library at Yale University. We would like to express our appreciation to Patricial Willis, the Curator of the American Collection, who contributed significantly to this project.

We recognize the Gloria Loomis Agency for granting us permission to quote from Wharton's books and archives.

A Forward Glance

Introduction

American novelist of international fame. . . . She holds a universally recognized place in the front rank of the world's living novelists. . . . We are proud . . . to enroll her name among the daughters of Yale.
—Professor William Lyon Phelps, New Haven, 1923

When I get glimpses, in books & reviews, of the things people are going to assert about me after I am dead, I feel I must have the courage & perseverance, some day, to forestall them.
—Wharton, Salsomaggiore, May 1924

IN JUNE 1923, EDITH WHARTON, WHO HAD NOT SET FOOT ON NATIVE soil since before the First World War, came home to accept an honorary degree from Yale University. As she explained to her cousin, Tom Rhinelander, it was the first Doctorate of Letters offered to a woman by "one of our great universities."[1] Having "loved Letters all [her] days," she did not think of refusing.[2]

In retrospect, everything about the day—apart from the heat—seemed "beautiful & impressive." The ceremony, which commemorated Yale's two hundred and twenty-second year, transported Wharton to "another world."[3] And, in a sense, the child who had surreptitiously read books in her father's library, and who had been educated by governesses and tutors at home, had entered another world, dramatically symbolized by her presence on the stage of Woolsey Hall.[4] With her sat fourteen other honorary degree recipients, including five "sons of Yale" and one other woman, Mary Emma Woolley. An authority on biblical history, higher education, and labor legislation, Woolley had served as president of Mount Holyoke College since 1901 and had received an honorary Master of Arts from Yale in 1914. Breaking from precedent, Yale would now confer upon her an honorary Doctorate of Laws. In the words of Professor William Lyon Phelps, this second degree made Woolley the "equivalent of a Yale man" ("Commencement, 1923," 1234).

Imagine Wharton, who liked to call herself "a self-made man," trying to suppress a smile.[5] Contemptuous of suffrage, not to

13

mention lesbians,[6] she found herself paired with an accomplished woman who in many respects was ideologically and emotionally her opposite.[7] Was Wharton also laughing at herself? Having viewed university women with disdain—"they'd much better stay at home and mind the baby"[8]—she had joined their ranks.

As Yale's faculty paid tribute to Woolley's efforts for women's rights and the American Peace Society, they recognized Wharton for elevating "the level of American literature." "For nearly twenty-five years," Phelps observed,

> she has produced novels, some of the most notable being "The House of Mirth," "Ethan Frome," [and] "The Age of Innocence." ... She writes short stories and full-length works with equal skill. ... She is a realist in the best sense of the word, revealing the inner nature of men and women without recourse to sensationalism and keeping ever within the boundaries of true art. ("Commencement, 1923," 1234)

Years later, Wharton's niece, Beatrix Farrand, emphasized how "deeply [her aunt] appreciated the honour given her by Yale and as a recognition she wished all her manuscripts, letters, etc., deposited at the University Library."[9] Gaillard Lapsley had first suggested this possibility to Wharton. Within a year of her death, Lapsley, acting in his role as literary executor, arranged for Wharton's papers to be donated to Yale with one stipulation— that her "correspondence and biographical material" remain sealed for "a period of years, roughly corresponding to a generation, ... until 1965." Pleased by this "magnificent" bequest, Yale University President Charles Seymour readily agreed: "I can understand the wisdom of postponing a formal biography until a future generation and the necessity of guarding against the danger that the material might fall into incompetent or unwise hands in the meantime."[10]

Looking to the future, Wharton took a precaution to insure her literary reputation. Only months before the ceremony at Yale, she had informed her publisher about a plan that "ha[d] been vaguely floating through [her] mind for some time." Although Wharton saw little connection between autobiography and fiction, she now told Rutger B. Jewett that she wanted to write her memoirs: "One of my objects in doing this would be to avoid having it inaccurately done by some one else after my death, should it turn out that my books survive me long enough to make it worth while to write my biography."[11]

Less than a year following her journey to New Haven, Wharton purchased a blue-covered exercise book used by Italian school-children. Under the title *Quaderno dello Studente,* she signed her name simply as "*E.W.*" and made her first entry in the note-book she kept sporadically from 1924 until 1934, the year in which her autobiography, *A Backward Glance,* appeared. On the title page, she left a directive: "If ever I have a biographer, it is in these notes that he will find the gist of me."

Many scholars would agree that the first biography to appear after her death, Percy Lubbock's *Portrait of Edith Wharton* (1947), did justice neither to the woman nor to the writer. Lub-bock presented Wharton as cold, calculating, and imperious; as a writer, she was a lesser Henry James. Wharton's worries about what her contemporaries would say of her after her death were, it seems, prescient. As Gaillard Lapsley correctly surmised, jus-tice to Edith Wharton would come only in a "future generation." That moment arrived nearly forty years after Wharton's death, when in 1975 R. W. B. Lewis's Pulitzer Prize–winning biography of Wharton appeared. Followed two years later by Cynthia Griffin Wolff's probing psychological study, *A Feast of Words: The Tri-umph of Edith Wharton* (1977), Lewis's biography heralded a Wharton revival that continues to this day.

In April 1995, friends of Wharton again convened at Yale. This time they not only came to honor Wharton but also R. W. B. Lewis on the twentieth anniversary of his book, *Edith Wharton: A Biography.* The conference, sponsored by Yale University, the University of Delaware, San Diego State University, and the Edith Wharton Society, featured presentations on biography and auto-biography, and on the autobiographical impulse in Wharton's fiction, poetry, and personal writings.

The essays collected in this volume represent a portion of the complex and varied scholarly work delivered at the Yale confer-ence. To borrow one of the titles she considered for her autobiog-raphy, these essays offer at once a "further glance" at Wharton and her work, and a "forward glance" as well. Highlighting previ-ously unpublished work from the Wharton collection at Yale's Beinecke Rare Book and Manuscript Library—for example, Wharton's correspondence with Beatrix Farrand and an unfin-ished short story composed in Italian—this collection is the first to focus on Wharton and questions of autobiography, biography, and aesthetics. Although the following essays treat well-known novels, such as *The House of Mirth, The Custom of the Country,* and *The Age of Innocence,* they also examine a number of overlooked books, including *In Morocco, The Fruit of the Tree,* and *The Children,* to locate Wharton through a series of influential cultural contexts: American, European, and African.

The shape of *A Forward Glance: New Essays on Edith Wharton* moves outward, first exploring issues of biography, autobiography, and aesthetics; then extending those discussions to Wharton's fiction and nonfiction, with particular attention to gender, race, and class.

In the opening essay, which in many ways serves as an introduction to the ideas behind this collection—and behind the Yale conference also—Susan Goodman provides an overview of Wharton as she has been presented by her best-known biographers: Percy Lubbock (*Portrait of Edith Wharton*), R. W. B. Lewis (*Edith Wharton: A Biography*), Cynthia Griffin Wolff (*A Feast of Words*), Eleanor Dwight (*An Extraordinary Life*), and Shari Benstock (*No Gifts from Chance*). Noting that Wharton herself "devoured biographies" but feared biographers, Goodman situates both the subject and the biographer within a theoretical discussion that illumines the interrelationship of biography, autobiography, and fiction. "A paradigm of human yearning, suffering, and creativity," biography is a means to practice the autobiographical gift as well. As Goodman reveals, Wharton's biographers are also autobiographers "whose personal narratives develop within, alongside, or in opposition to the subject's."

Mia Manzulli adds a chapter to Wharton's evolving biography by turning to a previously neglected moment in Wharton's life: her little-known correspondence with her niece, noted landscape architect Beatrix Farrand. Manzulli's reading of their letters stresses the warmth of this friendship in a manner that undermines Lubbock's claim that Wharton disliked women and favored "the company of men." Through their long correspondence, Wharton and Farrand "created a shared space . . . where novelist and landscape gardener could achieve 'exquisite collaborations,' fruits of a rare partnership of creative equals."

Fruits of a more forbidden kind are the focus of Denise Witzig's deconstructive analysis of another, this time fictional, exchange of letters described in "His Father's Son," a complicated story of homosexual desire in which Wharton acts as literary "cross-dresser." Regarding Wharton's biographers and critics, Witzig claims that many "have emphasized sexuality, *her* sexuality, as the primary motivation or location of narrative choices," assumptions that Witzig's "homotextual" analysis of "His Father's Son" persuasively refutes.

The relationship of gender and genre is central to Katherine Joslin's analysis of Wharton's "gendered" aesthetics in *The Fruit of the Tree* and to Maureen Honey's interdisciplinary study of "Wharton's multilayered [fictional] presentation of women's bodies through sophisticated reference to Victorian painting." Joslin cites an oft-quoted passage from Wharton's correspondence in which she admits that *The Fruit of the Tree* is flawed: "I conceive my subjects like a man . . . , architectonically" but "execute them like a woman, episodic[ally]."[12] Relating Wharton to prominent women of her day who challenged "scientific" masculine models—among them, Jane Addams, Florence Kelley, and Charlotte Perkins Gilman—Joslin reinterprets this problem novel as a necessary failure that finally enabled Wharton to reject masculinist abstractions and "celebrate the [feminine] episodic" in the incidental tales that followed. Focusing on three novels, *The House of Mirth, The Custom of the Country,* and *The Age of Innocence,* Maureen Honey also maps the evolution of Wharton's aesthetics. Each novel "juxtaposes images of female strength with erotic poses of vulnerability making it difficult for male characters to see the living woman who compels their attention."

Other essays reexamine Wharton's ties to individual artists, notably, Henry James, and to the dominant literary movements of her time: naturalism, realism, and modernism. Upsetting a critical commonplace that holds only "The Master," not his "pupil," was a font of literary influence, Jerome Loving offers a new slant on James's revisions for the 1908 New York edition of *The Portrait of a Lady.* That "the story of the later Isabel is more compelling than its predecessor" owes much to James's response to "Wharton's [naturalist] 'portrait' of Lily Bart" and to his knowledge of Wharton's personal troubles at the time. As Loving argues, "The problem James faced as he revised *Portrait* for the twentieth century was that he could not credibly write—or rewrite—a realistic novel in an age of naturalism." In a different vein, Frederick Wegener chronicles Wharton's "venomous" critique of modernist tenets and unveils the conservative ideology that underlies her aesthetics. Through copious references to Wharton's neglected critical essays and unpublished letters, Wegener documents that "Wharton's often regressive social and political views . . . are closely intertwined with her convictions about the writing of fiction and the making of art."

Essays on the rarely studied travel writing, *Fighting France, from Dunkerque to Belfort* and *In Morocco,* also conjoin Wharton's politics to her aesthetics. Mary Suzanne Schriber traces the origins of *Fighting France* to Wharton's war correspondence and to her repeated journeys to the Front. These trips enabled Wharton to document the devastation for an American readership still unconvinced that the United States should enter the war. By analyzing how Wharton both relies upon and deliberately inverts "the conventions of the travel genre," Schriber establishes that *Fighting France* is "travel writing in the grotesque." As such, this combined elegy and call-to-arms effectively marks the end of an historical era and of "an epoch in women's practice in travel writing."

An examination of Wharton's sexual and textual politics leads Judith L. Sensibar to interpret Wharton's dual role as travel writer and wartime correspondent more critically. She maintains that *In Morocco,* like Wharton's other wartime "propaganda," "consciously identifies with and supports hegemonic and Western attitudes toward race and class, particularly the imperialist nature of the war itself which she explicitly ties to France's ongoing colonization of North Africa." Judging this travel book as both "capitalist" propaganda and "fictional" narrative, Sensibar interrogates Wharton's colonialist response to African "blackness" and Muslim "other." Stephanie Batcos approaches *In Morocco* differently, viewing the book as a lens through which to "glimpse . . . Wharton's ideas about culture, civilization, and the self." Connecting this work with Wharton's later, more veiled self-portrait in *A Backward Glance,* Batcos posits that *In Morocco* is at times less travel literature than autobiography, self-writing that enables the author to "successively lose, fragment, and recover her self," a process which culminates in Wharton's chapter on "Harems and Ceremonies." Having to some extent "lost" her self in her Moroccan travels, Wharton in this chapter "draws attention to herself as a [western] woman." Gender thus "becomes the means by which she re*orients* herself through 'unknown' Africa and journeys back to the 'known.'"

Though *The Age of Innocence* may seem on the surface far removed from Wharton's wartime literary and "cultural work," Anne MacMaster argues, rather, that this novel "registers the central crux of American identity . . . the history of slavery in the land of the free, the fear of the foreign in a nation of immigrants, the drive toward conformity behind the creed of individualism." MacMaster demonstrates that in this novel

Wharton's characterization of the "dark" heroine, Ellen Olenska, "addresses her class's anxieties about race after the Great War . . . by making racial doubling into a narrative strategy."

Focusing on class, Gianfranca Balestra studies an unpublished short story that Wharton wrote in Italian, perhaps to improve her knowledge of the language. In addressing Wharton's expertise in Italian and in Italian art and literature, Balestra relates this incomplete tale to other "memorable lower-class" portraits of servants in Wharton's fiction. Analyzing this story both as a language exercise and as a work of art, Balestra concludes that this fragment "presents one of [Wharton's] best attempts at depicting the life of a servant, whose plight in a class-ridden Italian society is portrayed with sensitivity and acute attention to detail."

In the final essay in this collection, on the late novel *The Children,* Ellen Pifer argues that Wharton practices a form of "self-criticism," "dramatiz[ing] and critiqu[ing] herself as a character" to "recast her relationship to the society that shaped her" and adapt to the brave new world of postwar Europe. Departing from critics who typically associate Rose Sellars with her creator, Pifer links Martin Boyne to Wharton: "Through the eyes of her male 'other,' . . . Wharton conveys a sympathetic, if ambivalent vision of the wilderness she dreaded." In this way, *The Children* serves as a vehicle by which Wharton could confront her fears about the future that awaited her, not only including worries about old age and death, but also anxieties about how later generations of readers would respond to her work.

In the sixty years since her death, Wharton's reputation has followed a dramatic trajectory somewhat like the life of the title character in David Graham Phillips's *Susan Lenox: Her Fall and Rise* (1917), a novel in the naturalist tradition, which the New York Society for the Suppression of Vice attacked and which Wharton much admired. As Wharton knew, reviewers may be capricious, tastes may change, and reputations may rise and fall—sometimes, as in Wharton's case, to rise again.

Anticipating her death, Wharton was understandably concerned with her literary legacy and with the disposition of her literary estate. Yet whatever doubts she may have had about the future or about her writing, her general opinion of reviewers remained firm. In her 1924 notebook, she lamented:

> Reading most reviews of my books—the kindest as well as the most disapproving—is like watching somebody in boxing-gloves trying to

dissect a flower. I don't mean to suggest that my novels are comparable to flowers—real ones—but they are certainly more nearly like them than they are like the conception of my work in the mind of the average reviewer. (St. Brice, June 7, 1925)

As Professor Phelps proclaimed that afternoon at Yale long ago, and as the essays in *A Forward Glance* attest, Wharton does, indeed, merit recognition as an American novelist of international fame. In the centennial year since the publication of her first book, Wharton continues to draw new readers, readers not preoccupied—as she feared—with "bits of vanished life," but readers intent on understanding the "welter" she called life and on preserving, however inadequately, both the flower and the conception of her art.

Notes

The first epigraph is from "Commencement, 1923," *Yale Alumni Weekly*, July 6, 1923, 1234. Subsequent references are cited in the text.

The second epigraph is from Edith Wharton, 1924 Notebook, *Quaderno dello Studente*. Passages from this notebook and from unpublished letters are reprinted by permission of the Yale Collection of American Literature, Beinecke Rare Book and Manuscript Library, Yale University; and the Estate of Edith Wharton and the Watkins/Loomis Agency. Unless otherwise indicated, all subsequent citations to unpublished materials are from the Wharton papers at Yale.

1. Wharton to Tom Rhinelander, May 4, 1923. Shari Benstock notes that in future years Wharton's poor health led her to decline additional offers of honorary doctorates from Columbia and Rutgers (*No Gifts from Chance: A Biography of Edith Wharton* [New York: Scribner's, 1994], 380).

2. Wharton to Bernard Berenson, quoted in Benstock, *No Gifts from Chance*, 380.

3. Letter to Henrietta Haven, June 28, 1923. Wharton's letters about this occasion frequently refer to the heat. Dressed in full academic regalia and fearing sunstroke, Wharton marched about the courts of Yale for nearly an hour. She later compared the climate of Connecticut to that of Salsomaggiore: "It has been so hot," she wrote a friend from Italy, "that once or twice, on waking in the morning, I have taken my dressing-gown for an Academic toga, & thought another degree was awaiting me. And so it was, but only Fahrenheit!" (Letter to Walter Maynard, May 29, 1924). In its commencement issue, the *Yale Alumni Weekly* also noted the heat: "The weather . . . was all that could be desired, and Commencement Day was perfect—if the heat be excepted" ("Commencement, 1923," 1231).

4. The *New York Morning Post* reported that "the exercises adhered strictly to precedent, with the procession of officers, faculty, candidates for degrees, and alumni from the college campus, through New Haven Green to Hewitt Quadrangle, and thence into Woolsey. The Harkness Tower Chimes played the music for the march, beginning with York tune and ending with 'America.'

In the hall the New Haven Symphony Orchestra ... played from Bizet and Mendelssohn" ("Yale Gives Women Honorary Degrees," June 20, 1923, n.p.).

5. Quoted in Percy Lubbock, *Portrait of Edith Wharton* (New York: Appleton, 1947), 11.

6. On Wharton's attitude toward lesbianism and male homosexuality, see Shari Benstock, *Women of the Left Bank: Paris, 1900–1940* (Austin: University of Texas Press, 1986), 87; and Robert A. Martin and Linda Wagner-Martin, "The Salons of Wharton's Fiction," in *Wretched Exotic: Essays on Edith Wharton in Europe,* ed. Katherine Joslin and Alan Price (New York: Peter Lang, 1993), 106. For a letter that illustrates Wharton's general displeasure "with the new gomorrahs" and her more particular distaste for "a lady" admirer who found Wharton "*irasistable*" (*sic*), see Wharton's May 13, 1922 letter to Gaillard Lapsley (*The Letters of Edith Wharton,* ed. R. W. B. Lewis and Nancy Lewis [New York: Scribner's, 1988], 451–52).

7. For a biographical account of Mary Woolley's fifty-two-year relationship with Jeanette Marks, see Anna Mary Wells, *Miss Marks and Miss Woolley* (Boston: Houghton, 1978). Wells argues that the scandal caused by this "companionship" ultimately led to Woolley's removal from the presidency of Mt. Holyoke in 1937 and the appointment of the University's first male president. Marks, an English professor at Mount Holyoke, published an adulatory (and guarded) portrait of the *Life and Letters of Mary Emma Woolley* (Washington, D.C.: Public Affairs, 1955).

8. Wharton to Minnie Cadwalader Jones, 23 May 1923, quoted in Shari Benstock, *No Gifts from Chance: A Biography of Edith Wharton* (New York: Scribner's, 1994), 387.

9. Farrand, notes appended to a letter to Wayne Andrews, December 3, 1958.

10. Seymour to Gaillard Lapsley, February 22, 1938.

11. Wharton to Rutger B. Jewett, February 21, 1923, *The Letters of Edith Wharton,* ed. R. W. B. Lewis and Nancy Lewis (New York: Scribner's, 1988), 465.

12. Wharton to Robert Grant, November 19, 1927, ibid., 124.

Edith Wharton's Composed Lives

SUSAN GOODMAN

Writing lives is the devil!

—Virginia Woolf

EDITH WHARTON DEVOURED BIOGRAPHIES. ACTUAL LIVES, ESPE-cially those of women writers and intellectuals, fascinated her even more than fictional ones. She especially liked *The Portrait of Zélide* (1925), written by her friend Geoffrey Scott. Wharton responded to the story of the Dutch girl Belle de Zuylen turning into Madame de Charrière, an eighteenth-century novelist whose intimate friends included Boswell and Constant, for one obvious reason: She saw a kind of double whom she could own or disown at will. Scott's description of Madame de Charrière might be of Wharton herself: "Madame de Charrière was not of marble, emphatically, nor even of the harshness of Houdon's clay. But the coldness of Houdon's bust—its touch of aloofness—corresponds to an intellectual ideal, more masculine than feminine, which she set before herself."[1]

No less than poetry, biography involves what Virginia Woolf called a "secret transaction" in which a voice answers a voice.[2] Ellen Glasgow, a contemporary of Edith Wharton and herself an autobiographer, worried about the validity of her own inner voice: "How can one tell," she asked, "where 'truth' ends and imagination begins?"[3] Dorothy West echoes Glasgow when she admits that she could no longer tell what had or had not happened in her autobiographical novel, *The Living Is Easy*. She had written too many versions of her parents' lives to know whether she had made them all up, or whether one was true.[4] Writing lives *is* the devil because the subject, no matter how close to the bone, must in large part remain unknown. The process itself raises doubts about the construction of identity and the nature of biography. The "truth" of biography like that of autobiography must be, of necessity, evolving. It grows from a process of amendment and revision.

22

The biographer has the almost impossible task of sacrificing neither literary instinct nor historical conscience. For one biographer, truth might finally depend on historical accuracy; for another, on "the divination of an inexplicable presence, whether a verbal mood, or an emotional aura" of facts or deeds.[5] In "great" biographies, the social, material, and relational aspects of a subject's life reflect a reality beyond the everyday realities recorded. Woolf observed that "biography is considered complete if it merely accounts for six or seven selves, whereas a person will have as many thousand." What we call the "true self" may be a compact of all these selves, "commanded and locked up by the Captain self, the Key self, which amalgamates and controls them all" (Woolf, 309, 310). However we conclusively define the self, personality can be nothing more than a collaboration between ourselves and the world at large.

Biography, like art, tends to marry history and fiction.[6] Personal memory—whether that of the subject and/or the biographer—develops into a kind of public history even as it calls accepted myths or histories into question. In his discussion of autobiography and the meaning of history, Wilhelm Dilthey raises an issue crucial to biography. Humanity, he argues, can understand itself "only in history, never through introspection," because the distance between past and present leads to a more authentic representation.[7] Biography partly exploits Dilthey's notion of historical accuracy in its representation of a socially informed collective memory, and frequently judges it irrelevant in its pursuit of the idiosyncratic. The popularity of biography may have something to do with its offering a double perspective, both a long and a close look, a factual account and a personal interpretation.

When it most matters, biography seems more than a compilation of facts and dates; it is a paradigm of human yearning, suffering, and creativity. It calls not for the supposedly dispassionate eye of the historian or scientist but for passionate engagement. If we accept that any writer tells his or her own disguised story, then the biographer is also an autobiographer, whose personal narrative develops within, alongside, or in opposition to the subject's.[8] Leon Edel describes the biographer's dilemma as twofold: "[H]e must apprise the life of another by becoming that other person; and he must be scrupulously careful that in the process the other person is not refashioned in his image."[9] The biographer has at least two selves: one belonging to the writer who consciously or unconsciously reveals his or her

prejudices and values, and the other belonging to the critic who
must shape and winnow the detritus of a life into a coherent
identity. Think of Edith Wharton trying to piece together the
lives of her female relatives: "I know less than nothing of the
particular virtues, gifts and modest accomplishments," she confessed, "of the young women with pearls in their looped hair or
cambric ruffs round their slim necks, who prepared the way for
my generation. A few shreds of anecdote, no more than the faded
flowers between the leaves of a great-grandmother's Bible, are
all that remains to me."[10] Wharton's attempt at biography, her
"effort of the heart,"[11] highlights a very human desire to place
our own lives within the context of other lives. Nevertheless,
undertaking a biography can have its perils, when the act of
writing separates us from ourselves, when the process of self-
revelation, whether autobiographical or biographical, leads us to
conclusions at odds with who we think we are.

Any narrative exists to some extent independently of its
author, especially when private dialogue, that inner voice, becomes translated into public discourse.[12] The biographer must
also be a linguist, who speaks at least three languages: his or
her native tongue, that of the subject; and a hybrid dialect of
the two, which informs a biography's tone. For the biographer
no less than the creative writer, one's soul often feels a stranger,
closer, as Wharton wrote, "than one's bones and yet with a face
and speech forever unknown to one."[13]

Questions of voice aside, the relationship between biographer
and subject—subtle, intimate, and ambivalent—is complicated
by any number of personal and political factors. A biographer
may choose a subject who seems a soul mate in need of rescue
or who represents the values of a secretly envied (or despised)
class.[14] Telling the life of a woman may present a particular set
of problems. Linda Wagner-Martin cautions that the biographer
has to resist telling the same old story, in which the roles of
wife, mother, or mistress govern,[15] without discounting the importance of those roles in the subject's life. Not only must the
writer come to terms with the stories embedded in our culture
itself, but he or she must further resist the story subjects wanted
told. A biographer is a thief of sorts, someone who slips into the
subject's mind intending to peek behind closed doors and make
away with the gold.

Writers may be among the most difficult subjects for biographers. Even the belief, which many writers share, that all writing
is an extension of personality does not necessarily inhibit some-

one from doing a certain amount of self-editing. And those who believe that books live on the personalities of their authors as much as merit have been known to create what they think the public wants: an easily grasped, virtually stereotyped, personality. We just have to think of Benjamin Franklin, Ernest Hemingway, or Wharton herself. For the biographer, art always contends with life, the art of your subject and also the art of all those who have written about the subject before.

The act and process of writing alters the biographer's identity no less than that of the subject. Marjorie Kinnan Rawlings, best known as the author of *The Yearling,* serves as an example. Long before she accepted a commission to write a never completed biography of her friend, Ellen Glasgow, she had a dream that eerily captures the ambiguous relationship between biographer and subject. "You came to live with me," she told Glasgow after visiting her in 1914:

> I was away when you came, and on my return, to one of those strange mansions that are part of the substance of dreams, you were outside in the bitter cold, cutting away ice from the roadway and piling it in geometric patterns. I was alarmed, remembering your heart trouble, and led you inside the mansion and brought you a cup of hot coffee. You had on blue silk gloves, and I laid my hand over yours, and was amazed, for my own hand is small, to have yours fit inside mine, much smaller. You chose your room and suggested draperies to supplement a valance. The valance was red chintz and you showed me a sample of a heavy red brocade of the same shade. I told you from now on I should take care of you, and you must not do strenuous things, such as cutting ice in the roadway. James Cabell came into the room and asked what the two of us were up to. (As of course he would!) (*WW,* 294)

Mythologizing the subject and empowering the dreamer, Rawlings's dream reveals the complexities inherent in literary friendships and their posthumous extension in literary biography. From Rawlings's point of view, the relationship encompasses burden and privilege because she must come to terms with a predecessor whom she would like to supplant. If the dream underscores a certain anxiety about influence,[16] the younger generation's desire to topple its predecessors, it also explores its opposite. As the younger woman takes the older woman's shrunken hand and leads her into the strange mansion—what Henry James called the house of fiction or academics have come to call the canon—the generational roles reverse.

Rawlings's skeptical relationship to Glasgow and the tradition she represents finds expression in the "chintzy" decor of Glasgow's room. In contrast, Glasgow's plan to complement the valance with panels of brocade, a richer and more durable material, models for Rawlings a way of accommodating individual talent within other traditions. Rawlings's promise to nurture Glasgow—and by extension her work—disturbs Cabell because he intuits his own exclusion from female traditions history has increasingly honored.

Like Rawlings, the biographers of Edith Wharton have had to contend with a formidable subject, one who purposefully teased and inevitably frustrated the readers of her autobiography, *A Backward Glance* (1934), with the warning that she had to make the most of "unsensational material" (*ABG*, xx). Wharton understood the importance of biography, and, wanting no postmortems on the basis of guesswork and gossip, she destroyed many of Walter Berry's letters and left other materials, including correspondences and diaries, clearly marked for her biographer. "When I get a glimpse, in books and reviews, of the things people are going to assert about me after I am dead," she wrote, "I feel I must have the courage and perseverance, some day, to forestall them."[17] In the end, however, she, like all subjects, could not escape a kind of tyranny. "The wants of others," she explained, "the wants of the dead and one's predecessors . . . have an inconvenient way of thrusting their different habits and tastes across the current of later existences."[18] Wharton showed a kind of prescience. The sealing of her papers suggests that she imagined more sympathetic readers decades hence, though she probably did not guess that what she called the "pornographic fragment" of Beatrice Palmato would lead more than one critic to see her as a possible survivor of incest.[19]

Wharton's autobiography did not prevent competing biographies. The title of her autobiography, which she borrowed from Walt Whitman, hints at another, perhaps, secret or sensual self as it guides us toward a reading of her place in American letters. Wharton has fixed herself historically, her "backward glance" suggesting a link to the past and a move with or toward life. The titles of the principal Wharton biographies similarly reveal how their authors have conceived their subject's life. Percy Lubbock's *Portrait*, R. W. B. Lewis's *Biography*, Cynthia Griffin Wolff's *A Feast of Words*, Eleanor Dwight's *An Extraordinary Life*, and Shari Benstock's *No Gifts from Chance* situate both the subject and the biographer, offering us an abridged overview of major biographical approaches from the 1940s to the turn of the twentieth century.

As Lubbock's title, *Portrait of Edith Wharton* (1947), suggests, his book is a kind of palimpsest of friends' memories collected, edited, and woven together with his own commentary. The truth of the memoir rests on its firsthand testimony from Wharton's closest associates. In truth, the memoir differs little from Lubbock's other books on women writers, including Elizabeth Barrett Browning and Mary Cholmondeley, in which he pairs his female subject with a male counterpart to her disadvantage.[20] *Portrait of Edith Wharton*, for example, places Wharton's "little literary talent, pretty as it was," in the frame of Henry James's genius.[21]

Unlike many biographies written primarily for the general reading public, Lubbock's *Portrait* had another audience: its immediate circle of contributors. Although this second group knew of Lubbock's troubled history with Wharton, who openly critiqued his wife and subtly disparaged his work, none found the composite mosaic wanting—perhaps because they each read their portrait as "the" portrait.

The strength of Lubbock's memoir lies in its intimacy and its form. Although the plot of Wharton's life is distorted by Lubbock's obvious sexism, its amorphous shape could serve as a model for telling women's lives, often a tally of private routines, rather than public events. Before critics debated the fictionalizing of biography and the merits of genre divisions, Lubbock wrote what Edith Wharton called "uncategorizable" books: "I wish that he'd write books that go into categories," she told Gaillard Lapsley, "the public always takes to them more readily."[22] His *Portrait*, which blurs the distinctions between history and fiction, memoir and literary criticism, follows the same pattern. Foreshadowing recent biographies of women, such as Ann J. Lane's study of Charlotte Perkins Gilman,[23] the chronology of Wharton's life and its individual incidents are of far less importance than the puzzle of her personality. Slices from Wharton's life highlight what we might see as her major phases, such as her remove to Europe or her growing interest in Catholicism. The reader functions as a voyeur, surreptitiously eavesdropping on each memoirist's soliloquy about the subject. Because Lubbock's skeleton primes readers to construe these vignettes uncharitably, they find themselves sympathizing with the narrator, who tolerated and forgave Wharton, rather than with Wharton herself. Lubbock's commentary highlights a crucial concern of biography, for readers cannot help questioning whether he functions as a disinterested observer or has become, in the process, the main character.

Although *Portrait* attempted to answer the basic question that propels biography ("Who was this person?"), it did not demonstrate why the life remained worth noting. That task fell to R. W. B. Lewis, whose biography appeared in 1975, nearly thirty years after Lubbock's. Lewis possesses a "historic imagination,"[24] and his hermeneutic approach places Wharton in the social, cultural context of her time. He gives us what Bernard Berenson called an "assimilable and inspiring ideated personality":[25] a woman of genius. Repudiating Lubbock's portrait of Wharton as a cold grande dame writing between social engagements, Lewis makes accessible "one of the most intelligent American women" (Lewis, xii). Lewis treats Wharton as "subject," "a person of high literary accomplishment" (i), the fascinating author of *The House of Mirth* (1905), *Ethan Frome* (1911), and *The Age of Innocence* (1920), someone of central importance to American letters. "Her writings," in Lewis's estimation, "find their larger human implications out of a vast imaginative report on one segment of American social history and on Americans glimpsed . . . amid the international community" (Lewis, xiii). In making his argument, Lewis holds Wharton the woman at arms' length. The legend of her life does not overshadow her accomplishments. Instead, she becomes what we might think of as "a cultural term of reference."[26]

Lewis's Wharton has ineradicable ties to specific historical movements and to a larger, sometimes imagined history of European civilization. Her life becomes emblematic of the eras it spans: postbellum old New York, Edwardian London, and Paris from *la belle époque* through the First World War. And it is peopled with the makers of history: Theodore Roosevelt, Henry Adams, William Dean Howells, Aldous Huxley, and Kenneth Clark—to name a few. The biography revolves around a central paradox: How could a person brought up in a home that offered no opening into contemporary history arrive at the center of so much of it? Her life moves from the almost instinctive making of fiction, which from the first mirrored the emotional constellation of her immediate family, to a life drawn almost solely from her writings.

If Lubbock emphasized the woman and Lewis the author, Wharton's next biographer, Cynthia Griffin Wolff, found them inseparable. To her, the problems of becoming a novelist were inextricable from the problems of becoming a woman. *A Feast of Words: The Triumph of Edith Wharton* deviates from traditional biographies of famous men by focusing on the subject's interior life, her way of making meaning. As in many biographies and in Wharton's own autobiography, Wharton's public life never overshadows her private self. The book's prologue, which briefly sketches the facts of a conventional life, works like Wolff's own explanation of the frame story to *Ethan Frome;* what follows is a vision or a version of Edith Wharton. The story, as the narrator of *Ethan Frome* tells us, lies in the gaps.[27]

Wolff's story of Wharton's psychological and artistic development portrays a self expressed in and shaped by language. "How could she have written so well?" Wolff asks. "Why did she write at all?"[28] In the tradition of Wordsworth's *Prelude, A Feast of Words* traces the growth of an imagination. Wolff pictures Wharton's life not as a discrete and separate entity, but as evolving, separate selves accreting one upon the other, enriching the fabric of the whole. Like a detective, Wolff tracks Wharton through the signs she leaves or the language she uses, structuring the story around the dichotomous metaphors of feast and starvation. Wharton's life falls into four parts, characterized by section titles that underscore its relationship to her fiction: "A Portrait of the Artist as a Young Woman"; "Landscapes of Desolation: The Fiction, 1889–1911"; "Studies of Salamanders: The Fiction, 1912–1920"; and "Diptych—Youth and Age: The Fiction, 1921–1937." Wharton the writer dominates this biography even more than Lewis's. For this reason perhaps, Wolff remains the only biographer of Wharton to call her by her last, rather than her first, name. That choice underscores a different relationship between Wolff and her subject, one that honors Wharton's personal and professional autonomy as well as Wharton's own sense of decorum. It also grants the biographer a measure of sovereignty, which keeps at least theoretically, if not emotionally, a necessary boundary between selves intact.

Shari Benstock had the daunting task of writing a life largely defined for most readers and scholars by Wolff and Lewis, whose book won a Pulitzer. Her enterprise raises the issue of what makes another biography worth writing. Benstock rests her case on new facts and in some cases on the lack of facts. Her accumulation of documented and disputed evidence about Wharton's life—ranging from the circumstances of her birth to the nature of her alleged neurasthenia—makes us read, as Henry James did, "*re*constructively." As both cultural critic and feminist biog-

rapher, Benstock challenges the received views of her subject
influenced by stereotypes about a woman's nature or, for that
matter, her business acumen. Benstock, who wanted to "lay
down a better factual framework" about how Wharton worked,
saw Wharton's life separate from her books and her books separate from her life.[29] In other words, she tried to let the facts
speak for themselves, and because her biography includes me-
ticulous annotation, any intrepid reader with time may track
the real Wharton him- or herself. *No Gifts from Chance,* then,
is the story of a strong woman who does her best to exercise
free will, while caring deeply about others, including other
women, such as Sara Norton, Elisina Tyler, Minnie Cadwalader
Jones, and Beatrix Farrand. Benstock provides a context for analyzing Wharton's own myths about her life without doing any
editorializing. Lucretia Jones emerges from these pages a misguided and sometimes insensitive mother but no monster;
Teddy Wharton becomes an almost tragic figure when we learn
of his father's psychotic interludes and suicide nine years before
the onset of his own bipolar illness; and Walter Berry, here
gentle and engaging, becomes someone we can understand Edith
Wharton loving and Marcel Proust admiring.

If Benstock's revisionist biography emends Lewis's image of
Wharton, Eleanor Dwight's extends Cynthia Griffin Wolff's, emphasizing her visual, rather than her verbal, precocity and aesthetics. *Edith Wharton: An Extraordinary Life* (1994) has two
complementary texts, one written, the other pictorial. Ultimately commanding, the pictorial text supplements the narrative, while opening it to objections. The pictures both encourage
and limit the reader's own interpretation, as they suggest un-
wonted plots of their own.

Dwight envisions Wharton's self evolving from places charged
with personal and cultural significance—so much so that Wharton's love of William Morton Fullerton seems wedded to her love
of France. The defining characteristics of Wharton's personality
become her visceral response to beauty and ugliness, her tendency to see the world as a series of pictures, and her instinct
to please by "making the picture prettier" (Dwight, 19). Not surprisingly, Dwight imagines Wharton's self as a house full of
rooms. "A woman's nature is like a great house full of rooms,"
Wharton herself wrote in "The Fullness of Life":

> there is the hall, through which everyone passes in going in and
> out; the drawing room, where one receives formal visits; the sitting

room, where the members of the family come and go as they list; but beyond that, far beyond, are other rooms, the handles of whose doors are never turned; no one knows the way to them, no one knows whither they lead; and in the innermost room, the holy of holies, the soul sits alone and waits for a footstep that never comes.[30]

Dwight views Wharton's life, as she does Wharton's novels, through the filter of her books on decoration and architecture. Wharton "always had to be 'situated' in a particular way to the world" (177). Berenson's complaint about Wharton's insistence on the exact arrangement of her room when traveling has long been seen as a sign of her unreasonableness. Dwight, however, understands the importance of the morning sun to someone who writes each morning in bed. Where Lewis emphasizes Wharton's friendships with other writers, Dwight emphasizes her relationships with the designer, Ogden Codman, and the landscape architect, Beatrix Farrand. The principles that inform the books on decoration and gardens also inform the novels in which a primary design is "*born* and not *built*" (Dwight, 104). The architectonic nature of *The House of Mirth*—or, as Katherine Joslin argues (in an essay that follows), of *The Fruit of the Tree*—makes Lily Bart's descent from Mrs. Peniston's parlor to a boardinghouse's common room predestined.

A book, as Percy Lubbock cautioned in *The Craft of Fiction* (1921), is never solely the affair of the author.[31] Neither is the subject solely the property of any one biographer. Wolff, for example, places her biography in relation to a tradition by acknowledging her indebtedness to Lewis, who, in turn, credits her finding of the "Fragment of Beatrice Palmato." Long before reader-response or deconstructionist theories became popular, Lubbock argued that books are written by those who interpret them. These biographies of Wharton suggest an analogous transformation of subjects' lives, composed and decomposed by each new narrator in each new time.

Who, we might ask, is Edith Wharton? The question may sound irrelevant or naive in an age that discounts the very idea of continuous identity, what Wharton herself called the "irreducible core of selfness" (*HRB*, 272). Yet biographies continue to attract fresh generations of readers drawn like moths—or perhaps ferrets—to personalities that resist summation. "We are all prompted by the same motives," Samuel Johnson reminds us, "all deceived by the same fallacies, all animated by hope, obstructed by danger, entangled by desire, and seduced by plea-

sure."[32] For most readers, this belief in a "universal"—whether
illusionary or unfashionable—makes biography relevant.

As the subject of multiple biographies, Wharton has attracted
(to use one of her titles) a cadre of "angels at the grave." This
abundance of present, and assuredly future, biographies seems
fitting for someone who came to believe:

> The world is a welter and has always been one; but though all the
> cranks and the theorists cannot master the old floundering monster,
> or force it for long into any of their neat plans of readjustment, here
> and there a saint or a genius suddenly sends a little ray through the
> fog, and helps humanity to stumble on, and perhaps up. (*ABG*, 379)

Theories, as Wharton knew, cannot master that floundering
monster she called "life." Marjorie Rawlings learned this lesson
when she began to research the life of Ellen Glasgow. The more
Rawlings learned about the dynamics of the Glasgow family, the
more its members reminded her of little adders she had once
seen living under a floribunda rose.[33] Listening to Richmond
gossip over glasses of sherry and cups of tea, she lost heart.
Glasgow's autobiography, *The Woman Within* (1954), seemed as
much fiction as fact. Rawlings wondered if she could recount
what Glasgow had left out: the more disagreeable, even brutal,
aspects of her life. Some facts simply did not bear discussing.
The unpleasant realization that Glasgow could be spiteful and
manipulative particularly dismayed Rawlings. She no longer recognized the woman whom she had dreamed of rescuing from
the cold. In a sense, Rawlings floundered before the monster.
She could not come to terms with another's life, as she had
with the lives of her neighbors in *Cross Creek* (1942), without
exercising the liberties that fiction grants.

Lives always contain elements of fiction, whether they are re-
counted in autobiographies or autobiographical novels, such as
George Borrow's *Lavengro* (1851), D. H. Lawrence's *Sons and
Lovers* (1913), Virginia Woolf's *To the Lighthouse* (1927), or
Wharton's own *Hudson River Bracketed* (1929) and *The Gods
Arrive* (1932).[34] When Wharton looked at the welter of her own
life in *A Backward Glance,* she may have been confirming only
a small part. Can any autobiography or biography, even one as
rich and full as Lewis's of Wharton or Edel's of James, ever corral
that slippery monster? Can biographers know their subjects better than she or he knew themselves? Rawlings discovered that
you can do just so much with facts. The problems that Rawlings

faced as a biographer, a writer such as Jean Paul Sartre faced in his autobiography, *Les Mots,* which reduces experience to words. His response to the insubstantiality of fact or the integrity of personality—another way of describing Wharton's welter—suggests that neither autobiography nor biography are fixed forms.

For the biographer, as for the reader of her fiction, a subject as complex and compelling as Edith Wharton must ultimately project our own consciousness—"only out of reach," as Berenson assures us, "whence answers may not be expected" (Dwight 282) or even desired. As theories about the self rise and fall, as intellectual fashions change and cultural emphases shift, new interpretations, along with new facts, will be needed. In the end, there can be no definitive biography of Wharton, because the welter will and should remain.

Notes

The epigraph is from a letter of Woolf to her sister, Vanessa Bell, in *Letters of Virginia Woolf,* ed. Nigel Nicolson and Joanne Trautmann, vol. 6 (New York: Harcourt Brace Jovanovich, 1980), 245.

1. Geoffrey Scott, *Portrait of Zélide* (New York: Charles Scribner's Sons, 1927), 1–2.

2. Virginia Woolf, *Orlando: A Biography* (New York: Harcourt Brace Jovanovich, n.d.), 325 (hereafter cited as Woolf).

3. Ellen Glasgow, *The Woman Within* (New York: Harcourt Brace, 1954), 281 (hereafter cited as *WW*).

4. Katrine Dalsgard, "Alive and Well and Living on the Island of Martha's Vineyard: An Interview with Dorothy West, October 29, 1988," *Langston Hughes Review* 12 no. 2 (1993): 40.

5. Willa Cather, *On Writing: Critical Studies on Writing as an Art* (New York: Knopf, 1949), 41–42.

6. See, for example, Elspeth Cameron, "Truth in Biography," in *Boswell's Children* (Toronto: Dundrun Press, 1992), 27–33; and David A. Nock, "Biographical Truth," in *Boswell's Children,* ed. R. B. Fleming 33–37.

7. Wilhelm Dithey, *Meaning in History: Wilhelm Dilthey's Thoughts on History and Society,* ed. H. P. Rickman (London: Allen & Unwin, 1961), 80.

8. For a discussion of this process, see Bell Gale Chevigny, "Daughters Writing: Toward a Theory of Women's Biography," in *Between Women: Biographers, Novelists, Critics, Teachers, and Artists Write about Their Work on Women,* ed. Carol Ascher, Louise DeSalvo, and Sara Ruddick (Boston: Beacon Press, 1984), 356–79. Also see Janice Dickin McGinnis, "Aimee Semple McPherson: Fantasizing the Fantasizer? Telling the Tale of a Tale-Teller," in *Boswell's Children,* 45–57.

9. Leon Edel, *Literary Biography* (Bloomington: Indiana University Press, 1973), 11.

10. Edith Wharton, *A Backward Glance* (1934; New York: Charles Scribner's Sons, 1964), 15 (hereafter cited as *ABG*).

34   SUSAN GOODMAN

11. Marcel Proust, *Contre Sainte-Beuve,* ed. P. Clarac (Paris: Gaillimard, Pléiade, 1971), 221–22.

12. Maurice Merleau-Ponty, *Themes from the Lectures at the College de France, 1952–1960,* trans. John O'Neill (Evanston, Ill.: Northwestern University Press, 1970), 12–25.

13. Edith Wharton, *Hudson River Bracketed* (New York: Charles Scribner's Sons, 1985), 45 (hereafter cited as *HRB*).

14. See Robert Skidelsky, "Only Connect: Biography and Truth," in *The Troubled Face of Autobiography,* ed. Eric Homberger and John Charmley (New York: Macmillan, 1988), 7.

15. Linda Wagner-Martin, *Telling Women's Lives: The New Biography* (New Brunswick, N.J.: Rutgers University Press, 1994), x.

16. Harold Bloom, *The Anxiety of Influence: A Theory of Poetry* (New York: Oxford University Press, 1973).

17. R. W. B. Lewis, *Edith Wharton: A Biography* (New York: Harper & Row, 1975), xii (hereafter cited as Lewis).

18. Edith Wharton and Ogden Codman, Jr., *The Decoration of Houses* (New York: Charles Scribner's Sons, 1897), 18.

19. See, for example, Barbara White, *Edith Wharton: A Study of the Short Fiction,* Twayne's Studies in Short Fiction Series 30 (New York: Twayne, 1991); David Holbrook, *Edith Wharton and the Unsatisfactory Man* (New York: St. Martin's, 1991); and Gloria Erlich, *The Sexual Education of Edith Wharton* (Berkeley: University of California Press, 1992), 35, 40, 100, 126, 182 esp.

20. Susan Goodman, *Edith Wharton's Inner Circle* (Austin: University of Texas Press, 1994) 85–92, 86 esp.

21. Percy Lubbock, *Portrait of Edith Wharton* (New York: D. Appleton, 1947) 243–44.

22. Letter of Edith Wharton to Gaillard Lapsley, December 17, 1923, Beinecke Library.

23. Ann J. Lane, *To Herland and Beyond: The Life and Work of Charlotte Perkins Gilman* (New York: Meridian, 1991).

24. See "Mary Johnston and the Historic Imagination," *Southern Writers: Appraisals in Our Time,* ed. R. C. Simonini, Jr. (Charlottesville: University Press of Virginia, 1964), 74.

25. Bernard Berenson, *The Bernard Berenson Treasury,* ed. Hana Kiel, with an introduction by Nicky Mariano (New York: Simon and Schuster, 1962), 138 (hereafter cited as *BBT*).

26. Eleanor Dwight, *Edith Wharton: An Extraordinary Life* (New York: Harry N. Abrams, Inc.), 282 (hereafter cited as Dwight).

27. See Edith Wharton, *Ethan Frome* (New York: Macmillan, 1987), 1, 17.

28. Cynthia Griffin Wolff, *A Feast of Words: The Triumph of Edith Wharton* (New York: Oxford University Press, 1977), 5.

29. Augusta Rohrbach, "An Interview with Shari Benstock," *Edith Wharton Review* 12 no. 2 (fall 1995): 17–19.

30. Edith Wharton, "The Fullness of Life," in *The Collected Short Stories of Edith Wharton,* ed. R. W. B. Lewis, vol. 1 (New York: Charles Scribner's Sons, 1968), 14.

31. Percy Lubbock, *The Craft of Fiction* (New York: Peter Smith, 1947), 77.

32. Samuel Johnson, *The Rambler* (60), ed. W. J. Bate and Albrecht B. Strauss, vol. 1 (New Haven: Yale University Press, 1969), 323.

33. Elizabeth Silverthorne, *Marjorie Kinnan Rawlings: Sojourner at Cross Creek* (Woodstock, N.Y.: Overlook Press, 1988), 335.

34. See Susan Goodman, *Edith Wharton's Women: Friends and Rivals* (Hanover, N.H.: University Press of New England, 1990), 126–134.

"Garden Talks": The Correspondence of Edith Wharton and Beatrix Farrand

MIA MANZULLI

> It is cold here [Ste. Claire] for the first time this winter, and
> I envy you the more equable climate of California. I wish I
> could hover over you while you are planting the garden for I
> have no doubt that I could suggest many things that are not
> quite hardy enough for our own uncertain weather, but
> which you would revel in. . . . I should love to send you a lot
> of plants, but alas I suppose that is quite impossible. At any
> rate we must compare notes by letter whenever you have
> time, unless & until we have a chance to talk, which is infi-
> nitely more satisfying.
> —Wharton to Farrand, February 7, 1931

DISTANCE SEPARATED EDITH WHARTON AND HER NIECE, BEATRIX
Farrand, for much of their lives. By 1920, Wharton was dividing
her time between Pavillon Colombe at St. Brice, just north of
Paris, and Ste. Claire in Hyères on the French Riviera; while
Farrand, a noted landscape architect, split her time between
Reef Point in Maine, and the Huntington Library in California.
Letters thus became a substitute for what Wharton, in another
letter to Farrand, calls "garden talks": "We've been too long without seeing each other & you've been too long without seeing the
other side of the world. And oh the garden talks we're going to
have!" (October 6, 1920).

Although Wharton's extensive letter writing has been well
documented, her affectionate and in many ways revealing correspondence with Farrand has been largely overlooked. A reading
of the Wharton-Farrand correspondence suggests first an extension of Susan Goodman's argument in *Edith Wharton's Women,*
in which she dismantles the perception of Wharton as "a woman
who did not really care for women."[1] Second, the Wharton-
Farrand letters reveal a particular awareness of the idea that
a woman's creativity is linked to her sexuality. Perhaps most
important, the letters between the aunt and her niece created

a shared space, a verdant "kind of letter"—to use Wharton's phrase—where novelist and landscape gardener could achieve "exquisite collaborations,"[2] fruits of a rare partnership of creative equals.

The term "exquisite collaborations" comes from a letter Wharton wrote to her lover, Morton Fullerton, on August 26, 1908:

> when you spoke of your uncertain future, your longing to break away & do the work you really like, didn't you see how my heart *broke* with the thought that, if I had been younger & prettier, everything might have been different—that we might have had together, at least for a short time, a life of exquisite collaborations—a life in which your gifts would have had full scope, and you would have been able to do the distinguished & beautiful things that you ought to do?[3]

Wharton's correspondence with Farrand suggests that in her niece she found a companion who was "able to do the distinguished & beautiful things" that this talented young woman was meant to do.

Farrand's collaboration with her aunt at The Mount, Wharton's home in Lenox, Massachusetts, is an early example of their partnership. Although Wharton designed most of the landscaping, Farrand was responsible for the two thousand–foot approach to the house and The Mount's kitchen garden as well. Of Farrand's contribution to the design of The Mount's gardens, Farrand's biographer Jane Brown has commented:

> Edith decided that she knew exactly what she wanted, and Beatrix knew her aunt too well, and loved her too much, to interrupt her in full flight. The Mount's garden was born from Edith's assumptions about Italian gardens, made *before* she researched and wrote her articles. . . . It was no less than a designed disaster, and Beatrix must be absolved from anything to do with it.[4]

However, it is of crucial importance that Wharton never felt that The Mount was a "designed disaster." In a letter to Fullerton in July 1911, she writes: "Decidedly, I'm a better landscape gardener than novelist, and this place [The Mount], every line of which is my own work, far surpasses the House of Mirth."[5] A number of Lenox neighbors, who subsequently commissioned Farrand to landscape their estates, agreed. Wharton's belief in her niece's talent led her to support Farrand's burgeoning career by procuring several important commissions: "Eastover," which was the Harris Fahnestock estate; the flower garden at "Elm-court," for Mrs. Emily Vanderbilt Sloane; and Giraud Foster's "Bellefontaine" (Brown, 210). Wharton would even introduce her niece to Robert and Mildred Bliss, owners of Dumbarton Oaks, the property that would become the site of Farrand's most famous garden.

The relationship Farrand shared with Wharton transcended that of aunt and niece; they were close friends, garden enthusiasts, and professional equals. Only ten years her senior, Wharton was nearer in age to Farrand than she was to either of her own brothers, and she remained closer to Farrand and her mother, Minnie Cadwalader Jones, than to any of her immediate family. If anything, Minnie Jones's separation from Wharton's brother, Frederic, in 1882, and eventual divorce in 1896, confirmed the intimacy between the women. Wharton, it must be remembered, was never close to her mother, nor did she have any sisters. She once commented to a friend that "Minnie and Trix make up to me for my own wretched family" (*Letters,* 405). Farrand and Wharton were (along with Minnie Cadwalader Jones) each other's primary family, with one extravagantly related series of progeny: their gardens. As neither of the women had children, it is easy to read the garden as a substitute for family. Upon the marriage of Beatrix Jones to Max Farrand, Wharton advised her niece:

> Blessedness gives such a bloom even to chairs and tables—and how the sunlight strikes on a bowl of flowers, when one looks at it through a haze of happiness! Fasten with all your might on the inestimable treasure of your liking for each other and your understanding of each other—build your life on its serene foundations, and let everything you do and think be a part of it. And if you have a boy or girl, to prolong the joy, so much the better. (January 18, 1914)

Wharton's language, with its images of blooms and flowers, evokes the garden, yet also hints at a wistfulness for the children she never had. At times, Farrand referred to Wharton's flowers as her family, implying perhaps that Wharton found in her role as gardener a means to fulfill her maternal desire:

> Are you in the market for any more American iris? There are some good ones, especially of the yellows and coppers which have appeared within the last few years. And as your Ste. Claire iris children seem to be thriving may they not have a few newcomers added to

them in whatever colors would fit into the rest of the family? It amuses me to hear that Fulva has flowered well with you as she is usually a persnickety lady. (July 20, 1936)

On occasion, Wharton herself indeed anthropomorphizes her flowers, imagining her "children"'s "hurt":

Every day for the last week I have longed for you, for your beautiful irises are in their glory. You will remember that when you were here you were disappointed that they had not made a more vigorous growth, and I was depressed because I felt that I must in some way have hurt their feelings, and that they were going to be sulky about it. But their only grievance was the cold wet weather, and as soon as the sun came back they burst into vigorous growth, and for the last few days they have been a glorious spectacle. (May 4, 1933, Ste. Claire)

For both women, gardening not only becomes "a glorious spectacle" of maternal ambition, but a means to express a woman's professional aspirations as well. When Farrand procured a landscaping commission from Yale University, where her husband was a professor of history, Wharton congratulated her:

It's a great satisfaction, isn't it, to find one's work recognized, and know that the dedicated sense one had within one corresponds to an outward reality? I know the feeling, and am sure you'll agree with me that it's about the best there is, in this world of uncertainties. I'm very proud of your success, and perhaps in my pride there is more understanding of what it means than if I hadn't my own trade to measure your achievement by.[6]

To Wharton, Farrand was a kindred spirit, a woman of strong opinions and professional drive. However, the two women shared more than a family connection; each emerged as an artist from a "provincial society [in which] authorship was still regarded as something between a black art and a form of manual labor."[7]

In many ways, at the turn of the century, landscape gardening remained even more of a "black art" than writing. Largely dominated and defined by men, it seemed no place for a lady from a prominent family. Farrand's sex and old New York background seemed—as it had with Wharton—a mixed blessing. To some extent, Farrand's social status gave her a certain cachet: "Although fond of tennis and golf, and in love with her profession, she yet finds time for society" (Brown, 59). Headlines such as

"New York Society Girl a Landscape Architect" or "Miss Beatrix Jones's Vocation—She does landscape gardening of all kinds from the ground up," could have come from the pages of Wharton's *The Custom of the Country* (1913). Such publicity led one male colleague to speak of Farrand as having a "bedroom practice," meaning she did a little work between cards and tea. Although a charter member of the American Society of Landscape Architecture, she found herself excluded from consideration for large-scale public commissions awarded to Frederick Law Olmsted and Jens Jensen.[8] Nevertheless, Farrand persisted, and by 1911, she had a large office in Manhattan at 124 East and 40th Street. Fully aware of the sexism inherent in her profession, she made a point of hiring only women to handle production.

In a 1916 lecture at Bryn Mawr on "Landscape Architecture as a Profession for Women," Farrand suggested that "no one should undertake to practice landscape architecture who has not already income enough to keep her alive without the practice of her profession as the money return is not large."[9] In another speech, she cautioned that "the profession therefore is not for those who must count on a steady increasing income, since it is peculiarly dependent on the prosperity of the country and is almost entirely a profession of luxury" (Balmori, 109). The financial security attached to Farrand's social status allowed her to pursue a career as a professional landscape architect in much the same way that inheritances permitted Wharton to embark on a writing career.

For Farrand, landscape gardening seemed the ultimate expression of creativity. As Brown has suggested, Farrand "had grown up loving and needing the beautiful Mount Desert landscape in a way perhaps she did not quite understand herself. [There] she had acquired her landscape 'eye,' her ability to understand the quality of place" (27). What began as a summer hobby at Reef Point developed into a lifelong passion. Gardens challenged her: She "had a marvelous time being fully alive to the scale, geometry, landscape settings" (Brown, 49).[10] A letter to Wharton, dated July 20, 1936, illustrates Farrand's visionary "eye":

It occurs to me that you might like to try at St. Brice the lovely but very ramping Mongolian creeper.... The flowers are like vine-flowers and the same color and scent. The longest truss outside my balcony now measures thirty-five and a half inches (Why couldn't it have been the full yard!) The leaves are rather like bitter-sweet but larger.... The seeds are, as its name implies, three winged and quite ornamental in the last season. Would you like some seed sent you for a place where it can be allowed to galumph and gallop?

Like Wharton, Farrand had an eye for detail, an appreciation of order; a respect for the civilizing effects of nature (influenced by Ruskin); and, above all, a "galumphing" sense of fun.

Wharton's letters to Farrand are similarly marked by an easy familiarity, a frolicsome tone, and a warmth of affection:

> Your description of the meanders of the Reef, with its "happy colonies" of this, that, & the other have filled me with a dark despair for which you will see the reason when you see the photos of my squalid "borders." I might have found some consolation in my espaliered fruits; but how can I when you flaunt your dwarf apples in my face, you brute? (October 6, 1920)

Wharton at times envied Farrand's talent, and a vague and friendly "rivalry" surfaced occasionally.[11] Both women enjoyed teasing one another, and their gardens—which they always had in common—were a constant source of friendly competition.

Wharton and Farrand each published a number of articles related to gardening. Wharton combined her interests in gardens and writing with a series of articles for *Century* magazine on "Italian Villas and Their Gardens" (later published as a book), but was dismayed when her *writing* came under attack by certain critics as "too dry and technical" (*A Backward Glance,* 138). Farrand's biographer speculates that Farrand stopped writing gardening articles after 1907 either because she found writing difficult or because she was wary of competing with her aunt. Farrand's early articles, "Le Nôtre and His Gardens" and "The Garden as Picture," appeared in *Scribner's* magazine in 1905 and 1907, respectively, but further articles of significance were not published until the late 1930s. Not a confident writer, Farrand still kept extensive journals. Like Wharton, she recognized a certain connection between gardening and writing. In "The Garden as Picture," she observed that gardening "is like composing in French alexandrines with their measured rhythm and subtle caesura."[12] In an extensive letter to Wharton, Farrand writes:

> Have you got any good petunias? We have some California seed of which we are quite proud. Salmon and lavender with a purple throat, a deep rose red with a black throat, and a white with a green throat, all singles, which seem to us good. Should you like any of

these seed? . . . But if the reins are not laid on the neck of my horticultural horse you would have a twenty page typewritten letter instead of what is already too long a one for your sufferance. (July
20, 1936)

Farrand, the hesitant writer, must have found her aunt a formidable correspondent at first. Yet the women's exchange tended
to merge, rather than delineate, their styles. If Wharton rambled
on for pages, Farrand sometimes borrowed her metaphors. But
Farrand seems unnecessarily worried about the length of her
letter, given that her aunt was prone to rambling pages of prose.
In fact, Farrand is well suited to her writing partner: Like Wharton, she is equally playful and generous and, as in the letter in
which she speaks of "reining in" her "horticultural horse," answers her aunt in a descriptively literary style.

Significantly, one of Farrand's early articles, "The Garden in
Relation to the House" (1897), anticipates Wharton's *Italian Villas and Their Gardens;* Farrand asserts that the "arts of architecture and landscape gardening are sisters, not antagonists."[13]
Like Farrand, Wharton believed that the garden should be designed "in relation to the house"[14] and that architecture and
landscape gardening should complement one another. In *Italian
Villas and Their Gardens*, Wharton takes up the garden as subject most explicitly, but she returns to it again and again in her
writing, using it as an extended metaphor for female creativity
and sexuality, as much as for setting.

Wharton frequently made this connection between gardening
and writing: If the woman author can write herself into existence, then the gardener, too, can construct an identity in the
laying out of her garden. In *A Backward Glance,* she reflects on
the mysteries of her own writing processes in a chapter tellingly
called "The Secret Garden":

> My impression is that, among English and American novelists, few
> are greatly interested in these deeper processes of their art. . . .
> Therefore I shall try to depict the growth and unfolding of the plants
> in my secret garden, from the seed to the shrub-top—for I have no
> intention of magnifying my vegetation into trees! (198)

In her chapter entitled "Little Girl," Wharton recalls her "secret sensitiveness to the landscape" (54), as well as the "secret
ecstasy of communion" (69) she experienced when reading literature: "I say 'secret', for I cannot remember ever speaking to
any one of these enraptured sessions" (69–70). From an early

age, Wharton sensed that she was intimately connected both to
the landscape and the written word, a relationship that she
chose to keep private:

> There was in me a secret retreat where I wished no one to intrude,
> or at least no one whom I had yet encountered. Words and cadences
> haunted it like song-birds in a magic wood, and I wanted to be able
> to steal away and listen when they called. . . . For the moment that
> was enough of ecstasy; but I wanted to be always free to steal away
> to it. (70)

The "sensitiveness," "ecstasy" (repeated twice), and "enraptured"
nature of the creative process links woman's creativity—as a
writer or a gardener—to her sexuality.[15] The garden's potential
as a space for sensual expression surfaces in Wharton's letters
to Farrand as well. In a letter of October 23, 1920, Wharton
yearns for Farrand's physical presence and expresses a desire
for a shared sensory and even sensual excess: "I want awfully to
see you after all these years, and I'm already garden-Talking with
you in the spirit. Oh what orgies we'll have on my 23 terraces!—"
(October 23, 1920). Of course, Wharton in no way proposes a
literal orgy for aunt and niece, but she most certainly situates
the garden as a place where such sexual freedom might be experienced.[16] The sculpted hedges, shaded paths, and inevitable *gi-
ardino segreto* (literally, the secret garden with high hedges,
flowers, benches, and statues) in Wharton's garden afford privacy. At once protected and exposed, the garden stands in opposition to the constraints of domestic space. There a woman can
be "dangerously feminine" and "sexually mobile": "Her sexuality
is no longer controlled by the house."[17]

Wharton felt comfortable sharing her garden-fantasies with
Farrand. Wharton's vision of Farrand in her new garden at St.
Brice, "roll[ing] in my new grass with laughter,"[18] recalls Charity
Royall in *Summer,* lying in the grass, letting the wind tickle
and seduce her. Although there is no evidence to suggest that
Wharton experienced sexual desire for Farrand, the erotic qual-
ity of her language is striking.[19] In another letter, Wharton
writes:

> Here, at present, the whole country is gushing with roses . . . which,
> after one outburst in Dec., and then a gentle steady flowering all
> winter, have now cast aside all restraint, and are smothering walls,
> house-fronts & balconies in white and crimson and golden breakers
> of bloom.—It is getting to be *agony* not to talk of all this . . . with

you face to face; & whatever Max decides for the future, I do hope you & he will dash away for a few weeks before 1920 is over & come & embrace . . . the chrysanthemums. (March 25, 1920; Wharton's italics)

Wharton "talks" to Farrand as though she were a lover, perhaps because she knows that Farrand was the self-proclaimed "product of five generations of garden lovers"[20] and would understand her "agony."

Tension in the letters comes from the combination of thwarted and indulged desire—thwarted in the sense of the women's separation; indulged by their playfully erotic "garden talks." One such example is Wharton's letter from the French Riviera:

While I was at Cannes I took myself . . . over to the Cap Ferrat . . . where the best gardens on the Riviera are known to be found in a little group . . . & I came back absolutely dazzled—I never saw anything in England even remotely approaching these as pure *flower-gardening.* Such colour—harmonies, & such sheets of radiant colour—. . . such Botticellian effects of narcissus, tulip & crocuses (all miraculously in bloom at once) took my breath away & made me feel ready to shake you for not being with me, you idiot! (March 16, 1922; Wharton's italics)

Evoking the enticing landscapes of Botticelli and perhaps his flower-bedecked goddess of *Primavera* as well, Wharton here captures the "dazzling" sensuality of "pure *flower-gardening.*"

The breathtaking highs that gardening produces in these women are sometimes accompanied by devastation. Wharton writes during a particularly bad winter:

As for me, I'm such in deeper and deeper depths of sloth & I wallow & gloat in it—shamelessly. Even gardening has ceased to occupy me actively, as the plants have all stopped growing, & my daily occupation of watching for bulb[s] . . . & peony shoots & unfolding rose-sprays has ceased. . . . Nature is as perverse as mankind since the war. (January 15, 1922)

After the war, Wharton's letters to Farrand lose their sensual overtones. They show her "need to restore both continuity and rootedness to her life. Toward that end . . . she took steps at once practical and imaginative. The practical measure was to establish herself in the first home of her possession since The Mount" (Lewis, 419). Once established at Pavillon Colombe, and then also at Ste. Claire, Wharton turned to her garden for stability and comfort. But the garden would sometimes fail her, and present her with "a blow . . . with which Trix [would] deeply sympathize."[21] Talk of the garden became more a means to talk of other, more dangerous things: old age and encroaching death.

In times of despair, Wharton knew that she could complain to Farrand who, better than anyone else, understood how the failures of a garden affected her. Near the end of 1922, she would tell her niece:

> I'm plunged in distress by the definite & unconcealable discovery that my poor Bérard, who grows stone walls like chick-weed, kills flowers much more successfully & effectually than he does their enemies, such as caterpillars & green fly. He has managed to blast my garden from garret to cellar this year—but luckily his antagonism doesn't include shrubs or creepers, or sea & sky & sunshine—so there's a good deal left. However, I've got the hard task of gardener-hunting ahead of me, & with all my "littery" waiting & champing to be done, it's rather a bore—Next year I hope you'll see successful results. (Ste. Claire, December 12, 1922)

She had recently finished *The Glimpses of the Moon* and *A Son at the Front* and was overseeing the vastly different gardens at Ste. Claire and St. Brice. Like her aunt, Farrand managed two distinct garden properties, each with its unique dilemmas. She writes to Wharton:

> Just as your two Saints, Brice and Claire, vary so do our two places, California and Reef Point. Winter annuals, acacias, iris, oranges, South African bulbs all thrive & enjoy themselves in California. Here [Reef Point, Maine] sturdy perennials, a few delphiniums, all the heaths . . . blueberry, mayflower, lily of the valley, and five foot osmunda ferns thrive. The two problems are so totally unlike that it does not seem as though both of them could be equally horticultural. (July 20, 1936)

The exchange of problems, along with thoughts on gardening and suggestions for improvement, characterizes much of the correspondence between Farrand and Wharton. In this way, the letters might be read as a distinct aspect of Wharton and Farrand's creative, *collaborative* practice.

A spirit of generosity characterizes the letters to Farrand written in the later years of Wharton's life. In a letter dated February 7, 1931, Ste. Claire, Wharton writes:

> [Your letter] arrived in hand with the wonderful irises. I am overcome by this magnificent gift. . . . Since you wish to have a share in

the flowering of Sainte-Claire, I gladly accept a third of the price. . . .
I have just been out with the gardener placing the treasures in our
very best soil, and can hardly wait to see them in bloom. . . . It is
delightful to think that my enjoyment of them will be associated
with you.

Wharton eagerly accepts Farrand's gift and immediately plants
Farrand's irises, as though in their blooming a part of Farrand
will come to life. Farrand, in a letter from Reef Point dated
October 24, 1936, says:

Our little Madeiran gardener in Calif. writes me excitedly that some
new South African bulbs are already up & abloom and as he does
not specify what they are, I am twittering to set out to see them. If
the Lachenalias bloom out of doors in California, I shall twit you
with them and ask you if you want any, as we have an enterprising
bulb farmer who is trying a good many of the Africanders. Do you,
for instance, have the Gladiolus Tristes hybrids and the vari-colored
sparaxis hybrids? These are quite splendid with us and should I
think do well with you provided you can bake them in the summer.

Farrand's horticultural learnedness is evident in her writing,
but so again is her playfulness. The excitement of both gardeners is contagious. They send bulbs back and forth, offer ad-
vice and consolation, and most significantly, recognize each
other's presence in their own gardens. Here are those "garden
talks" Wharton longed for, an extended collaboration which allowed them to share in the artistry of each other's gardens.
    The ultimate manifestation of Wharton and Farrand's exqui-
site collaboration may well be the impact the correspondence
had on Wharton's fiction. The letters may perhaps have influenced Wharton's fictional portraits of gardeners. Though Wharton's female characters are rarely writers, they are, on occasion,
gardeners. There is Justine Brent, the amateur botanist; Anna
Leath, whose "flower baskets and gardening implements" (*The
Reef*, 147) suggest that she has had a hand in maintaining the
large landscaped park of Givré; and Halo Tarrant, whose artistry
is reflected in the gardens that she creates and rehabilitates in
The Gods Arrive. Wharton's fictional female gardeners, in the
spirit of Beatrix Farrand, maintain a commitment to the principles of design and a love of the garden.
    Shortly before her death, Edith Wharton remarked: "I like to
love, but not to [be] loved back, that is why I like so much
gardens [*sic*]."[22] Though other "loves" in Wharton's life may not

have loved back, Farrand clearly did. At Wharton's death in 1937, Farrand mourned, "We have lost an incomparable friend. We shall find it an empty, queer world without her, and already one feels the void where one could ever before rely on her wisdom, keenness, appreciation, and justice."[23] The letters of Edith Wharton and Beatrix Farrand reveal a loving, reciprocal relationship that flourished like their gardens. What these letters say, on a very basic level, is that these women shared a remarkable friendship. There is a playfulness, a rivalry, a desire to share and be involved with each other's lives and work, but since distance made meetings infrequent, then a desire to write. These letters cut through any pretense of reserve and reveal a passionate intensity as well as a deep intimacy. When Wharton writes that she wants "to wallow in flowers . . . all the year round,"[24] she tacitly invites Farrand to share in a conversation that explores what it means to be a woman, an artist, a friend.

Notes

The correspondence of Edith Wharton and Beatrix Farrand is reprinted by permission of the Yale Collection of American Literature, Beinecke Rare Book and Manuscript Library, Yale University, and the Estate of Edith Wharton and the Watkins/Loomis Agency.

1. Susan Goodman, *Edith Wharton's Women: Friends and Rivals* (Hanover, N.H.: University Press of New England, 1990), 4.

2. Deborah Williams pointed out to me the suggestive phrase, "exquisite collaborations," which Wharton first used in an August 26, 1908 letter to W. Morton Fullerton in reference to what she had hoped their relationship might have been.

3. Letter quoted in Alan Gribben, "'The Heart Is Insatiable': A Selection from Edith Wharton's Letters to Morton Fullerton, 1907–1915," *Library Chronicle of the University of Texas at Austin* n.s. 31 (1985): 31.

4. Jane Brown, *Beatrix: The Gardening Life of Beatrix Jones Farrand, 1872–1956* (New York: Viking, 1995), 79. Subsequent references will appear directly in the text.

5. R. W. B. Lewis, and Nancy Lewis, eds., *The Letters of Edith Wharton* (New York: Scribner's, 1988), 242. Subsequent references will appear directly in the text with the designation *Letters*.

6. Letter quoted in Louis Auchincloss, *Edith Wharton: A Woman in Her Time* (New York: Viking, 1971), 165–67.

7. Edith Wharton, *A Backward Glance* (New York: Appleton, 1934), 69. Subsequent references will appear directly in the text.

8. Diane Kostial McGuire, "Beatrix Farrand's Contribution to the Art of Landscape Architecture," *Beatrix Jones Farrand: Fifty Years of American Landscape Architecture, edited by McGuire Fern and Lois Fern* (Washington, D.C.: Dumbarton Oaks, 1982), 31.

9. Quoted in Diana Balmori, "Beatrix Farrand at Dumbarton Oaks: The Design Process of a Garden," *Beatrix Jones Farrand: Fifty Years of American Landscape Architecture,* ed. McGuire Fern and Lois Fern (Washington, D.C.: Dumbarton Oaks, 1982), 109. Subsequent references will appear directly in the text.

10. Wharton, too, was alive to scale, geometry, and landscape setting—not only in her gardening but in her fiction as well. *The Reef* in particular attests to this. Henry James, of course, praised it for its "Racinian" unity (*Henry James Letters,* vol. 4, ed. Leon Edel [Cambridge: Harvard University Press, 1984], 644). *The Reef*'s tightly drawn relationships and its deliberate shifts between interiors and exteriors reflect Wharton's attention to geometry; in fact, she plays with geometry, replacing the familiar love "triangle" with a decided "square." Each corner is occupied by one of the four primary figures in the novel: Anna Leath, George Darrow, Sophy Viner, and Owen Leath. Furthermore, the title of the novel itself, *The Reef,* calls to mind the Reef Point gardens in which Farrand cultivated her skills as a landscape gardener.

11. See Goodman's discussion of "ambivalence" in Wharton's relationships with women in *Edith Wharton's Women* (31–32).

12. Beatrix Farrand, "The Garden as Picture," *Scribner's* 43 (1907): 7–8.

13. Beatrix Farrand, "The Garden in Relation to the House," *Garden and Forest* (April 7, 1897): 133.

14. Edith Wharton, *Italian Villas and Their Gardens* (1904; New York: De Capo, 1988), 6.

15. Eleanor Dwight has noted a connection between sexuality and gardens, particularly in relation to the Beatrice Palmato fragment (*Edith Wharton: An Extraordinary Life* [New York: Abrams, 1994], 258).

16. The gardens in *The Reef* most explicitly evoke the sexuality so often reflected in the letters of Wharton to Farrand. Wharton describes the court beyond the Givré as "very still, yet full of a latent life," and moments later remarks that "Just such a latent animation glowed in Anna Leath" (Edith Wharton, *The Reef* [1912; New York: Scribner's, 1965], 85). The design of the landscape is also suggestive: "Beyond a gate in the courtyard wall the flower-garden drew its dark-green squares and raised its statues against the yellowing background of the park. In the borders only a few late pinks and crimsons smouldered" (86). In this carefully planned landscape, with its neat squares, its "escutcheoned piers," its "level avenue of grass," and its "rectangular yews," something smoulders (83, 85). That such a well-ordered garden might have smouldering borders suggests that such a well-ordered life, like that of Anna Leath, might have room for more burning emotions than one would suspect. Subsequent references will appear directly in the text.

17. Mark Wigley, "Untitled: The Housing of Gender," *Sexuality and Space,* ed. Beatriz Colomina (New York: Princeton Architectural Press, 1992), 335.

18. Letter to Farrand, June 30, 1919.

19. R. W. B. Lewis has noted that Wharton "entered a new mood of sensuality" in her seventies: "[O]ne sign of it was the way her opinion of contemporary writing was sometimes guided by the degree and kind of sexuality in it. She looked upon ... Colette as ... a woman who could communicate directly to her about the infinitely subtle nature of female passion" (Lewis, *Edith Wharton* [1975; New York: Fromm, 1985], 520). Subsequent references will appear in the text with the designation Lewis.

20. Beatrix Farrand says this about herself in the posthumously published autobiographical note "Beatrix Farrand, 1872–1959," *Reef Point Gardens Bulletin* 1 no. 17 (n.d.).

21. Letter from Wharton to Minnie Cadwalader Jones, December 26, 1920 (*Letters,* 436).

22. Quoted from "Les Derniers Mots," quoted in Gloria Erlich, *The Sexual Education of Edith Wharton* (Berkeley: University of California Press, 1992), 118.

23. Letter from Beatrix Farrand to Gaillard Lapsley, August 18, 1937.

24. Letter from Wharton to Farrand, November 19, 1919.

The Writer's Wardrobe:
Wharton Cross-Dressed

DENISE WITZIG

> ... every text is esoteric, not because it hides a secret but
> because it constitutes the secret, that which has yet to be
> revealed is never exhaustively revealable.... *Who are you?*
> is probably the most relevant question to ask of a text, as
> long as one isn't requesting a kind of identity card or an
> autobiographical anecdote.
> —Luce Irigaray, *Sexes and Genealogies*

WHETHER FRAMED AS BIOGRAPHY, POSTCOLONIAL STUDIES, PSYCHO-
analysis, or queer theory, identity politics figures dramatically
in textual practice and interpretation, placing the body and its
representation in culture at the center of critical discourse. Textual identification is reader identification, engaging the desire
for narrative authentification, for language as lived experience.
Certainly, the centrality of the body and of identity-in-language
is at the heart of feminist criticism and its aims and has long
been so. The material effects of identity politics, the convergence
of the culturally inscribed female body and historical gender
upon language, are the basis for feminist literary criticism.
Thus, a writer's sexuality, her femininity, and her grounding in
culture as female can be seen to constitute her identity within
literature as a historical subject and a producer of literary texts.
Feminist criticism has allowed generations of readers and critics
to engage texts written by women in new and startling ways,
contextualizing a place for the woman writer within language
and literary history marked by difference as well as specificity.

But to some extent, current feminist literary criticism persists
in a nostalgic, and even conservative, gesture toward institutionalizing the feminine by conflating real life—the lived life of a
particular body, the author's—and textual production. This
methodology posits the woman author as a biographical detail
of writing, knowable because "readable," through the mimetic

correspondence of life to text(s). Some of this interpretive strategy naturally arises from the problematics of theorizing gender
within the constructs of historical experience. As Judith Butler
observes of feminist practice itself,

> ... the identity categories often presumed to be foundational to
> feminist politics, that is, deemed necessary in order to mobilize
> feminism as an identity politics, simultaneously work to limit and
> constrain in advance the very cultural possibilities that feminism is
> supposed to open up.[1]

In textual considerations, the feminine body or subject natural-
ized as an interpretive strategy restricts identity to an organizing
principle which becomes the sum of experience. Within literary
criticism, the woman who writes runs the risk herself of being
rewritten as the text of the "womanwriter," a character in her
own narrative.

The kind of totalizing gesture that privileges sexual biography,
a particular kind of body politics, over any other interpretation
can be seen in recent critical attention to Edith Wharton. Clearly,
interest in Wharton scholarship has reached a new peak, particularly with current mass culture marketing, in film and publishing, of several of her many novels. (For some time now, a
reader has been able to buy *The Age of Innocence,* with a writh-
ing Michelle Pfeiffer on the cover, in line at the local Safeway.)
Although the feminist literary critic may rejoice at the long-
overdue popular attention to this writer, she may also speculate
on the role gender plays in the criticism. For, in addressing the
culturally and socially coded determinants of Wharton's work,
critics in both popular and academic venues have also emphasized sexuality, *her* sexuality, as the primary motivation or location of her narrative choices. Frequently, Wharton's plots and
characters are seen as workings-through of problematic filial
or sexual relationships, oedipalized narratives of anxiety and
transference. Through this kind of psychoanalytic reading, a familiar Freudian Masterplot,[2] the critics say we may locate the
nature of Edith Wharton's particular authorial anxiety and the
authentic author herself.

Although such speculations or revelations are of particular
interest to the feminist critic eager to deconstruct femininity as
a cultural discourse (that is, to situate the female body within
critical practice), they fail to take into account the systematizing
nature of critical interpretation in general, and the totalizing

effect of sexual biography, particularly for the woman who writes. By fashioning itself as a kind of literary pattern-making, criticism frequently configures the sexual body of the writer as an authentic text whose nudity is covered by a thin narrative tissue. Reading performs the stripping away of false selves (or characters), leading us to the true and essential writer and to the nature of writing itself. Sexuality, then, rather than operating at a level of narrative discourse, becomes the meaning and point of reference, the end of all narrative, the true story of the text.[3]

If the woman writer's story is always a story about being a woman, occupying a woman's body, then every character and every plot is a working-through of personal integration. The female text becomes restricted to psychodrama, contextualizing the anxieties and fears of the author, writing its own kind of "talking cure." Both writing and reading are then performed as a circular therapeutic exercise, the goal of which is to deliver the author back to herself (and inevitably to us). As Mary Jacobus observes, "The assumption [of this interpretation] is of an unbroken continuity between 'life' and 'text'—a mimetic relation whereby women's writing, reading, or culture, instead of being produced, reflect a knowable reality."[4]

Clearly, the writer cannot and should not be divorced from the woman. Understanding the nature of female experience biographically and historically, as body or class, allows the reader to understand the cultural inscription of gender on language and narrative. But the danger in assigning the writer's life to her text is in fixing the writing to a kind of literary symptomology, reducing every text to episode or anecdote—Irigaray's "identity card"—nostalgically privileging an authentic or originary "female identity" over literature or language. Although this critical practice is surely intended to provide a feminist and sympathetic reading of Wharton, it succeeds mainly in fixing her as *womanwriter*: textual hysteric.[5]

My question concerns how the feminist critic can propose a theory of language and of gender which takes account of the body (thus, sexuality) and the writer's life without institutionalizing the writer within those determinants; I see that possibility in the play of textual language itself. If feminist criticism is to be read as the story of women or a woman writing, then textuality—the ways in which writing and reading engage and perform female subjectivity—must be interrogated. I read in Edith Wharton's work, particularly in her short stories, an interrogation of the limits and possibilities of language and narrativity and a performance of gender and feminine subjectivity beyond signature or biography. Wharton's narrative language calls into question the writing/reading exchange in the production of meaning and of female identity in many of her stories, and it does so dramatically, consistently offering alternative possibilities for interpretation.

In her suggestive essay on Wharton, Amy Kaplan traces the writer's "different route toward professionalism, one which does not treat the writing process as a dyadic one—primarily between the author's self and the object she creates—but instead emphasizes the mediating social context in which art is produced."[6] Kaplan sees Wharton as a social reconstructionist firmly rooted in nineteenth-century realism, exploring the profession of authorship through the medium of the literary marketplace. As she creates an identity in that sphere, argues Kaplan, Wharton evades the historical paradigm of the woman writer in its domestic trappings and subtly disrupts the boundaries marking masculine and feminine, public and private.[7]

I would add to this reading the contention that Wharton's writing works to deconstruct or dismantle realist models of sociohistorical identity through language itself. In this way Wharton constructs the category of gender as an interrogation of genre, creating a specifically literary discourse which engages and subverts the realist commodification of identity as the product of writing. In particular, she explores the "exchange value" of literary production (between writer and critic as well as writer and reader), and its part in collapsing personal and social identity boundaries, through the epistolary motif, which acts as an alter-text or commentary on narrativity and the writing process. The impact of Wharton's strategy is both literary and theoretical, allowing these narratives to slip out of mainstream realism and mimetic textuality into a premodernist engagement of the limits and possibilities of language itself. Wharton uses the letter as synecdoche, metaphor, metonym—a detail that disrupts and alters the narrative line in her stories. The effect is to challenge the realist text, its meaning and discursive value to the reader. In Wharton's stories, the letter engages a matrix of dialogues about genre, the reading practice, the feminine, as identity, gender itself, and language. It provokes a debate about writing.[8]

Throughout her narratives, Wharton's letters work to disperse image and identity, unsettling realist interpretation, at once dramatizing and cloaking the writing act as a kind of performance or masquerade, an inverse striptease.[9] This is not to say the letter may not unveil or strip away identity to reveal another narrative meaning; it may. Frequently, however, it serves to cover up or disguise the text and the narrative in an engagement of possibilities—multiple meanings, identities, desires—diffuse and unassimilated bodies of evidence.

Wharton's subversion of identity can be found in a number of her short stories and novellas; certainly the epistolary motif has been discussed at length in regard to her own published letters which reveal a speculative, lifelong correspondence between the profession of authoring and the author herself.[10] The letter assumes a major role in stories such as "Mr. Jones," "The Letters," "Pomegranate Seed," and "The Muse's Tragedy," among others. This essay takes a look at "His Father's Son," a lesser known and early story, one that particularly dramatizes writing and the character of the writer. In "Son," the discursive position of "writer" is a literary guise or masquerade that plays with the *idea* of interpretation, ultimately claiming it and its inherent value as a product of the reading exchange. The story involves the performance of narrative masquerade as a way in which to evade textual meaning, and identification, resisting appropriation as commodity in the literary marketplace. Here, as elsewhere in her stories,[11] Wharton interrogates gender as a fixing of signature or identity, forcing a series of readers—both internal and external to the narrative—to confront a more subversive meaning to the text at hand and to their own participation in it.

"His Father's Son," first published in 1909, and included a year later in *Tales of Men and Ghosts,* is the story of business tycoon Mason Grew and his aesthete, upwardly mobile son, Ronald. The elder Grew is a character seemingly rooted in generic and historic realism: Plain-talking and crude, he represents the triumph of entrepreneurial and industrial technology through his invention and manufacturing of the "Secure Suspender Buckle." He's made his fortune keeping men's pants up. Young Grew, the beneficiary of his father's ambition, has received a cultural education which has enabled him to move out of his class into social circles beyond his father's purview. More refined than the rough Mason, Ronald has "grown" into a comfortable and secure middle-class milieu of operas, parties, and good family names.[12] For all critical purposes, father and son are the only two characters in the story, and the narrative serves as a history of their relationship. As in the much later "Roman Fever," the dialogue between these two central figures consummates the narrative moment and delivers a revelation to the reader.

Young Grew has come into possession of his deceased mother's letters, letters that dramatically reveal a passionate, sexually charged, intellectually engaged relationship with famed European pianist Fortune Dolbrowski. Reading between the lines of this correspondence, Ronald Grew deduces he is not "his father's son," but rather the product of this literarily documented desire. This reading makes sense; certainly it authenticates his own aesthetic impulses and sensibilities, poetic demeanor, and general dissimilarity from the elder Grew. It authorizes his own reading of himself, and his reading of Grew, creating a correspondence between the two. "I always thought you gave me the letters," says the son, "as a way of telling me—."[13] This unfinished admission is a common Wharton device, alluding to a subliminal or submerged textual reading or understanding that the internal reader has apprehended. On a critical level, it is also a reading that exchanges one law of patriarchal identity, the name of the father, for another, seminality.

The truth of the letters, however, is more subversive than this apparently legitimate reading, and here Wharton surely alludes to and parodies the convention of epistolarity as a feminized discourse of romantic excess. For the father counters the son's claim to authentic or "real" identity with his own unmasking: *He* is the true participant in the correspondence with Dolbrowski; *he* is the writer who provoked and sustained this passionate engagement, performing and documenting his desire on paper. The exchange is enabled, indeed authenticated, by Grew's use of his wife's signature, a ruse that ensures the letter-text's safety within the boundaries of heterosexuality, but that also masks a pervasive and disruptive homotextuality, a desire in language that cannot be contained. (It's a love that dare not speak its [own] name.)[14] On one level, this reading reveals another, more aesthetic and romantic, facet of Mason Grew's identity, one comically at odds with his crass businessman role and class. Simultaneously, it relocates Ronald Grew's paternity within the letter-exchange itself. "I'll tell you where the best of those letters is— it's in *you*," says the father to the son.[15] A product of textuality, of his father's aesthetic impulses and identifications, infused with sexual energy, Ronald's very being is at the matrix of desire and language. He literally "grew" from words.

This story performs many familiar themes seen in Wharton's later narratives, particularly those of class hierarchies and their legitimacies. In this vein, both Cynthia Griffin Wolff and Gloria Erlich find biographical significance in the story's central question of the nature of paternity as social identity, critically privileging the oedipal plot.[16] But, once again, this narrative works to diffuse identity rather than locate it squarely in mimetic representation and biography. Instead, Wharton veils subjectivity through her language and through her dismantling of the regulatory categories of gender and genre. As noted above, the oedipal exchange that is the machine of plot engages a provocative homotexuality which poses more interpretive questions than it answers. In Shari Benstock's reading, the epistolary works on one level as an economy which masks homoeroticism, fetishizing both the letter and the woman (as the letter substitutes for sex, the object of desire, the body of the lover).[17] Through letters (which activate or mimic an "artificially invaginated" text), the two Grews and, by implication, Dolbrowski, engage in a patriarchal circuit which exchanges desire and meaning, seemingly erasing the feminine (or a feminine body) from the circuit altogether. Inevitably, the feminine seems relegated to signature only, a corollary to the disruption of textual authenticity. Just as the letters give Grew and Dolbrowski to each other, they give father and son to themselves in oedipal reproduction, the story's title prefiguring the revelation as it emphasizes product, resemblance, identity.[18] Playing with this notion of identity (its loss or absence and reification), the characters "find" it and each other in a literary performance of the relationship between castration and fetish, a resolution determined between (father's) text and (mother's) signature.[19] Furthermore, on a narrative level, resolution ostensibly reasserts the phallocentric claims of signature, authority, and the name of the father. "[Y]ou're your father's son, every inch of you!" says Grew to Grew.[20]

This is not to say, however, that the feminine is elided from plot. The "Name of the Father," argues Naomi Schor, "obscure[s] a fact whose significance is only beginning to be measured: the writer is someone who plays not only with mother's body, as Barthes has written, . . . but also with her name."[21] Mrs. Grew's name activates and authenticates the epistolary exchange in the narrative, as it provides a necessary cover or disguise for Mason's writing excess—his desire or "imagination," as Wharton calls it. "Large and literal," Addie Grew is characterized by her husband as dull and inexpressive, "placid," "unperceiving," "obtuse." She is "waked into a momentary semblance of life" by the performance of Dolbrowski, an event the couple has found "transfiguring."[22] Indeed, as this moment precipitates the letters, it produces "the miracle of Ronald," "a changeling" whose mystery derives from the "dull endearments" and "conjugal indifference" of his parents.[23] For Mason Grew, the transfiguring event, shared with his wife, of Dolbrowski's performance represents "the only exquisite hour of his life save that of Ronald's birth."[24] It also represents recognition and shared knowledge between husband and wife, for it is with Addie's full consent that Mason uses her name. Clearly, the act of marital consummation is literally determined by and resonant of an inchoate desire, finally articulated, which transforms the participants and produces a miracle text and a miracle child. It is no wonder, then, that Ronald misreads mother, father, and himself; like the letters, he is the issue physically marked by pseudonym and masquerade.

But if we return to Wharton's language about the relationship between Mr. and Mrs. Grew, we can see that Ronald is not the only poor reader.[25] Although Mason is "Old Buckles" to his son, trapped in the "disguise in which he walked,"[26] Addie is, as noted above, placid and unperceiving to her husband. In a dialogue early in the story, an exchange remembered by Grew, which prefigures the later, revelatory exchange with his son, the large and literal Mrs. Grew remarks upon the dissimilarity between father and son:

> "[T]he way you took hold was in business. . . ."
> Mr. Grew's chest collapsed, and he became suddenly conscious of his comic face in its rim of sandy whisker. "That's not the only way," he said, with a touch of wistfulness which escaped his wife's analysis.
> "Well, of course you could have written beautifully," she rejoined with admiring eyes.
> "*Written?* Me!" Mr. Grew became sardonic.
> "Why, those letters—weren't *they* beautiful, I'd like to know?"
> The couple exchanged a glance, innocently allusive and amused on the wife's part, and charged with a sudden tragic significance on the husband's.[27]

It is no small point that it is Addie who first names Mason as a writer, before he even names himself. Although her recognition of this identity is amused, while his is tragic, Mrs. Grew clearly is the instrument through which Mr. Grew finally realizes the possibilities of his nature. After all, the disguised text is produced under her name and by her consent. It is also produced under her pen. "Your mother always copied the letters and signed them," reveals the father to the son.[28] Ironically, Mrs. Grew's complex part in the masquerade, including her reading of it, isn't fully recognized by Grew; but it is through her name and her body that Grew is delivered: to his desire, to language, to his son, to his true name. If the writer plays with the mother's body and her name, the progeny of this performance is inevitably the writer. Can the Name of the Mother be erased in the process?

Although paternity and product are clearly recuperated in Wharton's story, it is gender itself that energizes and transfigures textual production, reproducing and dispersing meaning on multiple levels of reading. Mason Grew throws on the costume, the masquerade, of femininity to call into play his own desire as well as the institution of gender in language and sexuality (mediated through the configurations of class). In her landmark essay, "Womanliness as a Masquerade," Joan Riviere asserts that "Womanliness [or cultural femininity] . . . could be assumed and worn as a mask . . . used as a device for avoiding anxiety" by women seeking power in male-identified occupations.[29] In the feminized textual economy of the epistolary, Mason Grew disguises his motives in a woman's name which serves to represent a woman's *body:*

> "But why write in my mother's name? Why make it appear like a sentimental correspondence?"
> Mr. Grew reddened to his bald temples. ". . . when I saw that the first letter pleased and interested him, I was afraid to tell him— *I couldn't* tell him. Do you suppose he'd [have] gone on writing if he'd ever seen me, Ronny?"[30]

Literary transvestism is its own transfiguration.

Mason Grew's letters mark out the middle ground of sexual mobility, the boundary between liberation and constraint. This textual cross-dressing is a performance authenticated by signature, ultimately revealed to be a writing act, a ruse, a pose, a mask. If, as Judith Butler says, "drag fully subverts the distinction between inner and outer psychic space,"[31] then Grew's letter-writing dramatically performs the instability or mutability of identity as it engages both the fantasies of self-evasion and self-recognition, just as it sublimates and transforms social and sexual authority. The letters configure identity as a ritualized posture which straddles the line between public and fantasy personae, and they reveal the machine of genre as it produces multiple images and multiple readings. The literary drag-performance of the letter in "His Father's Son" doesn't so much mock the law of gender or genre, as Butler might assert, as it dramatizes these categories and subverts them, allowing the reader to see writing as mimicry and play. In this, the *Author* is also most certainly a fiction.

In "His Father's Son" Wharton engages in a satiric and ironic play with language and with sexuality which confounds the reader's expectations of realistic correspondence by turning the oedipal plot, and its claims of identity, on its head. The act of writing and the persona of the writer are dramatically displayed and foregrounded, but instead of the "real" or authentic Author, we are met with the costumes and devices of performance and identity production and proliferation. In this way, gender and sexuality, like narrative meaning, are part of the writer's discursive wardrobe. We can see this story, and others, as "cross-dressed texts," more about the dispersion and instability of subjectivity than the fixing of identity. In "From Work to Text," Roland Barthes says, "The word 'bio-graphy' re-acquires a strong, etymological sense, at the same time as the sincerity of the enunciation—[a] veritable 'cross' borne by literary morality—becomes a false problem: the *I* which writes the text, it, too, is never more than a paper-*I.* "[32] Clearly, many of Wharton's stories are bio-graphies, but they cross the reader at every turn. For, across the lines of life and art lies the veil of language. Writing is masquerade, Edith Wharton seems to say, although the critic may never stop searching for the body—the author, the meaning—enfolded within the textual drapes.[33]

Notes

1. Judith Butler, *Gender Trouble: Feminism and the Subversion of Identity* (New York: Routledge, 1990), 147.

2. See Peter Brooks, "Freud's Masterplot," *Literature and Psychoanalysis: The Question of Reading: Otherwise,* ed. Shoshana Felman (Baltimore: Johns Hopkins University Press, 1982): 280–300. "Narrative must ever present itself," say Brooks, "as repetition of events that have already happened" (281).

3. For discussion of the contradictions of psychobiographical criticism, see Rosalind Coward's "Are Women's Novels Feminist Novels?" (*The New Feminist Criticism: Essays on Women, Literature, and Theory,* ed. Elaine Showalter [New York: Pantheon, 1985]: 225–39).

4. Mary Jacobus, "Is There a Woman in This Text?" *Reading Woman: Essays in Feminist Criticism* (New York: Columbia University Press, 1986), 108.

5. I am particularly in mind of Cynthia Griffin Wolff's well-known critical diagnosis of Wharton's sexual/authorial anxiety in *A Feast of Words: The Triumph of Edith Wharton* (Oxford: Oxford University Press, 1977), as well as more recent sexual-biographical interpretations represented by Sandra Gilbert and Susan Gubar's *No Man's Land: The Place of the Woman Writer in the*

Twentieth Century, 2 vols. (New Haven: Yale University Press, 1988 and 1989); Gloria Erlich's *The Sexual Education of Edith Wharton* (Berkeley: University of California Press, 1992); and Barbara White's *Edith Wharton: A Study of the Short Fiction*, Twayne's Studies in Short Fiction 30 (Boston: Twayne, 1991). All these works rely heavily on biographical psychoanalysis as literary interpretation.

6. Amy Kaplan, *The Social Construction of American Realism* (Chicago: University of Chicago Press, 1988), 66–67.

7. Ibid., 67.

8. For discussion of epistolarity as a particularly feminized genre, see Shari Benstock, *Textualizing the Feminine—On the Limits of Genre* (Norman, Oklahoma: University of Oklahoma Press, 1991); and Linda S. Kauffman, *Special Delivery: Epistolary Modes in Modern Fiction* (Chicago: University of Chicago Press, 1988).

9. In this, I am in mind of Naomi Schor's conception of literary interpretation as a striptease, an "erotics of hermeneutics," or text-pleasure. See *Reading in Detail: Aesthetics and the Feminine* (New York: Methuen, 1987), 130. I would suggest that narrativity itself traditionally is read by critics as a kind of striptease performed by the author to reveal, in a way that is both pleasurable and empowering, the "self" behind the writing. In my reading, Wharton clearly plays with these critical expectations and uses them to engage a more complex textual relationship.

10. See R. W. B. Lewis and Nancy Lewis, eds., *The Letters of Edith Wharton* (New York: Collier, 1988). For an illuminating discussion of Wharton's use of letters in her fiction, see Candace Waid's *Edith Wharton's Letters from the Underworld: Fictions of Women and Writing* (Chapel Hill: University of North Carolina Press, 1991); and the collection of essays edited by Annette Zilversmit, "Reading the Letters of Edith Wharton," *Women's Studies* 20 no. 2 (1991).

11. See my essays, "'The Muse's Tragedy' and the Muse's Text: Language and Desire in Wharton," *Edith Wharton: New Critical Essays,* ed. Alfred Bendixen and Annette Zilversmit (New York: Garland, 1992); 261–70; and "Letter(s) from an Unknown Woman: Edith Wharton's Correspondence with Authority," *Women's Studies* 20 no. 2 (1991): 169–76, for a fuller discussion of this critical reading.

12. As is frequently the case with Wharton's characters, names add dimension and significance to their narrative positions and functions. While Mason Grew literally "grows" himself out of his hard work and ambition, he will always retain an affiliation with the labor class, the bricklayer of his own fortune, resigned to his "brick house with its sandstone trimmings" (36). Ronald, however, as befits his more refined given name, grows out of and beyond his father's aspirations: ". . . from the start he *was* what Mr. Grew had dreamed of being" (39). The pianist, Fortune Dolbrowski, whose signature comes to represent new possibilities for identity and self-recognition for both father and son, bears a surname that is European, foreign, exotic. And "Fortune" signifies everything from wealth to luck to destiny. Inevitably, he is the Grews' "good fortune."

13. Edith Wharton, "His Father's Son," *The Collected Short Stories of Edith Wharton,* vol. 2, ed. R. W. B. Lewis (New York: Scribners, 1968), 45.

14. Certainly, Lewis Danyers's interest in Mary Anerton in "The Muse's Tragedy" belies a similar homotextual correspondence, or desire for correspondence, on the part of the critic for the poet, Rendle, through the translative

figure of Sylvia. This is another kind of economy at play in the literary market-place, one theorized as the locus of "sociocultural order" in Luce Irigaray's essay, "Commodities among Themselves," *This Sex Which Is Not One,* trans. Catherine Porter (Ithaca: Cornell University Press, 1985), 192–97.

15. Wharton, "Father's Son," 49.

16. In *A Feast of Words,* Wolff says, "'His Father's Son' is a gentle story in which many variations of real and shadow self are blended together with the reassuring harmony of a resonant chord" (155). But a later note presents a reading which is more biographically directed: "For many years a rumor had intermittently circulated that Edith Wharton was not Frederic Jones's daughter, but the product of a liaison between Lucretia and the tutor of Wharton's two older brothers. . . . Edith Wharton thought the whole thing a silly joke. . . . However, 'His Father's Son' may be her most direct statement on the matter; who could doubt her heritage—she was so unmistakably her father's daughter, just exactly in the way that Mr. Grew's son is unmistakably his father's son" (426). For her part, Erlich observes that "Wharton never quite relinquished the notion that artistic gifts are inherited from the paternal side. If her father's poetic leanings were minor, perhaps he was not the father of her talent" (141). Both critics infuse Wharton's story, and many other of her narratives, with a strong oedipal fixation which to them consistently motivates characterization.

17. Wharton's attitude toward homosexuality is difficult to determine, although she clearly characterizes it as subversive in stories such as "The Eyes" and "A Bottle of Perrier." But late nineteenth- and early-twentieth-century texts display a variety of scientific and literary discourses about the mutability of sexuality and eroticism, with particular interest in homosexuality. As Chris Craft observes, "the preferred taxonomic label under which these writers [Tennyson and Whitman, among others] categorized and examined such sexual desire was not, as we might anticipate, 'homosexuality' but rather 'sexual inversion,' a classificatory term involving a complex negotiation between socially encoded gender norms and sexual mobility that would seem at first unconstrained by those norms" (220). "Significantly, this displaced repetition of heterosexual gender norms contains within it the undeveloped germ of a radical redefinition of Victorian conventions of feminine desire. The interposition of a feminine soul between erotically associated males inevitably entails a certain feminization of desire since the very site and source of desire for males is assumed to be feminine" (223). Wharton seems to be exploring this kind of "sexual inversion" in her story, based on Romantic concepts of soul or imagination-excess. In "Son," the homosexuality is *homotextual*—aesthetic, literary, discursive.

18. See Susan Winnett's critique of Peter Brooks's Oedipal Masterplot in "Coming Unstrung: Women, Men, Narrative, and Principles of Pleasure," *PMLA* 105 no. 3 (1990): 505–18.

19. "Only those who have it can play with not having it," says Nancy Miller in "The Text's Heroine: A Feminist Critic and Her Fictions," *Conflicts in Feminism,* ed. Marianne Hirsch and Evelyn Fox Keller (New York: Routledge, 1990), 118.

20. Wharton, "Father's Son," 46. The circuitry of the letter dramatizes a doubling and redoubling of several mirrored pairs of characters—Father/Son, Mason/Dolbrowski, Ronald/Dolbrowski—as well as their imagined counterparts—outer Mason/inner Mason, inner Mason/ Ronald, inner Mason/ Dolbrowski, Ronald (son of Mason)/ Ronald (son of Dolbrowski). The split that

occurs between Addie's signature and her body or desire can also be configured as double. Although the letter-text clearly reflects doubling in the exchange of writing and reading, it also refracts the doubling effect into myriad identities or selves. This fracturing parallels Mason's double image of himself, and his identification with his son: "Ronald's resemblance to Mr. Grew's early conception of what he himself would have liked to look might have put new life into the discredited theories of prenatal influence . . . from the start he was what Mr. Grew had dreamed of being . . . the real Ronald had the same cosmic vision as his parent" (38–39). This emphasis on vision as both literal (physical) and metaphorical (intellectual) configures a mirror relationship between father and son, recalling the Romantic split between self and other and suggesting Lacan's theory of mirror-stage development in the psychoanalytic subject, which occurs between mother and infant. Much can be made here of Mason occupying the place of Ronald's mother in the letters, a position that inevitably leads to a better understanding of subjectivity in both father and son. For the purpose of this discussion, however, it is important to stress that it is the letter-mirror that inevitably reflects the "true" natures of writer (Mason) and reader (Ronald) back to themselves and to each other.

21. Naomi Schor, *Breaking the Chain: Women, Theory, and French Realist Fiction* (New York: Columbia University Press, 1985), 50.

22. Wharton, "Father's Son," 43.

23. Ibid., 41.

24. Ibid., 42.

25. We can only speculate about the interpretation(s) of Mason's letters by Dolbrowski, an unseen reader of that text. As correspondent in the epistolary exchange, the pianist is also an unseen writer and, it goes without saying, a participant in the discursive masquerade. As noted above, Dolbrowski can be read as an implicit double or refraction of Mason Grew.

26. "The souls of short thick-set men, with chubby features, mutton chop whiskers, and pale eyes peering between folds of fat like almond kernels in half-split shells—souls thus encased do not reveal themselves to the casual scrutiny as delicate emotional instruments. But in spite of the disguise in which he walked Mr. Grew vibrated exquisitely in response to every imaginative appeal; and his son Ronald was always stimulating and feeding his imagination" (38). The body as disguise for the soul can be read, of course, as Romantic (and Christian) conceit. But I am also interested in Wharton's use of "instrument" to describe Mason. Obviously, Dolbrowski plays upon this instrument and is met with the resonance of Mason's desire and imagination, the erotic aspect of which cannot be overlooked.

27. Wharton, "Father's Son," 40.

28. Ibid., 47.

29. Joan Riviere, "Womanliness as a Masquerade," *Psychoanalysis and Female Sexuality,* ed. Hendrik M. Ruitenbeek (New Haven: Yale University Press, 1966), 28.

30. Wharton, "Father's Son," 48.

31. Butler, *Gender Trouble,* 137.

32. Roland Barthes, "From Work to Text," *Image-Music-Text,* trans. Stephen Heath (New York: Hill and Wang, 1977), 161.

33. I'd like to thank the Faculty Development Fund at Saint Mary's College for making it possible for me to present a version of this paper at the conference, "Edith Wharton at Yale," in April 1995. I'd also like to thank Gloria-Jean Masciarotte for her limitless enthusiasm, insight, and ideas on this essay, and Laura Green for her incisive and witty reading over endless cups of coffee.

Architectonic or Episodic? Gender and *The Fruit of the Tree*

KATHERINE JOSLIN

WRITING TO ROBERT GRANT ON NOVEMBER 19, 1907, EDITH WHARTON thanked him for his criticism of her industrial novel, *The Fruit of the Tree,* then puzzled over how she went wrong:

> The fact is that I am beginning to see exactly where my weakest point is.—I conceive my subjects like a man—that is, rather more architectonically & dramatically than most women—& then execute them like a woman; or rather, I sacrifice, to my desire for construction & breadth, the small incidental effects that women have always excelled in, the episodical characterisation, I mean.[1]

She envisions her work as a struggle between conception and execution, two suggestive metaphors, and reproaches herself for spoiling her manly design by behaving "like a woman." Then she turns midsentence and reverses herself, suggesting that sacrificing a female impulse to a male design may be what ruined the novel. Wharton, as the tension in her sentence implies, fears that an episodic female narrative lacks the intellectual seriousness of a male architectonic structure and doubts that she can be a successful novelist, lodged as she is between genders. "This is the reason why," she confessed, "I have always obscurely felt that I didn't know how to write a novel." Examining the failure of *The Fruit of the Tree* in light of Wharton's anxiety tells us much about the pressure on her and the strategy she used to lessen it.

Wharton thought tirelessly about structure—the design of a row of flowers, the placement of a door in a room, the shape of her day—but she assigned "architectonics" (even the term is cumbersome) to men, "master" builders. Although she co-authored *The Decoration of Houses* (1897), with its stress on aesthetic ordering, she did not think of herself as the architect in the project; Ogden Codman held the credential. The word architectonic belongs as well to philosophy and science, where professionals systematized knowledge into abstraction, territory that Wharton similarly considered male. Woman's territory—"incidental" and "episodical"—appears fragmented, tentative, conditional, a region not clearly defined by any profession and, therefore, possessing neither intellectual nor aesthetic cachet.

Her letter to Grant weighs the value of abstract or theoretical discourse, what Mary Poovey calls the language of "disinterested knowledge." In her essay "The Social Constitution of 'Class': Toward a History of Classificatory Thinking," Poovey argues that political thinkers adopted the discourse of natural philosophers "in order to lend prestige to a political theory."[2] Her analysis of the writings of Adam Smith, one of her examples, sheds light on Wharton's dilemma. Smith claimed "disinterested knowledge" or the objectivity of science, Poovey theorizes, because it signified a gentleman's world of contemplation. A man of social rank and privilege lives a comfortable distance away from the working world and possesses, perhaps above all else, a considerable amount of time for reflection. A man's ability to use abstract and theoretical knowledge signifies his social as well as intellectual status:

Because it required the capacity to see objects in terms of their formal properties or relationships or as common members in a representative category, the ability to generate theory was a sign of a man's gentlemanly education, just as a liberal education produced this capacity in gentlemen.[3]

Disinterested modes of discourse differentiated the gentleman from the common man, who worked with his hands and, according to Smith in *The Wealth of Nations*, possessed little intellect:

The torpor of his mind renders him, not only incapable of relishing or bearing a part in any rational conversation, but of conceiving any generous, noble, or tender sentiment, and consequently of forming any just judgment concerning many even of the ordinary duties of private life.[4]

For Smith, education might lift the individual laboring man out of his social class by giving him the tools to use the gentleman-like discourse of abstraction, theory, and inquiry.

A gentleman's claim to disinterested knowledge separated him quite clearly from a woman, who was housed in the domestic sphere and whose intellect was limited by her emotions, tied as she supposedly was to her body. Smith explains a woman's education in *The Theory of Moral Sentiments*:

> There are no public institutions for the education of women, and there is accordingly nothing useless, absurd, or fantastical in the common course of their education. They are taught what their parents or guardians judge it necessary or useful for them to learn; and they are taught nothing else.[5]

Education cannot change the essential female condition, cannot raise any woman, regardless of her social class, out of her state because her essence derives from nature not society. The gentleman, therefore, can separate his intellect from that of the uneducated working man and from that of all women by producing and valuing abstract knowledge over concrete particulars.

Constructing a novel architectonically, employing the disinterested knowledge of the scientific man, attested to Wharton's intellectual place in the leisure class, in spite of her gender. The social sciences, professionalizing in the late nineteenth century and coming of age in the Progressive era with ideas for social, economic, and political engineering, attracted Wharton, a social historian and would-be social scientist herself. "*No* novel worth anything can be anything but a novel 'with a purpose,'" she wrote to Morgan Dix in 1905 as she was planning *The Fruit of the Tree*:

> Social conditions as they are just now in our new world, where the sudden possession of money has come *without* inherited obligations, or any traditional sense of solidarity between the classes, is a vast & absorbing field for the novelist.[6]

It is that "vast & absorbing field" that Wharton felt compelled to enter.

If we look at Wharton in the context of other professional women during the first decade of the twentieth century, a generation that included Jane Addams in sociology, Florence Kelley in industrial relations, and Charlotte Perkins Gilman in economics, we see that they all experimented with the authority of masculine discourse and its (supposedly) scientific muscle. Addressing Rockford Female Seminary in 1882, Jane Addams admonished her classmates to avoid Cassandra's fate by figuring out how to talk like a man. Women, that is to say, were destined to be ignored by men unless they could educate themselves in the mysteries of male discourse. If women would study "at least one branch of physical science," she posited, they might acquire the insight of male thought and the power of male expression, and by adding male modes to the innate female trait of intuition, women might surpass men in public discourse.[7] Later when Addams's own writing combined disinterested knowledge with interested, episodic, decidedly female discourse, Florence Kelley chided her for ignoring the masculine discourse of sociology. Kelley's education at Cornell and Zurich was based on a masculine model; she had joined the Socialist Labor Party and translated Engels and Marx before joining Addams at Hull House, the social settlement in Chicago. *Hull-House Maps and Papers,* written with Kelley and in the discourse of economics and sociology, remained Addams's only attempt to write in a male mode. We can see a similar bifurcation in the writings of Charlotte Perkins Gilman, whom we remember primarily for her episodic tale, "The Yellow Wallpaper," rather than her social and economic analysis of American culture, *Women and Economics.*

Not unlike these other women, Wharton spent much of her time schooling herself in the sciences: "There is nothing like the joy of a good scientific book," she admitted to Sara Norton in a long series of letters that mixed casual chatting about weather and friends with comments on their reading of philosophical and scientific texts. As she was writing *The Fruit of the Tree,* she was reading *Individuality and Immortality,* by the German scholar Wilhelm Ostwald, and *Introduction to Philosophy,* by Friedrich Paulsen, and criticizing William James, who had written the foreword to the translation of Paulsen's book. James insisted, "Humanity will never be satisfied with scientific knowledge to explain its inward relation to reality." Irritated as she frequently was with his ideas, Wharton responded to Norton, "What other kind of knowledge is it capable of receiving?" During 1906, 1907, and 1908, Wharton's reading of scientific and philosophical books was especially intense; she refers in letters to Vernon Kellogg's *Darwinism Today* and Robert Lock's *The Recent Progress in the Study of Variation, Heredity and Evolution.*[8] She claims as "formative influences" Darwin, Taine, Spencer, and Lecky, placing herself clearly within the gentleman's world of "disinterested knowledge."[9]

The tension between what she interpreted as masculine and feminine discourse surfaced often in her early fiction. *A Backward Glance* recorded the clash in her first long novel, *The Valley of Decision,* when she found herself torn between the

demands of structure and the urge simply to write. Walter Berry
sought to allay her fears by encouraging her, "Just write down
everything you feel like telling."[10] She claimed:

> The advice freed me once for all from the incubus of an artificially
> pre-designed plan, and sent me rushing ahead with my tale, letting
> each incident create the next, and keeping in sight only the novel-
> ist's essential sign-post; the inner significance of the "case" selected.

"Incubus," a trope fraught with masculine and sexual meaning,
embodies the pressure on her as a woman writer to create a
strong architectonic shape as she resisted the artificiality of the
task. In a letter to Sara Norton as the novel was appearing, Wharton calls it her "deformed child" (the sexual metaphor still lingering in her mind), an historical novel that does not manage
to conceal its structure: "I haven't fused my facts sufficiently
with the general atmosphere of the story, so that they stick out
here & there, & bump into the reader."[11]

The problem of novel-building continues to plague Wharton
as she took on the social history of New York in *The House of
Mirth,* a story close to her own experiences and, therefore,
perhaps more difficult to shape than the remote world of
eighteenth-century Italy. She writes to William Brownell in 1905
that she rejoices in his "seeing a certain amount of architecture"
in the novel:

> I was pleased with bits, myself; but as I go over the proofs the whole
> thing strikes me as so loosely built, with so many dangling threads,
> & cul-de-sacs, & long dusty stretches, that I had reached the point
> of wondering how I had ever dared to try my hand at a long thing—[12]

Her descriptions, full of bumps and dangles and dead-ends, reveal her frustration with herself as a master-builder.

Her inner battle between masculine and feminine modes of
presentation came to a crisis in *The Fruit of the Tree,* causing
the novel to fail. Could it be, I am asking, that she allowed the
male architectonic structure to fail in order to free the female
episodic impulse?

The early title of the manuscript, "Justine Brent," hints at
Wharton's initial desire to tell a more leisurely story about a
professional woman. Wharton wrote steadily on the novel in late
1905 and early 1906, then abandoned it for three months, while
she traveled in Europe. In 1906, she was savoring the victory of
The House of Mirth, collaborating on a play version of the novel,

working on *Madame de Treymes,* traveling through England with Henry James and through France with Teddy, writing travel essays for magazines, selecting a place in Paris, and meeting the intellectual world of Faubourg St. Germain. Reading through R. W. B. Lewis's and Shari Benstock's biographies, one senses the rapid movement of the year, the tremendous outlay of energy in travel and relocation, and one wonders how she managed to complete *The Fruit of the Tree* at all.[13]

Justine Brent, a nurse and the heroine, comes from the upper class, has read widely, developed her intellect, come to understand art and household decoration, yet she has sunk into the prosaic middle class of work and responsibility. Justine may be Wharton's most attractive professional woman, preferable in every way to Gerty Farish, the social worker in *The House of Mirth.* Many critics have noted Justine's likeness to Edith Wharton; she is intelligent, moral, beautiful, energetic, professionally trained, and committed to an active life. The hero repeatedly fails to recognize her out of her nurse's uniform because of her youthfulness, shapeliness, and style. Under her professional clothes, she is a lady.

Not only is she a lady but also a writer—Wharton flirts here with a portrait of the female artist. The heroine admits that she writes to "medicine her despair by turning it into fiction," a process perhaps close to Wharton's own.[14] After an early failed romance, Justine Brent had taken up the pen:

Her ready pen often beguiled her into recording her impressions, and she now found an escape from despair in writing the history of a damsel similarly wronged. In her tale, the heroine killed herself; but the author, saved by this vicarious sacrifice, lived, and in time even smiled over her manuscript.[15]

The key word is "sacrifice" or, more precisely, "vicarious sacrifice." Justine writes fiction to resolve tension, to "escape from despair," to "sacrifice" a heroine in order to live, to "smile over" the manuscript. She possesses an artist's sensibility, perceives the "imaginative side" of her work (144), creates "for herself an inner kingdom" (152), and considers the leisured society around her as having "missed the poetry of their situation" (221). Justine allowed her heroine to suffer as a type of therapy, to free the writer to go on with her life and her work. In this way, Wharton's portrait of the artist comes close to a self-study.

The manuscript "Justine Brent," however, gave way to an elaborately structured novel about mill reform. The idea of Edith Wharton, a daughter of the leisured New York elite, writing an industrial novel seems, on the face of it, absurd. Manufacturing, although including the labor of women and men, signifies a male industry, the very opposite of homemade or domestic labor, the topic of Wharton's earlier experiment with naturalist fiction, "Bunner Sisters" (1892; published 1916).

Critics have not particularly liked *The Fruit of the Tree.* Edmund Wilson noted it was a "confused" novel, not able to decide between its two themes, mercy-killing and mill reform; most critics who follow him agree.[16] For Irving Howe, it was "dull and earnest"; R. W. B. Lewis thought it should have been a novella; Cynthia Griffin Wolff reads the novel as a "way-station" on Wharton's route toward her affair with Morton Fullerton; Janet Goodwyn explores its "spurious coherence" and "awkwardness of composition."[17] Margaret McDowell and Deborah Carlin find their way around the unwieldy plot by reading it as a novel about marriage. McDowell concedes, "The structure evinces her recurring interest in the double plot, a technical device she never mastered," but goes on to discuss Wharton's portrait of a marriage as a yoking together of strangers.[18] Carlin links the elements of the plot by arguing that Wharton uses "marital incompatibility" as a "lens through which the novel examines a variety of other irreconcilable social issues."[19] Other critics use the novel to advance more general arguments about Wharton's fiction. Candace Waid, for example, refers to the novel primarily through the letter to Grant in a discussion of Wharton's resistance to the "feminine aesthetic," especially that used by New England's "local color" women writers.[20] Susan Goodman, without discussing the novel per se, notes that it resembles Mary Wilkins's novel *The Portion of Labor* (1901), much as Wharton wanted to separate herself from Wilkins and Jewett and to associate her work with the masculine structures of Theodore Dreiser and Sinclair Lewis.[21] No one feels very comfortable writing about the novel and only rarely has someone recommended it.

What makes *The Fruit of the Tree* a compelling book to read is not that it is a good book. Often sloppy in language and somber, even for Wharton, in tone, the narrative rarely relaxes into satire and hardly ever into humor; rather the story marches forward, bullying characters and assigning them improbable motivations and preposterous judgments. The novel opens in a hospital, after an industrial accident where a mill worker named

Dillon mangled his hand. The nurse Justine Brent concurs with the mill manager John Amherst that in such a case, the worker might as well be dead, because his wife, too frail to feed the family on her own, might as well have the chance to find another husband. One can see that Wharton, as Vernon Parrington had noted years ago, might have been a better writer if she "had been forced to scrimp and save and plan."[22] She clearly knows little about mill work and almost nothing about working-class life: Who would argue that a worker should be euthanized over the loss of a hand?

John Amherst woos and weds the mill owner, the widowed Bessy Westmore, and sets out to reform the factory and its surrounding community. By novel's end, he constructs cottages, to be privately owned, a school, a day care, a hospital, and finally a health facility; that is to say, the professional middle-class reformer manages a social revolution. Wharton does not record the clashes between owners and workers that led to the creation of labor unions, nor does she envision social change as a struggle between the wealthy and the poor; indeed, her novel avoids any mention of the radical and often brutal social change happening around her in industrial America. Amherst's energies produce a professionally engineered paternalism in "the hopeful air of a 'rising' residential suburb" (621). The mill workers, or so it appears, begin to rise into the middle class. Yet Wharton never tells us about the continued lives of the mill workers or how they respond to the reforms. She seems, in fact, not to care about that larger story she so meticulously and architectonically constructed for the novel, the story that interrupts and supersedes her more episodic portrayal of Justine Brent.

The architectonic lines of *The Fruit of the Tree* "stick out" and "bump into the reader," as did those of *The Valley of Decision*. Wharton constructs three social groups who must come to understand a "sense of solidarity between the classes": the workers, called rather pointedly "hands"; the owners, represented by the frivolous Bessy Westmore, who had inherited the mill from her dead husband but has not "inherited" a sense of responsibility in her ownership; and the professional middle class, represented by John Amherst, the mill manager, and Justine Brent, the trained nurse.

The novel looks, at times, like a piece of naturalism, Zolaesque in its blending of science and literature. Westmore, a New England mill town, is the typical monster of naturalist fiction:

> With sudden disgust [Amherst] saw the sordidness of it all—the poor monotonous houses, the trampled grass-banks, the lean dogs prowl-

ing in refuse-heaps, the reflection of a crooked gas-lamp in a stag-
nant loop of the river; and he asked himself how it was possible to
put any sense of moral beauty into lives bounded forever by the low
horizon of the factory. (22)

The hero doubts that the development of the mill will, in the
natural course of time, provide hope for the town:

in obedience to the grim law of industrial prosperity, it would soon
lose its one lingering grace and spread out in unmitigated ugliness,
devouring green fields and shaded slopes like some insect-plague
consuming the land. (24)

Human lives are governed, as they are in Zola's novels, by "grim"
surroundings in the control of prowling dogs and devouring ugliness. The scene reflects the fatalism of naturalist philosophy,
an outlook not unlike Wharton's own. Her view of the workers
and their limited lives might have come from the pages of Adam
Smith: the "torpor" of their minds, their incapacity for "rational
conversation," and certainly their lack of judgment in "even the
ordinary duties of private life."

The industrial accident claims the hand of the factory worker,
who must look to the Progressive reformer and hero John Amherst to make Westmore a better world. As the manager of the
mill, he counsels Bessy Westmore about an owner's responsibility to her workers and then proposes marriage, a coupling that
promises to place the manager in control of mill conditions. The
part of the novel that baffles and annoys readers and critics is
Bessy's death; she falls from her horse, rather obviously named
"Impulse," and crushes her spine. Justine Brent, her friend and
household manager, witnesses her suffering after the fall and,
with all family members out of the country, administers a lethal
dose of morphine to end Bessy's suffering as she believes a good
nurse should (remember the earlier discussion of euthanasia in
Dillon's case). Justine goes on to marry Amherst without first
explaining the mercy killing.

The plots and subplots, although I admit they are confusing,
cohere perhaps too well. The *hand* of labor is mangled and therefore helpless to effect social change; the *back* of the mill owner
is crushed and therefore incapable of supporting the responsi-
bilities of management in its relationship to labor; the *head* of
the mill, the manager, then weds the *heart* of the novel, the
nurse. John Amherst and Justine Brent represent the new generation of men and women who propose that social justice and

order be managed by middle-class, educated professionals, that is, the social engineers emerging from settlement houses such as Hull House and from universities at the turn into the twentieth century.

Emile Zola proclaimed in "The Experimental Novel" that once scientists discovered the rules governing the social mechanism, "experimental moralists" might ameliorate poverty and end exploitation of the working class. John Amherst, just such a moralist, believes it his duty to spend Bessy's money to correct the inequities of capitalism and, together with his second wife, Justine Brent, to transform Westmore into its "final shape," presented as a clear contrast to the grim naturalism of the opening scene:

> Westmore prospered under the new rule. The seeds of life they had sown there were springing up in a promising growth of bodily health and mental activity, and above all a dawning social consciousness. The mill-hands were beginning to understand the meaning of their work, in its relation to their own lives and to the larger economy. And outwardly, also, the new growth was showing itself in the humanized aspect of the place. (621)

The middle-class social reforms, financed with the profits of capitalism, nurture the prosperity of a nascent middle-class suburb that signals a penultimate happy ending for the novel.

Wharton, never a muckraker, remains aloof from her working-class characters, a fact that has irritated many critics. Why didn't she spend more time, for example, researching the textile mills of North Adams, Massachusetts? Blake Nevius reports that the din of the machines apparently appalled her and, more importantly, prevented her from getting the information straight.[23] The woman who had spent so many years researching Italian history and art for *The Valley of Decision* and who would later bristle at critics who claimed she had the facts wrong about New England in *Ethan Frome* seemed unconcerned about the criticism her story drew in its serial publication. She made changes for the novel edition but remained indifferent to the charge that she hadn't done her homework. Nevius recounts that in a letter to Burlingame, Wharton admitted that she had mistakenly used "ply-room" for "fly-room," "superintendent" for "manager," and "loom" for "card." A workman who had written to correct her errors explained to her that Dillon's accident could not have happened in a loom and that the "carder" was a man, not a machine. It may be, as Vernon Parrington and Alfred Kazin have charged, that she condescended to her lower-class characters.

One might argue, too, that the working class and even the middle class were beside the point Wharton wanted to make. At the novel's close, she gives her answer to labor problems and social reform. The working-class laborer has neither the power nor the brains to combat industrial capitalists; the upper-class owner wields power only for personal comfort, not social justice; the middle-class professional alone possesses the expertise to craft social, economic, and political reform. Wharton's architectonics deliver a novel with "a purpose" by analyzing the "sense of solidarity" so lacking in American culture.

Wharton makes this point, I would argue, so that she can discard the masculine text in favor of the feminine one. The episodic story of Justine Brent moves uncomfortably in tandem with the architectonic story of social reform. The heroine's work as a nurse seems more an avocation than a vocation; except for her part-time job that opens the novel and her stint in Michigan, she spends her time managing Bessy Westmore Amherst's household, the domestic equivalent of Amherst's job. In this position and in her later one as wife, she leads a leisurely life of reading and mulling. Wharton gives her a seemingly perfect marriage but only allows the true union to last about eight months (not bad as Wharton's portraits of marriage go). Justine's episodic story, if the early manuscript title means anything, is the one Wharton wanted to tell. And it is her story, after the elaborate depiction of mill reform, that ends the novel.

Wharton designs the whole novel to get to the supposed success of Amherst, the Progressive social engineer, so that she can undercut his public accomplishments by detailing the flaws in his private life. Wharton echoes the skepticism of her generation of American women toward a paternal model of reform. Jane Addams, for example, warns in *Democracy and Social Ethics* (1902) that paternalism may have deleterious effects on the reformer's private life: "To perform too many good deeds may be to lose the power of recognizing good in others."[24] Amherst, who learns belatedly of Justine's mercy-killing of Bessy, becomes increasingly alienated from his second wife, failing to recognize the "good" she rendered Bessy by putting her out of her misery. Following the logic of the schematized plot, Wharton delivers the hero's last "reform," based on his complete misreading of his first marriage and his insensitivity to his second wife. He salves his conscience over his troubled first marriage by constructing a health club for the working people of Westmore and deludes himself into believing that Bessy had planned the public facility before her death as a sign of her loyalty to his reforms. Justine knows that Bessy planned the spa for herself (anyone with a rudimentary ability to read character would draw that conclusion) but decides not to shatter her husband's illusion. Wharton assigns such obtuseness to her hero and such masochism to her heroine in order to place the final piece in the novel's structure—the last "accident."

Just as the hand of labor is severed, the back of ownership is broken, so the spiritual bond of marriage is destroyed: "Nothing was left of that secret union which had so enriched and beautified their outward lives" (623). The price of knowledge is silence for the heroine, a Cassandra after all, in spite of her scientific education and her forays into art. Perhaps in no other novel would Wharton say so clearly the single idea at the heart of all her fiction. It comes to us as Justine's thought: "[L]ife is not a matter of abstract principles, but a succession of pitiful compromises with fate, of concessions to old traditions, old beliefs, old charities and frailties" (624). Abstractions crumble in their encounter with everyday realities, the string of compromises and concessions we all have to make.

In delivering her message about the complexities of human experience and the inadequacies of human effort, Wharton deconstructs the architectonic shape of the novel and celebrates the episodic. As Justine had done with her early writing, Wharton "sacrifices" the female story to the "incubus" of the male design, a failure that freed her to work on other projects without the pressure of artificial construction. She allows herself to move away from disinterested knowledge toward interested, engaged, incidental narratives that she believed "women have always excelled in." At the same time, she was struggling with the design of *The Fruit of the Tree,* for example, she was making headway on several episodically structured projects: the novella *Madame de Treymes,* several short stories, and travel essays for *A Motor-Flight Through France.* She would go on to write *Ethan Frome* and *The Reef,* both structured more episodically around single incidents, and her next long novel, *The Custom of the Country,* would be picaresque. After writing her industrial novel, she smiled over her manuscript, flawed as it was, and moved on to the episodic tales she had to tell.

Notes

1. Edith Wharton to Robert Grant, 19 November 1907, in *The Letters of Edith Wharton,* ed. R. W. B. Lewis and Nancy Lewis (New York: Charles

Scribner's Sons, 1988), 124. She goes on to offer solace to Grant who claims he has reached a "blind alley" in his own writing. "But suddenly a door will open for you in the blank wall."

2. Mary Poovey, "The Social Construction of 'Class': Toward a History of Classificatory Thinking," in *Rethinking Class: Literary Studies and Social Formations*, ed. Wai-chee Dimock and Michael T. Gilmore (New York: Columbia University Press, 1994), 15–56.

3. Poovey, "Social Construction," 41.

4. Quoted in ibid., 44.

5. Ibid., 46.

6. *Letters,* 99.

7. For a discussion of Addams's discourse, see Katherine Joslin, "Literary Cross-Dressing: Jane Addams Finds Her Voice in *Democracy and Social Ethics*," in *Femmes de conscience: Aspects du féminisme américain (1848–1875)*, ed. Susan Goodman and Daniel Royot (Paris: Sorbonne, 1994), 217–38.

8. *Letters,* 146. See also 151, where she writes to her lover Morton Fullerton about Charles Dépéret's *Les transformations du monde animal* and Yves Delage's *L'Hérédité et les grands problémes de la biologie générale.*

9. Ibid., 136.

10. Edith Wharton, *A Backward Glance* (New York: Appleton-Century, 1934), 115.

11. *Letters,* 56–57.

12. Ibid., 94.

13. R. W. B. Lewis, *Edith Wharton: A Biography* (New York: Harper and Row, 1975), 159–80. Shari Benstock, *No Gifts from Chance: A Biography of Edith Wharton* (New York: Charles Scribner's Sons, 1994), 152–56.

14. Edith Wharton, *The Fruit of the Tree* (New York: Charles Scribner's Sons, 1907), 554. Other page references to the novel will appear parenthetically in the essay.

15. See Elaine Showalter, "The Death of the Lady (Novelist): Wharton's *House of Mirth*," *Representations,* 9 (winter 1985), for an interpretation of Wharton's own desire to kill off a heroine to free herself. Showalter argues that Lily Bart dies so that Gerty Farish, the new professional woman, may live, an interpretation that differs from my own.

16. Edmund Wilson, "Justice to Edith Wharton," in *Edith Wharton: A Collection of Critical Essays,* ed. Irving Howe (Englewood Cliffs, N.J.: Prentice-Hall, 1962), 21–22.

17. Irving Howe, "The Achievement of Edith Wharton," in *Edith Wharton: A Collection of Critical Essays,* 5. For Lewis's assessment, see *Edith Wharton: A Biography,* 180–82. Also see Cynthia Griffin Wolff, *A Feast of Words: The Triumph of Edith Wharton* (Oxford: Oxford University Press, 1977), 139–43; and Janet Goodwyn, *Edith Wharton: Traveller in the Land of Letters* (New York: St. Martin's Press, 1990), 67–73.

18. Margaret B. McDowell, *Edith Wharton,* Twayne's United States Authors Series 265 (Boston: Twayne Publishers, 1976), 53.

19. Deborah Carlin, "To Form a More Imperfect Union: Gender, Tradition, and the Text in Wharton's *The Fruit of the Tree*," in *Edith Wharton: New Critical Essays*, ed. Alfred Bendixon and Annette Zilvensmit (New York: Garland, 1992), 57–78.

20. Candace Waid, *Edith Wharton's Letters from the Underworld: Fictions of Women and Writing* (Chapel Hill: University of North Carolina Press, 1991), 9–10.

21. Susan Goodman, *Edith Wharton's Women: Friends and Rivals* (Hanover, N.H.: University Press of New England, 1990), 164, n. 15, and 168, nn. 8 and 9.

22. Vernon Parrington, "Our Literary Aristocrat," *Pacific Review,* II (June 1921), 157.

23. Blake Nevius, *Edith Wharton: A Study of Her Fiction* (Berkeley: University of California Press, 1953), 99–117.

24. Jane Addams, *Democracy of Social Ethics* (1902; rpt. Cambridge: Harvard University Press, 1964), 146.

Erotic Visual Tropes in the Fiction
of Edith Wharton

MAUREEN HONEY

EDITH WHARTON'S NEW YORK NOVELS, *THE HOUSE OF MIRTH* (1905), *The Custom of the Country* (1913), and *The Age of Innocence* (1920), are arguably her most discussed works. Although their settings and thematic treatments of old New York society, as well as their powerfully rendered women characters, have linked them in the minds of many critics, my approach examines their common sexual subject: ironic presentation of erotic tropes featuring women in fin-de-siècle painting.[1] In each of these novels, women seem to embody erotic vulnerability, represented by allusions to the art of Wharton's day, while they remain, at the same time, connected to specific paintings which announce their autonomous power. This ironic juxtaposition confuses male characters who desire these heroines but fail to perceive the strength behind their vulnerable poses until their romantic illusions lead them into emotional cul-de-sacs. Wharton's men safely compartmentalize their desire, yet they find themselves overwhelmed by women who both violate and manipulate erotic tropes of conventional female sexuality. Wharton's multilayered presentation of women's bodies through sophisticated reference to Victorian painting forms a narrative line in these texts, moreover, in which one character, Lily Bart, is victimized by the images that surround her; another, the engulfing Undine, victimizes others through manipulation of those same images; and a third, Ellen Olenska, merges autonomy with a sexual persona to achieve what seems a nonexploitative life of self-fulfillment. Viewing these three novels as a trilogy connected by their reliance on painting to articulate metaphors of erotic distance and suffocation, we can see their disparate heroines not simply as victims of male lust but as complex figures who appropriate postures of empowerment in a patriarchal cultural landscape. Indeed, men misread these women at their own peril.

As a woman writer drawn to sexual themes, Wharton found in art a useful backdrop for exploring the taboo. Art could represent the erotic to a public familiar with its visual tropes without offending the sensibilities of her readers. Supporting this view are art historians such as Paula Gillett who have identified the late nineteenth century as a time when public interest in the kind of art to which Wharton alludes was keen: "There was a high level of public awareness of painters and graphic artists, a high degree of interest both in their work and in their mode of life."[2] Writers commonly used painters' imagery because the popularity of painting gave them a visually literate audience well versed in iconographic presentation of familiar narratives.[3] Without assuming that Wharton had these particular pieces in mind when she wrote her novels, I would like to suggest that Wharton alluded to exotic tropes in Victorian painting as a way of exploring sexual tension with her characteristic irony.

The iconic construction of Wharton's first notable heroine, Lily Bart from *The House of Mirth,* rests on two popular subjects for fin-de-siècle painters. One of these is coded in Lily's name, a character from Alfred Lord Tennyson's *The Idylls of the King.* She is the "lily maid" Elaine who falls in love with Lancelot, nurses him back to health when he is wounded in battle, and finally dies when he does not return her love. Sensing herself near death, Elaine instructs her father to place her corpse on a barge to take her to Camelot, which he does after placing a lily in her lifeless hand. Late nineteenth-century artists painted many variations of Elaine's final journey just as they were preoccupied with two other literary heroines who die of unrequited love: Tennyson's Lady of Shalott and, more importantly for my purposes, Shakespeare's Ophelia. Art historian Bram Dijkstra connects these figures to what he calls "the cult of invalidism" among fin-de-siècle painters, and he comments on these artists' fascination with the death of a woman, a painterly subject Wharton incorporates into her plot. Dijkstra maintains that physical weakness in women was a sign of delicacy and spiritual cultivation; as she wasted away, a virtuous woman could both signal her devotion to a man without whose love she could not live and confer upon him the added power of her celestial purity. On a more practical level, the dying virgin or beautiful corpse could make no erotic demands: "The sleep-death equation had clearly become charged with morbid erotic implications, presenting the male with at least the fantasy of conquest without battle, of a life of power without constraints."[4]

Ophelia. John Everett Millais (1851–52).

Lily's neurasthenic descent into hopeless lassitude after Selden condemns her evokes the fate of both Elaine, Lancelot's spurned admirer, and Ophelia, who drowns herself amid water lilies when Hamlet rejects her. Diane Price Herndl, in fact, cites another such painterly subject, the figure of Albine who suffocates from the perfume of flowers, as she analyzes Selden's response to Lily's corpse at the novel's end: "Lily, too, becomes a dead but aesthetic object for a male viewer. It is only at her death, when she has literally embodied one of these paintings . . . that Selden . . . is able to love her."[5] The water lilies Selden and Lily encounter during their magical interlude at a fountain garden after the tableaux vivants, the heady perfume of violets emanating from the dress Lily wore that night just before she takes her fatal dose of chloral, and Lily's still-life beauty as a corpse all point to these commonly portrayed victims of unrequited love. Not only does Wharton skewer the fetishized artistic rendering of dead women with these references, but she also conveys the irony of Lily's association with erotic subjects when she is in reality sexually repressed.[6] For all her yearning to reach "beyond" her virginity, Lily can find no partner for her bed except the imaginary child she cradles in her final moments. Never aware of more than "faint stirrings in the blood" aroused in her by Selden, she is ambivalent about marriage to him, not merely because he does not have enough money (a convenient explanation for her conflicted feelings) but because she has mastered the art of seduction without visceral awareness of her sexual nature. Selden reinforces Lily's ambivalence through his own sexual inhibitions. Her tropic association with drowning and suffocation implies the cost of her sexual repression, just as her visually represented sisters have expired from intense yet thwarted desire.

When we regard Lily as a woman unconsciously mirroring the erotic cultural landscape that surrounds her, the central scene in which she impersonates the Sir Joshua Reynolds painting, *Mrs. Lloyd* (1776), takes on added complexity. In contrast to the nineteenth-century paintings Lily resembles on her deathbed, *Mrs. Lloyd* derives from the eighteenth century, an era Wharton valued for its privileging of simplicity, reason, and classical virtues. When juxtaposed with the prostrate virgins of fin-de-siècle art, Lily, posing as the soon-to-be Mrs. Lloyd of the portrait, takes on a healthier erotic cast. As Candace Waid notes, Lily holds a pen (instead of a lily) when she impersonates Mrs. Lloyd and becomes a writer.[7] Her natural setting, simplicity of dress, and

Mrs. Lloyd. Sir Joshua Reynolds (1776).

white complexion recall the ancient Greek and Roman period admired during the Enlightenment while evoking an ideal of equality associated with the French and American Revolutions. With her feet planted firmly on the ground, Lily as Mrs. Lloyd can escape the prison of her virginity and the Victorian world of gendered spheres to contemplate her partnership with a man of the Enlightenment. Selden's response to Lily's tableau illuminates such a reading of this scene. Certainly he acts as a voyeur, as Cynthia Griffin Wolff and others note, but his overwhelming transport at the sight of Lily, "detached from all that cheapened and vulgarized [her beauty]," suggests that he yearns to be with her on a plane of harmony outside "the trivialities of her little world." Reinforcing this positive interpretation of Lily's performance are the approving comments of Gertie Farish: "Don't you like her best in that simple dress? It makes her look like the real Lily—the Lily I know."[8] Selden is offended by the vulgar remarks of the men around him as they reductively associate Lily's representation with exhibitionism. The sexual response of the other men strikes him as obscene and inappropriate, another sign Selden understands that Lily hopes to portray something other than an erotic image for her audience. A representative of the Enlightenment man, he is the mate for Lily's Mrs. Lloyd.

Wharton's concluding scene in *The House of Mirth* provides a deadly counterpoint to the radiant eighteenth-century figure Lily creates in the tableaux vivants. It is a harsh reminder that the Victorian age is fascinated by women in a still-life pose, yet Selden's parodic response to Lily's dead body is framed by a narrative structure that transcends the other visual accounts of her objectification. While Selden remains true to form in his passionate embrace of a frozen object, he articulates to himself the actual reasons for the failure of their love, acknowledging his lack of courage in challenging the social codes that paralyzed him:

> That [Lily's corpse] was her real self, every pulse in him ardently denied ... the real Lily was still there, close to him, yet invisible and inaccessible; and the tenuity of the barrier between them mocked him with a sense of helplessness. There had never been more than a little impalpable barrier between them—and yet he had suffered it to keep them apart![9]

He berates himself for going through her papers and criticizing her, calls himself a coward, and recognizes the destructiveness

of his studied, emotional detachment and "spiritual fastidious-
ness." It is possible to doubt the sincerity of Selden's deathbed conversion, and perhaps we should; but Wharton clearly
condemns a social system that separates eros and love, a system
indeed Selden seems prepared to reject when he arrives at Lily's
flat that morning "—cut loose from the familiar shores of habit,
. . . launched . . . on uncharted seas of emotion; all the old tests
and measures . . . left behind."[10] The art metaphor Wharton employs in *The House of Mirth* underscores the inevitable impossibility of Lily's and Selden's love because their feelings are
sublimated into aesthetic appreciation of beauty at a distance.
Lily's very being, depicted with frank sensuality yet forever
chaste, calls into question their unconscious acts of sexual repression and erotic distancing. Her ultimate descent from living
to dead art indicts the society that has made women's bodies a
site of forbidden pleasure.

If Lily Bart's body functions as a cultural map of repressed
sexuality, Undine Spragg's suggests unmined virgin territory.
Unlike Lily, Undine consciously manipulates her body for the
benefit of men in *The Custom of the Country*. Ironically, men
view both women as maidens in need of rescue. Carol Wershoven
points out, for instance, that Selden blanches at the prospect of
being Lily's rescuer.[11] She cites as illustration the following passage from *The House of Mirth,* one that I see foreshadowing
Wharton's use of another painterly image in *The Custom of the
Country,* Andromeda chained to the rocks: "That 'Beyond' in
her letter was like a cry for rescue. He knew that Perseus's task
is not done when he has loosed Andromeda's chains, for her
limbs are numb with bondage, and she cannot rise and walk,
but clings to him with dragging arms as he beats back to land
with his burden."[12] Ralph Marvell similarly views Undine Spragg
as "a lovely, rock-bound Andromeda, with the devouring monster society careening up to make a mouthful of her; and himself
whirling down on his winged horse . . . to cut her bonds, snatch
her up, and whirl her back into the blue."[13] Here Wharton draws
on the many representations of Andromeda in fin-de-siècle
painting—nude, bound, helpless, and in need of rescue. Rife
with erotic connotations, the painted Andromeda's body is repeatedly depicted as exposed in an open landscape with her arms
often tied behind her back so she cannot hide herself.[14] Both
the sea monster and the threatening water itself are metaphors
of sexual ravishment poised to engulf this lovely virgin who has
been slated for sacrifice because of her beauty. Perseus, in con-

The Doom Fulfilled. **Edward Burne-Jones (1888). Second in Burne-Jones's Perseus and Andromeda series (1884–1888).**

trast, often portrayed safely on Pegasus in the air and clothed in armor, carries a protective mirrored shield while gripping a sword with which he has just decapitated the malevolent Medusa. Even when he is on the ground, the figure seems filled with a sense of his own power while Andromeda is at the mercy of overwhelming forces.

The erotic aura of paintings of Andromeda signals the openly sexual behavior of Undine, who, in contrast to the circumspect Lily Bart, mistakenly judged as a loose woman, is a sexually experienced woman misperceived as a naive innocent. Wharton extends this irony in her portrayal of Ralph Marvell, a man who dreams of being Perseus but is Andromeda in drag. Wharton associates Ralph with images of water, references to floating, and allusions to drowning that evoke depictions of Andromeda as well as other painted nude women in water. Lush paintings of a nude Venus or Aphrodite arising from the water were common in the nineteenth century as were representations of water nymphs and mermaids who float seductively or sit tantalizingly at the edge of water. Numerous as well are erotically charged portraits of drowned young women who demonstrate the fate of those unable to float or to find a rescuer. Linda Nochlin indicates that Victorian viewers understood these victims to be fallen women driven to suicide, a view that helps us understand Wharton's ironic placement of Ralph in this very position.[15]

Bram Dijkstra illuminates the meaning such paintings have for Wharton's narrative purposes as well when he discusses the many images of women who are floating in air or water during this era: "Woman's weightlessness was . . . a sign of her willing or helpless submission, allowed the male to remain uninvolved, permitted him to maintain his voyeur's distance from this creature of nature, this creature that was nature, who both fascinated and frightened him."[16] Wharton connects Undine to these images of women in water by her red hair, for these painted figures often have vivid red tresses, and by her name, that of Neptune's daughter and of mythical female creatures who lured men into the sea to their death.[17] Undines or nereids are also associated with Andromeda, for they are the ones who jealously insist she be sacrificed to the sea monster when they hear how beautiful she is.

Wharton's allusions to erotic images of floating women underscore Ralph's susceptibility and highlight his vulnerability to unmoored women. For instance, on their honeymoon Undine appears to float in Ralph's gauze-covered vision: "His eyes softened as they absorbed in a last glance *the glimmering submarine light* of the ancient grove, through which *Undine's figure wavered nereid-like above him*."[18] In rapturous contemplation of Undine's beauty, the poetry in Ralph's head takes the form of another weightless image, beautiful birds in flight, and he blissfully recalls those rare moments in his life when he could abandon himself to ecstatic union of mind and body: "As he lay there, fragments of past states of emotion, fugitive felicities of thought and sensation, *rose* and *floated* on the surface of his thoughts. . . . He had had glimpses of such a state before, of such

A Mermaid. J. W. Waterhouse (1901).

Sleep. Charles Chaplin (1886).

mergings of the personal with the general life that one felt one-self *a mere wave on the wild stream of being*"[19] (my emphasis). Undine intuitively reinforces Ralph's erotically romantic vision of her through her ability to appear ethereal, pliant, muselike in her skills to arrange fashionable dress. For instance, she attends the Driscoll fancy dress ball as Empress Josephine Napoleon, modeling herself explicitly after a portrait by Pierre Paul Prud'hon hanging in the Louvre, *Empress Josephine at Malmaison* (1805). The daring decolletage of this dress sexually entices, while the diaphanous gown and its association with a woodland setting suggest the pastoral romantic impulses on which Ralph depends for his poetry. Undine, whose name codes her as a seductress of the sea who lures men into her element, masquerades as a wood nymph, a dryad on safe ground.

Erotic representations of the water nymph, Andromeda, and drowned victims of male lust provided Wharton with a metaphoric canvas for ironic portrayal of both Undine and Ralph. In part, such images symbolize the danger of sexual abandonment, but if the floating woman stands for erotic submission and male conquest, Undine has no sexual desire and strikes a decidedly unsubmissive posture toward all her husbands. In contrast, Ralph's vulnerability to the myth of erotic detachment prepares him for a journey to oblivion. The female lost souls who fall into watery graves serve as ironic commentary on his fate as a seduced and abandoned lover. Wharton evokes these images when Ralph falls desperately ill while Undine carries on an affair with Peter Van Degen in Paris. Floundering helplessly as he attempts to rise from his sickbed, we are told:

> Everything slipped away and evaded him. It was like trying to catch at *bright short waves*. . . . He . . . felt himself moving about the room, in a queer disembodied way, *as one treads the air in sleep*, . . . [submerged in] *a dim pool of sleep* . . . a silent blackness far below light and sound; then he gradually *floated* to the surface with the *buoyancy of a dead body*. . . . Jagged strokes of pain tore through [his body], hands dragged at it with nails that bit like teeth. They wound thongs about him, bound him, tied weights to him . . . , but still he *floated, floated,* danced on the *fiery waves* of pain. . . . He became a leaf on the air, a feather on a current, a straw on the tide, the *spray of the wave* spinning itself to sunshine as the wave toppled over into gulfs of blue. . . . He woke on a stony beach, his legs and arms still lashed to his sides and the thongs cutting into him.[20] (My emphasis.)

Empress Josephine at Malmaison. Pierre Paul Prud'hon (1805).

Ralph has fallen into the sea, like Icarus, rather than ridden the air on a winged stallion, and his rhetorical position here as a bound figure floating on waves of pain draws him into the pool of desire from which he had felt safely distanced.

In *The Custom of the Country,* Wharton's use of the mirror—another version of Perseus's shield—and of water, nature's reflective surface, metaphorically encompasses the text itself. In many ways, this novel may be viewed as a mirror image of *The House of Mirth,* for the male gazer, rather than the female object of desire, drowns in the abyss of his romantic/sexual yearnings. The painting after which Undine models herself, Prud'hon's portrait of Josephine Napoleon, also resembles *Mrs. Lloyd.* But whereas Lily Bart in some sense inhabits Reynolds's portrait unmasked, Undine covers her vacuous interior, her absence of a stable self, when dressed as a classical figure. The real Undine loves luxury, as did the real Josephine, whose wardrobe of 673 velvet and satin dresses, 33 dresses of cashmere, 202 summer frocks, 785 pairs of shoes, and 980 pairs of gloves stood in sharp contrast to the woodland pose of simplicity captured by Prud'hon.[21] Wharton deftly demonstrates Undine's true nature by linking her to a deceptively simple and therefore false portrait of one of the most materialistic historical figures of the nineteenth century.

Undine's real self looks from the portraits she commissions of herself by Claud Walsingham Popple, a satirized figure who is a thinly veiled reference to John Singer Sargent.[22] Powerful, arrogant, ostentatious, and regal, these paintings counterbalance Ralph's alternative set of visual tropes which depict Undine in erotic, vulnerable poses. Set in sumptuous drawing rooms, Popple's studies of Undine show her fully clothed and far from beaches or clouds. Sargent's portrait *Mrs. George Swinton* (1896), in fact, uncannily recalls Undine's commanding presence in such portraits. Undine not only has red hair like the young rich woman in Sargent's painting, but she comes to possess an identical tiara of rubies at the novel's end when Elmer Moffatt fittingly procures Marie Antoinette's tiara for his bride. Here is the woman who planned her conquest of New York society under the tutelage of Marie Antoinette, whose portrait graced her hotel room.

In *The Age of Innocence,* Wharton transcends the negative duality regarding women's erotic presentation that we see in these earlier New York novels. Whereas Lily Bart is defeated by her culture's prohibitions against women's sexual freedom and

Mrs. George Swinton. John Singer Sargent (1896).

Undine Spragg claims her sexual power in a self-destructive way, Ellen Olenska combines sexual expression with moral and artistic sensitivity. To cast Ellen's erotic power in a positive light, Wharton eschews allusions to drowned, chained, or nymphic nudes in favor of a subtler sexual image painted by fin-de-siècle artists: women in the theater, the ballet dancers of Dégas, the stage performers of Toulouse-Lautrec, the beautiful young women in opera boxes of Cassatt and Renoir, as well as portraits of actresses by artists such as Georges Clairin, Alphonse Mücha, and Alfred Stevens. These images furnished Wharton with a metaphorical canvas that conveyed the concepts of erotic distance she wished to critique while affirming an autonomous, artistic life for women. One advantage provided by visual theatrical tropes in art for Wharton's narrative purposes is that their presentation of women's bodies avoided the morbidity of dead Ophelias, Elaines, and Albines. The female subject rests at ease, often smiling, and vibrant—she dances, sings, acts, or appreciates those who do while seated in an opera box. Moreover, she is clothed, unlike the naked Aphrodites, Andromedas, and Undines of more erotically charged art, and is thereby placed on a more equal plane with the male viewer.

At the same time, the theater's image afforded Wharton a sufficiently erotic gloss for Ellen's sexually sophisticated persona. Ellen inhabits a taboo world. As one historical account of the nineteenth century argues: "[T]he theater was not deemed a respectable place for a woman to be on either side of the curtain. . . . The ambiguous position of the actress was further compromised by any association with the New Woman and her philosophy of sexual self-determination."[23] Although these rigid views would change as the century wore on, Victorians still tended to link the theater with loose women, even with prostitutes. This libertine aura was enacted for the public by stars such as Sarah Bernhardt, for example, whose affairs and lifestyle violated standards of bourgeois morality. When Bernhardt visited New York in 1880 just six years after the time at which the novel begins, for instance, no women were allowed to attend a dinner in her honor at Delmonico's, nor were they admitted to an exhibit of her artwork because of her scandalous reputation.[24]

Wharton frames Ellen Olenska throughout *The Age of Innocence* with these images of women in the theater, conflates her character with actual fin-de-siècle actresses, and at one point connects her to a painted image strikingly like a portrait of Sarah Bernhardt. The novel opens, for example, on a scene at the opera

Woman with a Pearl Necklace in a Loge. Mary Cassatt (1879).

where singer Christine Nilsson is presented just before our first glimpse of Ellen in a box seat which occurs through the opera glasses of Lawrence Lefferts.[25] Wharton describes Ellen's revealing gown of dark blue velvet as "*theatrically* caught up under her bosom" (my emphasis): When she leans forward to watch the stage, she reveals "a little more shoulder and bosom than New York was accustomed to seeing."[26] This Josephine-style dress resembles the daringly low-necked gowns worn by models for painters of women in theater loges during the 1870s and 1880s, and it introduces the reader to Ellen Olenska whose name itself recalls that of the prominent nineteenth-century actress Ellen Terry. The theatrical eroticism that focuses male attention on Ellen at the opera is further underlined by Sillerton Jackson's recollection of Catherine Mingott's father, who deserted his wife for a Spanish dancer performing at another New York opera house.[27]

Ellen's ancestral association with the scandalous Spicer/Mingott family line, her open friendship with the adulterous Julius Beaufort, her erotically marked appearance at the theater, even the fact that she smokes, link her with Victorian stereotypes of stage women, a connection the novel emphasizes in other ways. For example, even as a child, little Ellen Mingott scandalized her family when she disembarked from an ocean liner dressed in crimson, "like a gipsy foundling," and entertained her relatives with Spanish dances and Italian love songs. Later, we see the adult Ellen again in red when Newland visits her apartment and finds her "half-reclined, her head propped on a hand and her wide sleeve leaving the arm bare to the elbow," a posture that approximates Georges Clairin's famous 1876 portrait of a languorous thirty-two-year-old Sarah Bernhardt. Indeed, Ellen here reminds Newland of a similar portrait by Carolus-Duran, a Parisian painter whose pictures were "the sensation of the Salon, in which the lady wore one of those bold sheath-like robes with her chin nestling in fur."[28]

The text identifies Ellen with yet another actress when Newland visits her after seeing *The Shaughraun*. He has responded emotionally to a scene in which the actress, Ada Dyas, sadly bids her lover adieu while resting her arms on a mantelpiece, cupping her face in her hands. Stealing to her unnoticed, the lover kisses an end of the velvet ribbon around her neck and then leaves. Although Ellen's erotic presentation as a woman of the theater is not his focus, James Gargano delineates the way this theatrical scene is reenacted when Ellen rests her elbows on the man-

Portrait of Sarah Bernhardt. **Georges Clairin (1876).**

tlepiece and one of her locks tumbles onto her neck, recalling
the actress's velvet ribbon. When Ellen articulates the impossibility of acting on their passion, Newland impulsively kisses her
shoe, simulating the stage lover's parting kiss.[29]

Wharton uses theatrical tropes as a frame for sexual encounters in both *The Custom of the Country,* when Undine displays
herself in an opera box and finds herself the object of Elmer
Moffatt's knowing gaze, and in *The Reef* (1912), where an aspiring actress captivates an older man in an opera box. Her fore-
grounding of such images in *The Age of Innocence,* however,
suggests a more complex approach to the notion of erotic attraction. Ellen's flamboyant clothing, notorious past, bohemian
lifestyle, and flagrant disregard for sexual convention arouse
Newland Archer. Yet Ellen does not destroy him, as Undine destroys Ralph in *The Custom of the Country;* nor does Newland
condemn Ellen as Selden does Lily in *The House of Mirth.* The

real danger lies in May whose sexual purity is announced by her white dresses and frozen demeanor.[30] So arid is his life with May that when Newland visits Paris after her death, he is overwhelmed by the vibrancy and beauty of "the life of art and study and pleasure that filled each mighty artery to bursting."[31] The theatrical stage and Ellen are intertwined once more in Newland's mind as he contemplates "the theatres she must have been to, the pictures she must have looked at," and the countess is again connected to erotic visual tropes when he thinks of her while gazing at "an effulgent Titian" at the Louvre.[32] In the novel's last scene, Ellen is positioned a final time as a woman on both sides of a theatrical curtain when Newland watches the shutters being drawn at her apartment balcony window, symbolically placing her behind a stage curtain. Its fifth floor placement, furthermore, recalls the opera box in which Ellen appeared at the novel's opening, but she has disappeared from his admiring vantage point. As a fifty-seven-year-old widower with erotic distance so well established in his life that he seems to have lost touch with eros completely, Newland Archer can no longer see the adventurous sophisticate who aroused his deepest sexual feelings.

In these three novels, Wharton explores the subject of erotic experience through reference to artistic tropes which frame the sensuality of female bodies in a recognizable visual vocabulary.[33] Each text features at least one specific painting connected to its female protagonist while naming other eighteenth- and nineteenth-century painters, and each novel shows women appropriating these or other painterly subjects to showcase their power. At the same time, an ironic subtext flows through these narratives, juxtaposing images of female strength with erotic poses of vulnerability making it difficult for male characters to see the living woman who compels their attention. Wharton unmasks the voyeur in these novels as a troubled lover desiring a fantasy woman who appears safe but is ultimately either too filled with life or a template of emptiness.[34] Pulled into the scene at which he gazes, Wharton's voyeur is either frightened by his erotic feelings or fatally misled by them. The female protagonists of these novels, in contrast, evolve from repressed victim to seductive victimizer to autonomous sexual rebel.

If we view these characters as aspects of Wharton's own sexual evolution from 1905 to 1920, we can detect her movement from sexual inexperience through a bittersweet erotic awakening to a measure of contentment with her liberated existence in

France as an accomplished artist comfortable with her sexuality. More importantly, perhaps, we can appreciate the artistry of a woman reared in a socially and sexually constricted world but drawn to a life of aesthetic exploration, sensual delight, and narrative adventure. Bringing the erotic woman of fin-de-siècle culture to life, Wharton was able to glimpse moments of sexual truth for her characters, even ecstasy in the case of her most inspired lovers as they battle convention and question the grounds of the cultural landscape that shapes their fate. Encouraged to put eros at a distance by the repressive social codes around them, Wharton's characters often fall prey to illusory fantasies of safety when they are in mortal danger. Nevertheless, Wharton seems to suggest, though their erotic knowledge is dearly bought, men and women must explore their deepest intimate longings to be truly alive.

Notes

1. Scholarship on the degree to which sexual attraction interested Wharton the artist and affected Wharton the private woman is now taking shape. Studies that I have found particularly useful include the following: Lev Raphael, *Edith Wharton's Prisoners of Shame: A New Perspective on Her Neglected Fiction* (New York: St. Martin's Press, 1991); Gloria Erlich, *The Sexual Education of Edith Wharton* (Berkeley: University of California Press, 1992); Barbara White, "Neglected Areas: Wharton's Short Stories and Incest" *Edith Wharton Review* 8 no. 1 (spring 1991): 2–12, 8 no. 2 (fall 1991): 3–10; Cynthia Griffin Wolff, "Cold Ethan and Hot Ethan'" *College Literature* 14 no. 3 (fall 1987): 230–45; Judith Fryer, "Women and Space: The Flowering of Desire," *Prospects* 9 (1984): 187–230; Clare Colquitt, "Succumbing to the Literary Style': Arrested Desire in *The House of Mirth*," *Women's Studies* 20 no. 2 (1991): 153–62; Adeline Tintner, "Mothers, Daughters, and Incest in the Late Novels of Edith Wharton," in *The Lost Traditions: Mothers and Daughters in Literature,* ed. Cathy Davidson and E. M. Broner (New York: Ungar Press, 1980). Cynthia Griffin Wolff's groundbreaking biography explores sexuality in Wharton's life and art as well, *A Feast of Words: The Triumph of Edith Wharton* (New York: Oxford University Press, 1977).

2. Paula Gillett, *Worlds of Art: Painters in Victorian Society* (New Brunswick, N.J.: Rutgers University Press, 1990), 192. See also Helene E. Roberts, "Marriage, Redundancy or Sin: The Painter's View of Women in the First Twenty-Five Years of Victoria's Reign," in Martha Vicinus, *Suffer and Be Still: Women in the Victorian Age* (Bloomington: Indiana University Press, 1972); and Daniel Walker Howe, "American Victorianism as a Culture," *American Quarterly* 27 no. 5 (December 1975): 507–32. A good overview of American images of women at the turn-of-the-century is Martha Banta *Imaging American Women: Idea and Ideals in Cultural History* (New York: Columbia University Press, 1987).

3. Helen Killoran attests to Wharton's extensive interest in and sophisticated knowledge of art while describing allusions to specific paintings in her novels. Although Killoran does not address the subject I do here, erotic tropes in visual art, her study provides a solid context for appreciating Wharton's use of art in her fiction. *Edith Wharton: Art and Allusion* (Tuscaloosa: University of Alabama Press, 1996). Philip Sevick calls our attention to the awareness among early twentieth-century writers like Wharton of the painting world, as well as the art of film and camera in *The American Short Story, 1900–1945* (Boston: Twayne Publishing, 1984), p. 19. Another study affirming the close association between literature and painting at this time is Laura Meixner, "The Best of Democracy': Walt Whitman, Jean-Francois Millet and Popular Culture in Post-Civil War America," in *Walt Whitman and the Visual Arts*, ed. Geoffrey M. Sill and Roberta K. Tarbell (New Brunswick, N.J.: Rutgers University Press, 1992).

4. Bram Dijkstra, *Idols of Perversity: Fantasies of Feminine Evil in Fin-de-Siècle Culture* (New York: Oxford University Press, 1986), 61. See also 37–47. Tennyson's centrality to Victorian culture is indicated in Jerome Hamilton Buckley, *The Victorian Temper: A Study in Literary Culture* (New York: Vintage Books, 1951), 66–86. Good examples of the other figures mentioned in this discussion are the painting *Elaine* by Toby Rosenthal (1874) and *The Lady of Shalott* by J. W. Waterhouse (1888).

5. Diane Price Herndl, *Invalid Woman: Figuring Feminine Illness in American Fiction and Culture, 1840–1940* (Chapel Hill: University of North Carolina Press, 1993), 136. See also Elisabeth Bronfen, *Over Her Dead Body: Configurations of Femininity, Death, and the Aesthetic* (New York: Routledge, 1992).

6. Gloria Erlich also views Lily Bart as a wrongly judged "loose woman" who is in fact repressed, but does not explore how Wharton encodes this irony in references to painting: "Virtually all circumstances in *The House of Mirth* conspire to focus sexual speculation about the person of Lily Bart, a woman who is unable to face her own sexuality, much less to act on it. Despite her skill at manipulating her image, she is almost invariably seen under compromising conditions that suggest she is a 'fast' woman if not a loose one. Her own unconscious or that of Edith Wharton inevitably places her in the spotlight of unacknowledged desire, causing her to lose control of the situations that matter most to her." *Sexual Education,* 72. Another analysis that reads Lily's resistance to marriage as a rejection of adult sexuality is Joan Lidoff, "Another Sleeping Beauty: Narcissism in *The House of Mirth,*" *American Quarterly* 32 (1980): 519–39.

7. Candace Waid, *Edith Wharton's Letters from the Underworld: Fictions of Women and Writing* (Chapel Hill: University of North Carolina Press, 1991), 28–30. In a dramatically different reading, Cynthia Griffin Wolff interprets Lily's impersonation of a painting as Wharton's metaphor for female as art object in a culture that forbids production of art to women; it is a moment of artifice and self-betrayal. *A Feast of Words,* 1977, 125–26.

8. Edith Wharton, *The House of Mirth* (1905; New York: Macmillan 1987), 179.

9. Ibid., 440.

10. Ibid., 438.

11. C. J. Wershoven, "*The Awakening* and *The House of Mirth*: Studies of Arrested Development," *American Literary Realism* 19 no. 3 (spring 1987): 27–41.

12. Wharton, *House of Mirth,* 211.

13. Edith Wharton, *The Custom of the Country* (1913; rpt. New York: Penguin 1987), 50.

14. Adrienne Auslander Munich explores the erotic nature of Andromeda paintings in *Andromeda's Chains: Gender and Interpretation in Victorian Literature and Art* (New York: Columbia University Press, 1989).

15. Linda Nochlin, "Lost and Found: Once More the Fallen Woman," in *Women, Art, and Power and Other Essays* (New York: Harper & Row, 1988). Other pertinent examples of paintings of drowned young women are *Virginia* by James Bertrand (ca. 1869) and *Found Drowned* by George F. Watts (1848).

16. Dijkstra, *Idols of Perversity,* 87. Examples of women floating on or in water or air include *Naissance de Vénus* by Alexandre Cabanel (1863); *Aphrodite* by Adolph Hirémy-Hirschl (ca. 1898); *The Oreads* by William Bouguereau (1902); *Dawn* by Walter Shirlaw (1886); *Twilight* by Jean-Louis Hamon (1867); and *Sleep and Poetry* by Edwin Howland Blashfield (c. 1886).

17. The water nymph of Victorian painting is described by Dijkstra in chap. IV, ibid., 83–118. Elizabeth Ammons discusses Undine's relationship to the myth of Undine the water nymph in *Edith Wharton's Argument with America* (Athens: University of Georgia Press, 1980), 115. Candace Waid delineates the irony of Undine's association with this figure in *Letters,* 1991, 145–48. The water nymph was ubiquitous in painting of this era. Some excellent examples include *The Sea-Maiden* by Herbert Draper (1894), *An Undine Playing in the Waves* by Pierre DuPuis (ca. 1896), and *The Green Abyss* by Aristede Sartorio (ca. 1895).

18. Wharton, *Custom,* 85.

19. Ibid., 82.

20. Ibid., 185. Candace Waid connects the language in this scene to Andrew Marvell's poem "The Unfortunate Lover." Waid conceptualizes Undine as an eagle who devours the organs of Prometheus while he is bound to a rock as well as the devouring monster of Andromeda mythology. *Letters,* 141–58.

21. Ernest John Knapton, *Empress Josephine* (Cambridge: Harvard University Press, 1964), 278.

22. Wolff, among others, notes this representation in *Feast of Words,* 1977, 113.

23. Vivien Gardner, and Susan Rutherford, eds., *The New Woman and Her Sisters: Feminism and Theatre, 1850–1914* (Ann Arbor: University of Michigan Press, 1992), 7. An earlier study confirms this view indicating that by midcentury, 70 percent of the American public disapproved of the theater and saw actresses as social outcasts because of their bohemian lifestyle. Albert Auster, *Actresses and Suffragists: Women in the American Theater, 1890–1920* (New York: Praeger Press, 1984), 18, 57. We see some of these notions at work in American fiction at the turn of the century, for example, Theodore Dreiser's *Sister Carrie* (1900), Stephen Crane's *Maggie, a Girl of the Streets* (1893), and Mary Austin's *A Woman of Genius* (1913).

24. Arthur Gold and Robert Fizdale describe these events in *The Divine Sarah: A Life of Sarah Bernhardt* (New York: Alfred A. Knopf, 1991), 171–72.

25. The prima donna, whom Wharton associates with Ellen, existed in a mythological tradition of a siren who lured sailors to their death with her seductive voice: "This powerful myth, associating women's singing with the death-hungry outpourings of a darkly erotic and hostile female sexuality . . . was still highly present in the art and literature of the nineteenth century.

That the prima donna of this era, commonly described as 'syren,' was ...
construed in the sensual terms of this predatory creature is demonstrated ...
by the publication of pornographic 'memoirs,' erroneously purporting to be
based on the sexual adventures of singers such as Elizabeth Billington, Lucia
Vestris, and Wilhelmina Schroder-Devrient." See Susan Rutherford, "The Voice
of Freedom: Images of the Prima Donna" in Gardner and Rutherford, *The New
Woman*, 1992.

26. Edith Wharton, *The Age of Innocence* (1920; rpt. New York: Macmillan,
1987), 9.

27. Ibid., 10.

28. Ibid., 104. Another painter of Bernhardt, Louise Abbéma, studied with
Carolus-Duran. Further connecting Wharton's allusion to Carolus-Duran with
portraits of Sarah Bernhardt is the fact that Henry James, Wharton's close
friend, reviewed both the Abbéma and Clairin portraits for the *New York Tribune*. Gold and Fizdale, *Divine Sarah*, 135–36.

29. James Gargano, "Tableaux of Renunciation: Wharton's Use of *The
Shaughran* in *The Age of Innocence*," *Studies in American Fiction* 15 (1987):
1–11. Gargano describes the way *The Shaughran* reference inscribes Wharton's central theme of renunciation, but he does not pursue the association of
Ellen with actresses or singers as I do here. Judith Fryer also discusses the
racapitulation of this scene from *The Shaughran* in other chapters of the
novel. *Felicitous Space: The Imaginative Structures of Edith Wharton and
Willa Cather* (Chapel Hill: University of North Carolina Press, 1986), 137.

30. The most prominent of these are Josephine Donovan, *After the Fall:
The Demeter-Persephone Myth in Wharton, Cather, and Glasgow* (University
Park: Pennsylvania State Press, 1989); Elizabeth Ammons, "Cool Diana and
the Blood-Red Muse: Edith Wharton on Innocence and Art," in *American
Novelists Revisited: Essays in Feminist Criticism*, ed. Fritz Fleischmann
(Boston: G. K. Hall, 1982); Fryer, *Felicitous Space*, 1986; and Gloria Erlich,
who suggests the sexual subtext of May's place in Newland's imagination when
she says: "Archer is a splitter of internal images—if Ellen signifies all that is
richly female and sexually desirable, May becomes to him a static icon of
permanent inviolability, a Diana-figure which he visualizes as an adolescent
boy." *Sexual Education*, 1992, 133.

31. Wharton, *Age*, 354.

32. Ibid., 359.

33. For a discussion of one such body of work and its revision by women
artists, see Carol Ockman, *Ingres's Eroticized Bodies: Retracing the Serpen-
tine Line* (New Haven: Yale University Press, 1995). Another useful study is
Anthea Callen, *The Spectacular Body: Science, Method, and Meaning in the
Work of Degas* (New Haven: Yale University Press, 1995).

34. Studies of Wharton's conflicted men include David Holbrook, *Edith
Wharton and the Unsatisfactory Man* (New York: St. Martin's Press, 1991);
and Lev Raphael, *Prisoners of Shame*, 1991.

The Death of Romance: *The Portrait of a Lady* in the Age of Lily Bart

JEROME LOVING

In his study of Henry James's revisions in *THE PORTRAIT OF A Lady* for the New York Edition, Anthony J. Mazzella argues that "there are two *Portraits,* not one, and that each is a different literary experience." In other words, "the Isabel Archer who faces her destiny is not the same young woman in both versions, nor is the quality of her destiny the same."[1] Given the subtlety of the textual changes, it is probably risky to argue for a significantly different book. Indeed, part of Mazzella's success in doing so—in suggesting a more cerebral, less emotional Isabel Archer in the later, 1908 version—may rest upon the critical consensus (in our time, not necessarily James's) that the later "Master" with his mannered style was the superior novelist. Yet it is arguable from Mazzella's detailed examination of the two books that the later Isabel is more conscious of the condition of womanhood and its perils, and this new emphasis on the main character's apprehensions necessarily alters the conduct of the supporting cast in her drama. *The Portrait of a Lady* was first serialized in 1880 and 1881, and published with slight revisions as a book in 1881. Here Mazzella finds a *jeune fille* of sorts, certainly a character who matches more the naive "American girl" first imprinted in *Daisy Miller* (1878). More is made of the twentieth-century Isabel's apprehension of men as domestic predators. This change in *Portrait,* Mazzella writes, is directly "related to [Isabel's] ideas on marriage, to the conventional proposals of marriage she receives from her three suitors, and to the fatality of money."[2] Isabel is more clearly fearful of sex, especially from Caspar Goodwood, whose name has a phallic ring to it. She fears "not what sex might do to her body but what it might do to her mind."[3] In other words, the character of the revised Isabel argues more persuasively than the original character for the plight of the female who—as James observed of American women at the beginning of the twentieth century—was all dressed up but with no place to go.[4] With regard to the fear of sex, in Isabel and the woman of the era she represents, married women also had no place to go. The story of the later Isabel, then, is more compelling than its predecessor as a sophisticated argument for women's rights.

James's popularity with readers, which never amounted to commercial success, decreased as his fictions became more complex.[5] Edith Wharton, one of his most enthusiastic readers, complained in 1904 that she found James's fiction of the past ten years almost impossible to read. His fictional stage, she later explained in A Backward Glance (1934), "was cleared like that of the Théâtre Français in the good old days when no chair or table was introduced that was not relevant to the action (a good rule for the stage, but an unnecessary embarrassment to fiction)."[6] Wharton may, however, have had another reason to dislike the later writings of the "Master," whom she personally adored. In the earlier complaint (from a letter to Scribner's in which she commented on the reviews of The Descent of Man [1904]), she objected to "the continued cry that I am an echo of Mr. James." As she told Scribner's, Wharton found herself in 1904 in an absurd situation: On the one hand, she was the female Henry James ("James and water"); on the other, she failed to write about "navvies & char-women."[7] She may have removed the later charge with The House of Mirth (1905), which includes a significant charwoman. The reality of the working world is also evident in the book's threat to those next-generation Madame Merles who do not know how to behave themselves as houseguests. And as to the first charge against her, the alleged tendency to "echo" the "Master," The House of Mirth not only revised that pattern, but it for once at least reversed the direction of influence. In other words, the "echo" reverberated back upon James as he read The House of Mirth and revised The Portrait of a Lady. In this case, the lady influenced the gentleman in the revision of the saga of Isabel Archer (whose sister, incidentally, is named Lily). Not only did Wharton's "portrait" of Lily Bart help to clarify James's Portrait of Isabel by encouraging him to locate more historically and realistically the source of his heroine's anxiety as she sought to "affront" her destiny, but Wharton's life also served James in his revision. As Millicent Bell observes, Wharton at first appeared to James "as only another writer, but soon emerged . . . as the kind of American woman who might have figured in one of his own fictions."[8]

Indeed, as R. W. B. Lewis remarks, James, privy to both the deteriorating state of Wharton's marriage and the affair she had with Morton Fullerton, which began in 1907, saw his friend of more than a decade in terms similar to those in which he had depicted Isabel Archer as she pondered the stifling circumstances of her marriage. "What comes to me most," he told Howard Sturgis, a close acquaintance of Wharton, "is the thought of how it must come to poor Edith, in these dark vigils, that she did years ago an almost—or rather an utterly—inconceivable thing of marrying him." James, Lewis argues persuasively,

> was exploiting his own fiction for an appraisal of actual life. The image of Edith Wharton in her dark Parisian vigil pondering her deadly marital imprisonment springs from what is perhaps the most brilliant narrative passage James ever wrote: the long vigil of Isabel Archer in *The Portrait of a Lady,* sitting late in the darkened room of her Roman palazzo meditating her disastrous choice of a husband and the course of her psychic incarceration by him."[9]

That James knew of neither the complete breakdown of Wharton's marriage nor her affair with Fullerton until late 1908 when the revised *Portrait* was finished and probably published does not discount the fact that he was *prepared* to see his friend in the light of such a "darkened room." Moreover, the evidence was fairly apparent for some years that Wharton's marriage ties were not strong. The first book of hers Wharton sent him and he read was *The Greater Inclination* (1899), a collection of short stories that showed the author to be probing the female condition in unprecedented and promising ways. In the best of the collection, "Souls Belated," Wharton depicts the protagonist as hopelessly imprisoned by the convention of marriage, if not the particular one Lydia Tillotson abandons in the story. More of a "feminist" in these earlier writings than the (much) later ones, Wharton was beginning to break the same new ground for the turn-of-the-century woman that Kate Chopin had unsettled the same year in *The Awakening.* We may assume that James continued to read Wharton (her books made available to him by the author's sister-in-law, Mary Cadwalader Jones, who first brought them together). We know positively that he read both her Italian novel, *The Valley of Decision* (1902) and *The House of Mirth.* After reading the first, he advised her to "DO NEW YORK!"[10]— which she did in the second.

According to one of Wharton's recent biographers, James was never able to appreciate *The House of Mirth* "as more than a lucky hit," preferring *The Fruit of the Tree* (1907), which failed as a commercial venture.[11] Yet as he recalled his own commercial failures, most dramatically evidenced by the play *Guy Domville* (1895), he may have reconsidered his judgment of *The House of Mirth* as he moved forward with his revisions for the New York Edition, especially for *The Portrait of a Lady*. Furthermore, James, whose female companions in his early and middle years had been predominantly older women, began in the last two decades of his life to feel the need for both younger and more intimate companions. In these years, according to Lyall H. Powers, James began to seek closer ties with various attractive younger people who admired him and whom he found "bright and interesting."[12] One of these was Fullerton, but another was Wharton, the first female of the younger generation to affect James acutely since Constance Fenimore Woolson, who committed suicide in 1894. Although (according to her autobiography) Wharton first met James as early as the late 1880s, their relationship did not become close until around 1903. It lasted without interruption—in fact, with increased intensity—until James's death in 1916. What may be inferred from the fact that James in his final years felt the need for more intimate and younger companions, including women, is that he was more in touch with the social circumstances of the post–Emerson American for whom (social) action was becoming as important as thought. In particular, as he revised *The Portrait of a Lady*, James was now in touch with a real-life version of an American woman living in Europe and unhappy in marriage.

I have argued elsewhere[13] that James's Isabel is not that different from his early male quester in Europe, Christopher Newman of *The American* (1877), nor (more generally) different from the other American questers who, before they ran back to Europe in James, ran off to sea (in Irving, Poe, and Melville), into the Gothic landscape or dark wood (in Brown and Hawthorne), to the West (in Cooper and Twain), or to war (after James, in Stephen Crane and Hemingway). Curiously, Isabel not only runs off to the Old World but to the old convention of marriage, the very institution from which she has fled when pursued by Caspar Goodwood and which will incarcerate her with Gilbert Osmond. Yet marriage in and of itself is not the central issue in *The Portrait of a Lady* (as it more clearly is in Chopin's *The Awakening* or Wharton's *The House of Mirth*). Rather, it is the American ideal of affronting one's destiny. Isabel's problem in such a romantic adventure is neither marriage nor Europe, but the deter-

mination to find someone (in marriage) whose actions she can
clearly influence, someone whose "boat" she can launch. Indeed,
as she faces in the aftermath the reality of her failed marriage—
in that "darkened room" of her Roman palazzo—she remembers
the "opportunity" Osmond's courtship had presented: "She had
felt . . . he was helpless and ineffectual." And thus: "She would
launch his boat for him; she would be his providence; it would
be a good thing to love him."[14] Isabel Archer—like the Isabella
who launched the first "American" boat with Columbus—does
not fail because she is a woman but because her American ideal-
ism leads her to expect something in Europe that exists only as
a dream in America—the "perfect" marriage in an imperfect
world.

This is as true in the 1908 version of *Portrait* as it is in the
earlier story. Yet the novels—or at least their heroines—are different. As Mazzella suggests, the New York Edition gives us a
better sense of Isabel's pending fate as a woman. In the original
version, when Osmond declares that he is "absolutely in love"
with her (his emphasis, the adverb itself, is somewhat threatening), we read: "The tears came into Isabel's eyes—they were
caused by an intenser throb of that pleasant pain I spoke of a
moment ago." In the revision: "The tears came into her eyes:
this time they obeyed the sharpness of the pang that suggested
to her somehow the slipping of a fine bolt—backward, forward,
she couldn't have said which." Mazzella comments: "The image
of the bolt as conceived by the later Isabel is ambiguously a
freeing and enslaving mechanism—a sense of unknown fate."[15]
We might go further to note the phallic imagery, which prefigures Osmond's psychological ravishment. Instinctively, Isabel
fears the loss of control that will come with her eventual acceptance of Osmond's proposal—that is to say, *his* impending power
over *her* and, of course, her money.

It is here that the character of Lily Bart influenced the remak-
ing of Isabel for James's twentieth-century readers. If it is clearer
in the 1908 version that Isabel's future as an individual is already preempted, the change may have come about from James's
reading of *The House of Mirth*. That story of the single woman
opens with an impending sense of doom for the female who
would "affront" her destiny, or try to avoid, as Lily does, the
"vocation" of marriage.[16] Lily Bart more resembles Madame
Merle than she does Isabel Archer, but she also suggests (as does
Madame Merle) the fate of Isabel. Like Madame Merle at age
forty, Lily at age twenty-nine is constantly in transit between

one acquaintance's home and the next. Both are "stranded," as it were, between domestic asylums that underscore the impossibility of marriage without male dominance. The source of this male control is money. In *Portrait*, it is the Touchett fortune, or the "Midas touch," that turns every human quality into a marketable commodity. In *The House of Mirth*, it is mainly the Trenor fortune, or Gus Trenor's lure of a "loan" to Lily, that ultimately controls her situation and seals her fate as a compromised woman. Indeed, Lily's life in the book opens in compromise. Literally stranded in a New York City train station between visits to other people's homes, she has no place to go before her next train but to Lawrence Selden's bachelor flat. There we learn that her time as a single woman instead of a kept or married one is fast coming to an end. Her most interesting male companion is Selden, and yet he resembles Ralph Touchett in his inability to marry Isabel. In both novels, the best male candidate for marriage is in one way or another disqualified, creating a vacuum to be filled with such boorish types as Caspar Goodwood or Percy Gryce.

The problem James faced as he revised *Portrait* for the twentieth century was that he could not credibly write—or rewrite—a realistic novel in an age of naturalism. As Powers observes, "Anyone familiar with James's earlier fiction up to the publication of *The Portrait of a Lady* . . . will notice in the fiction that followed a marked change both in subject matter and, more arresting, in narrative technique."[17] He cites such subsequent works as *The Bostonians* (1886), *The Princess Casamassima* (1886), and *The Tragic Muse* (1890), in which the focus is shifted away from the "international novel" and toward the middle and lower classes. Attention, of course, is also shifted away from the Howellsian (or realistic) idea that the individual might escape his situation with his dignity relatively intact—that the American "Silas" might "rise" in the fall that is his human destiny. In both versions of *Portrait*, Isabel is destined to return to Rome and to Osmond rather than "publish" her mistake in choosing a marriage partner; yet in the 1908 version, she senses this destiny from the outset, or at least earlier in the drama. In the twentieth-century version of the novel, Isabel is more "cerebral" because she is depicted with James's alterations as being more conscious of the restricting effects of her heredity and environment.

Isabel proclaims in both versions—in the scene in which she rejects Warburton's proposal of marriage—that she cannot es-

cape her unhappiness. However, there is—as Mazzella observes—an important change in this scene. In the first version,
Isabel is described as "young and flexible in her movement,"
which Warburton merely "noticed." In the revision, she is described as young and "so young and free in her movement that
her very pliancy seemed to mock at him."[18] In the second account of Isabel's affronting her female destiny in marriage, the
male with the money is visibly affronted—threatened and perhaps even shocked by her audacity to refuse the opportunity
that every woman was supposed to seek out. She was expected
to hope for and readily accept a marriage in which she would
strike the best economic bargain for her physical and social attributes. Not only is the later *Portrait* not a romantic portrait any
longer (in the adventurous sense of *Daisy Miller*), it is also not
influenced (even negatively) by Hawthorne's more romantic
treatment of the woman's plight. James had completed and published his 1879 study of Hawthorne for the English Men of Letters series shortly before writing the first version of *Portrait*.
There he had studied, of course, *The Scarlet Letter*, in which
Hester's beauty—after seven long years—returns from "what
men call the irrevocable past."[19] Of course, it comes back to a
self-"polluted priest" and guilt-ridden ex-lover. That, however, is
beside the point for our purposes here—except to note that Hester is allowed to exit the drama with her dignity not only intact,
but heightened. Her physical renewal is merely representative of
her increased stature—the "divine maternity" that Hawthorne
hints at in the beginning of his story. Isabel, on the other hand,
concludes as the "mother" of the illicit child she never had with
Osmond. This is true in both editions, but the difference is that
in the second version Isabel anticipates her inability to escape
her unhappiness long before she broods in front of the fire at
her Roman residence and concludes that Madame Merle and
Osmond have made a "convenience" of her.

Most readers will agree that Warburton is Isabel's "best catch."
He is much more of a gentleman than Goodwood (the only other
viable option), who—if his sudden and uninvited embrace of
her at the end of the novel is any indication—no doubt would
have tried to dominate her in marriage. Yet Warburton, with his
titles and properties, is something of a perpetual adolescent.
Nearly forty, he entertains the possibility of courting (the even
more immature) Pansy—while at the same time hoping for a
second chance with Isabel. He is not threatening to Isabel, except for her concern that she would become merely another of

his lordly possessions. In other words, the "best catch," the best a woman even of Isabel's talent and looks can find, is boring, if not otherwise harmful. This is also the situation Lily Bart faces in *The House of Mirth,* where—it should also be observed—all the marriages are horrors. She entertains several such unexciting prospects for marriage, but the most memorable is probably Percy Gryce with whom, among other activities, she imagines she would have to go to church each Sunday:

> They would have a front pew in the most expensive church in New York, and his name would figure handsomely in the list of parish charities. In a few years, when he grew stouter, he would be made a warden. Once in the winter the rector would come to dine, and her husband would beg her to go over the list and see that no *divorcées* were included, except those who had showed signs of penitence by being re-married to the very wealthy. There was nothing especially arduous in this round of religious obligations; but it stood for a fraction of that great bulk of boredom that loomed across her path.[20]

Not only does Lily face the banality of upper middle-class marriage (that Isabel's sister Lily also experiences in an earlier New York society), but she would be enlisted in keeping other "single women" in line and out of the spheres of social influence. As one critic of the double standard depicted in *The House of Mirth* reminds us, "A society that expects women to compete against one another for a very few positions of prestige cannot encourage friendship, trust, and mutual sharing among women. Instead, jealousy must govern their relationships with one another. No woman—not even a married woman—can really feel secure."[21]

Working for the "enemy," of course, is exactly what Madame Merle does after *her* fall from social virginity. In the later version of *Portrait,* however, she has been transformed to resemble the conniving women in *The House of Mirth,* such as Bertha Dorset and Carry Fisher. In a comparative textual study, which complements Mazzella's, Nina Baym points out that the earlier description of Madame Merle as "a brilliant fugitive from Brooklyn" becomes in the twentieth-century novel a "perverted product of their [hers and Isabel's] common soil." Although she tells Isabel in the 1881 version that the English "were the finest in the world," in 1908 they are "the most convenient in the world to live with."[22] Indeed, without Madame Merle's interference, Isabel might well have made a better choice of a husband. And without the social slights of female friends in *The House of Mirth,* Lily might have survived her mistakes. Both heroines make mis-

takes, to be sure. Although Isabel's primary mistake is more
subtle—not the conscious (or even unconscious) avoidance of
marriage as it seems to be in Lily's case but the impractical
intention to redefine marriage (and thus launch her husband's
boat)—her error is perhaps more serious than Lily's because
she remains unrepentant. As in the case of Hawthorne's Hester
and Arthur, penance is not enough because it does not reduce
the character's sense of dignity but in fact enlarges it.

In his revision of *The Portrait of a Lady,* James faced the
difficult and perplexing problem of allowing Isabel to end up
with her individuality unfragmented. We have no evidence that
he read *The Awakening* or *Sister Carrie* (1900), two other major
novels of the time that showed the woman in defeat (Edna dead
and Carrie rich but rocking aimlessly). We know, of course, that
he read *The House of Mirth,* which treats essentially the same
class of people that *The Portrait of a Lady* depicts. Despite his
treatment of lower classes in his novels of the 1880s and his
qualified approval of Emile Zola's "scientific" experiments (he
admired the realism but regretted the Frenchman's necessary
but perhaps overdrawn sordidness), he could—or would—never
create an American Nana, such as Dreiser's Carrie. Chopin's
Edna might have influenced him, had he read *The Awakening,*
because that heroine is of the same social class as Isabel and
other more recognizable Jamesian heroines. Even Wharton's
Lily was beyond his reach because she is already too fallen for
the dignified conclusion of the original Isabel. Yet James must
have realized that Lily clearly depicted the situation of the
middle-class woman in the twentieth century, the time zone for
the updated Isabel. For both Wharton's and Chopin's heroines,
however, the end is violent, suggesting the ultimate punishment
for the woman who defies the convention of marriage. In other
words, there was little or no (realistic) room for even the semiro-
mantic close, no room for the American romance in which, for
example, Hester exchanges her physical needs for spiritual (and
social) influence. There was also precious little room for Isabel
to renegotiate her future after failing to launch Osmond's boat.

If the American romance allowed for this crucial margin of
error, its time had passed. It had permitted its male questers to
escape danger and death, to wake up from their dramas and
treat them as "stories." Rip Van Winkle survives a twenty-year
coma (as the real-life characters in Oliver Sacks's *Awakenings*
ultimately do not) to tell his story; Arthur Gordon Pym survives
a giant cataract by way of the fiction of a "Symmes Hole" (in

which he and his companion are recycled through the center of the earth to tell their story); Ishmael alone survives Ahab's confrontation with the White Whale to tell his story; Emerson's persona in "Experience" survives the tragic death of his son to claim that grief "will make us idealists"; Thoreau's narrator in *Walden* forgets the harshness of nature (that Thoreau had found in the Maine Woods) to find its tranquility around a pond not a mile away from his mother's (and Emerson's) house; and Whitman's protagonist survives the limits of poetic language in "Out of the Cradle Endlessly Rocking" and "As I Ebb'd with the Ocean of Life" to find a passage "to more than India!" It is no wonder, therefore, that the first credible female quester in American literature might be expected to affront *her* destiny. Isabel not only is as bold as Ahab but as shrewd as Ishmael—in the nineteenth-century version of her character. She wakes up at the end of her drama as Emerson's "Whole Man," who steadfastly maintains that "Our life is not so much threatened as our perception."[23] In the twentieth century, however, she might ask more honestly and less rhetorically than Emerson, "Where do we find ourselves?"

In a sentence, the new Isabel wakes up where Lily Bart begins in the twentieth century. Here there is no American romance, no literary "Symmes Hole," to save her. Her potential suitors are essentially the same, but her new perception of them is seriously and tragically altered. Isabel is threatened by perception, which can no longer be explained away with the transcendentalism she had enjoyed in her first fictional life. James tells us in *Portrait*— in chapter 42—that Isabel "had never been able to understand Unitarianism!"[24] which is to say that she felt relatively free (potentially free in the Emersonian sense of self-reliance) of the social contraints that threatened to define her destiny. The revisions that highlight her anxiety suggest that James refitted his character for the age of Lily Bart. It is an era in which men and women are less conditioned by genteel standards and nineteenth-century quasi-romantic ideals in spite of their material needs. Gilbert Osmond is at least subtle and civil in his conflict with Isabel. [Whereas Gus Trenor nearly rapes Lily when she offers resistance to his will,] Madame Merle may have made a "convenience" of Isabel, but Bertha Dorset sets out to ruin Lily by inviting her abroad in order to set her up for the scandal involving Bertha's husband. It must have been clearer to James after reading *The House of Mirth* that Isabel simply could not survive the twentieth century on Emersonian principles. It was akin to asking—in a dangerous exaggeration of Emersonian-ism—that the slave free himself psychologically before his proper emancipation could take place. Self-reliance would not work without reliance upon social change. Add to this impression James's notions of American women in *The American Scene* (based on his tour after a twenty years' absence from the United States in 1904 and published in 1907), and we can better understand the influences he was working under when he revised the story of Isabel. The changed perceptions are manifested, of course, in *The Wings of the Dove* (1902) where the unselfish, poetically charming Milly Theale is literally and pathetically crushed by the ambitious plot of Kate Croy (who gets her lover Merton Denscher to propose to the terminally ill Milly so that he will inherit her money and thus have an adequate fortune to marry Kate).

Lily Bart is almost as helpless as Milly Theale. Possibly her one chance of protecting herself from Bertha Dorset is to black-mail her with the love letters from Bertha to Lawrence Selden that she mistakenly receives from the charwoman at the Bene-dick. It would be nice to think that she is above such sordid tactics—that, like Isabel, she should never stoop to such (modern?) chicanery. Yet she destroys the letters only because she cares for Selden. It is not, however, because she *loves* Selden, for it is clear in the novel that she would never marry him. Why? Probably because he does not have enough money. And this circumstance puts Lily in the same circumstance as Kate Croy, who finally sleeps with Denscher to push him into her plot against Milly. Kate is finally punished for her deeds in the Jame-sian (and Hawthornian) twist in which Denscher's Dimmesdal-ian conscience damns her. Just as ironically Lily is punished (indirectly, at least) for *not* going to bed (with Gus Trenor).

The point is that Lily is caught between the expediency of the twentieth century, in which a woman's body was perhaps more easily the object of male dominance in marriage, and the gentil-ity of the nineteenth century where the woman's virginity was still a vague source of power (e.g., in the romantic sense of Henry Adams's observations in "The Dynamo and the Virgin").[25] Lily, as far as the reader knows, retains her virginity but she is also powerless. Isabel, as far as the reader also knows, retains her virginity until marriage but James's heroine is just as power-less—at least in terms of affronting her destiny. "She had taken all the first steps in the *purest* confidence," Isabel recalls of her relationship with Osmond in chapter 42, "and then she had suddenly found the infinite vista of a multiplied life to be a dark, narrow alley with a dead wall at the end" (my italics).[26] This sentence remains unchanged in the revision of the novel, yet it demanded in the twentieth century a different story, if not a dramatically changed conclusion. (Indeed, the conclusion is already changed: Read in the context of Emersonian ideology, it might be concluded that Isabel will eventually leave Osmond after returning to Rome; whereas read in the wake of Lily Bart, the implication is clear that Isabel's option for independent action has largely disappeared.) The sentence resembles one in Emerson's "Experience," where political promises (and hopes for favorable change in general) are compared with "western roads, which opened stately enough, with planted trees on either side to tempt the traveller, but soon became narrow and narrower and ended in a squirrel-track and ran up a tree."[27] In this essay, Emerson is trying to reconcile the brutality of nature with its emblematic beauty and will conclude on the old optimistic note. After chapter 42, Isabel cannot afford the reconciliation, and neither could James after he returned to *Portrait* to revise her story.

James did a curious thing in trying to revise his works in the twentieth century—in the case of *The Portrait of a Lady* and probably in his other rewritten novels. He fell into the desire to revise these works *for* the twentieth century. In the case of Isabel, there were simply no longer "portraits" of ladies. Perhaps he sensed this change during the revision. For example, he chose for his frontispiece in the first volume of the 1908 version not a portrait but a house—the supposed mansion at Gardencourt (featured on the first [1975] Norton edition).[28] In fact, he also avoided using a portrait for the New York Edition of *The Wings of the Dove*—even though the heroine of that novel is compared with Bronzino's portrait of the beautiful Lucrezia Panciatichi, which still hangs today (as it did during the time of the novel) in Florence's Uffizi Gallery. Indeed, the painting's use as a frontispiece is so tempting that it appears on the cover of that Norton edition (though the negative is inverted). But—to put the matter much more bluntly than James himself would have—the "Dove" in that novel is a "dead duck" from the outset. Bronzino's idealized portrait of the woman would not have worked for the twentieth century as it did for the sixteenth (or even the nineteenth in America). His figure sits as aloof as Poe's Helen "in yon brilliant window-niche," which is to say statuelike and muselike. By the same token, the "new" Isabel dwells not in any portrait but in the "house" of Gardencourt. She inspires nobody in the novel, only the reader who would have Isabel transcend the experience of having her life negatively affected by human greed (namely, but not exclusively, Osmond's).

If any character in the novel—particularly any female character—survives both versions with her aspirations intact, it is Henrietta Stackpole. As Baym notes, Henrietta survives, especially in the revision where Isabel does not, through James's "systematic vulgarization" of the minor character. Dozens of revisions "make Henrietta harsher, more unpleasant, and more stupid."[29] There is, as Isabel observes in the twentieth-century revision of the book, "something of the 'people' in her." In both versions, Henrietta is described by Isabel as "a kind of emanation of the great democracy—of the continent, the country, the nation."[30] This is in response to Ralph's experimental criticism of the lady journalist. In a word, Isabel is defending Henrietta against being considered vulgar (as James, who valued his privacy and therefore disliked journalists, intended). Perhaps in revising, James felt his revised character's added "vulgarity," though unpleasant, was nevertheless in keeping with the twentieth-century woman who would survive the crush of matrimony, at least when marriage deprived her of professional and social advancement. Therefore, such revisions of this practical woman's lines were necessary to underscore Henrietta's difference from Isabel, who is finally deferential to male manipulation. For example, in the original version, when Isabel compares Henrietta to the "green" Pacific Ocean from which "a strong, sweet, fresh odour seems to rise," Ralph replies sarcastically that he is not so "sure the Pacific's so green as that" but that "Henrietta is decidedly fragrant." In the revision, she "smell[s] of the Future"—so much so that "it almost knocks one down!"[31]

Henrietta is—as she is described in both versions—"a proof that a woman might suffice to herself and be happy."[32] She is happy, however, only in (or coming from) a democracy and as a working woman. It appears that James was uncomfortable writing about such democratic women. It was perhaps painful to him that they were the ones who would survive in the new order of the twentieth century—not such romantic heroines as Isabel. Henrietta does not marry the artist (Osmond); she does not marry the lord (Warburton); neither does she marry the American (Goodwood)—all three on the surface, at least, admirable candidates for marriage. She marries instead Mr. Bantling, Ralph's friend and certainly a banterer. Yet Bantling is the only male in the novel who is prepared to accept a woman as an equal partner and who is not out to control her. And those who cannot meet Isabel on this basis not only include the three mentioned above but Ralph, who manipulates Isabel with the legacy, and Ralph's father, who agrees to the scheme and who also is smitten with Isabel.

Of course, Henrietta survives because she is driven by a more limited and thus more realistic ambition than Isabel. In this regard, Henrietta resembles Gerty Farish in *The House of Mirth*. Yet neither character is at any point a likely candidate for the heroine of a novel—anymore than a male character of the same standing (Bantling, for example) would make a good hero. And this indeed may be the point: In the twentieth century, neither sex could be romantically depicted without also being sentimentally depicted. Instead, they would have to "star" as one of Sherwood Anderson's grotesques in *Winesburg, Ohio* (1919) or be parceled out to the cast of John Dos Passos's *U.S.A.* (1938). Perhaps James was as prescient as Henry Adams in the *Education*, who saw that in the passing of the woman as symbolic virgin lay the demise of the American romance or Realism in the Howellsian mode. Woman could no longer be the object of the romantic notion, no longer its muse. Instead, she had become a part of the cast of human beings displaced by the metaphysical decline of humanism. Not yet deconstructed, Isabel had at least to be reconstructed in the first part of the twentieth century. And that necessity was, of course, the beginning of her end as a heroine and the end of her beginning again in the endless cycle, or series of "short stories," that punctuated the American novel before the 1890s and the influence of Zola. In the first version of *The Portrait of a Lady*, we are allowed, even encouraged, to think that Isabel will start over after she returns to Rome. In the revision, we can be fairly certain that this woman will return as Osmond's wife. In forcing us to reach this conclusion about the revised Isabel, James was eschewing the "happy ending" that Wharton herself had resisted in the unsuccessful stage adaptation of *The House of Mirth* (1906). As she recalled in her autobiography, "I knew that (owing to my refusal to let the heroine survive) it was foredoomed to failure." It was so foredoomed because of the American nostalgia (then and today) for the endless second chance or reawakening to life. This desire for a destiny without a destination was probably best summed up by Howells, who had accompanied Wharton to the opening night of the play in New York City and who had himself by this time learned the lesson of the twentieth century and the "fall" of the American Silas. As the two authors left the Savoy Theater, Wharton remembered, Howells "summed up the reason for the play's failure. 'Yes—what the American public always wants is a tragedy with a happy ending.'"[33]

Notes

1. Anthony J. Mazzella, "The New Isabel," in *The Portrait of a Lady*, ed. Robert D. Bamberg (New York: W. W. Norton, Inc., 1995), 597–619.

2. Mazzella, 601.

3. Ibid., 611.

4. *The American Scene* (1907); see Martha Banta, "They Shall Have Faces, Minds, and (One Day) Flesh: Women in Late Nineteenth-Century and Early Twentieth-Century American Literature," in *What Manner of Women: Essays on English and American Life and Literature*, ed. Marlene Springer (New York: New York University Press, 1977), 239.

5. *Henry James and Edith Wharton Letters: 1900–1915*, ed. Lyall H. Powers (New York: Charles Scribner's Sons, 1990), 84. James was visibly depressed over the poor sales of his New York Edition.

6. *A Backward Glance* (New York: Charles Scribner's Sons, 1934), 190–91.

7. *Letters of Edith Wharton*, ed. R. W. B. Lewis and Nancy Lewis (New York: Charles Scribner's Sons, 1988), 91.

8. *Edith Wharton and Henry James: The Story of Their Friendship* (New York: George Brazillier, 1965), 20.

9. Quoted in *Edith Wharton: A Biography* (New York: Harper & Row, Publishers, 1975), 317.

10. *Henry James and Edith Wharton Letters*, 33–34.

11. *Edith Wharton: A Biography*, 180–81.

12. *Henry James and Edith Wharton Letters*, 12.

13. *Lost in the Customhouse: Authorship in the American Renaissance* (Iowa City: University of Iowa Press, 1993), 160–76.

14. *Portrait*, 357.

15. Ibid., 263, 602.

16. Edith Wharton, *The House of Mirth*, ed. Elizabeth Ammons (New York: W. W. Norton, 1990), 10.

17. *Henry James and the Naturalist Movement* (Ann Arbor: University of Michigan Press, 1971), 1.

18. *Portrait*, 118.

19. *The Scarlet Letter*, ed. Seymour Gross, et al. (New York: W. W. Norton, 1988), 138.

20. *House of Mirth*, 47.

21. Cathy N. Davidson, "Kept Women in *The House of Mirth*," *Markham Review* 9 (1979): 11. For another version of this idea in Wharton, who cultivated and nurtured many of her female relationships, see Susan Goodman, *Edith Wharton's Women: Friends and Rivals* (Hanover, N.H.: University Press of New England, 1990).

22. "Revision and Thematic Change in *The Portrait of a Lady*," in *Modern Critical Interpretations of Henry James's "The Portrait of a Lady*," ed. Harold Bloom (New York: Chelsea House, 1987), 76.

23. "Experience," in *The Collected Works of Ralph Waldo Emerson,* ed. Joseph Slater, et al. (Cambridge: Harvard University Press, 1983), 3:27.

24. *Portrait,* 363.

25. *The Education of Henry Adams,* ed. Ernest Samuels and Jayne N. Samuels (New York: Library of America, 1983), 1070–72. Of course, Adams is making a distinction there between the symbolic power of the European woman's fecundity and the decreased influence of the "monthly-magazine" American woman, who was rendered sexless. In my adaptation of this distinction, I am asserting that the American woman of the nineteenth century was at least empowered (and thereby protected to some extent) by her position as the upholder of the "moral affections" in American life.

26. *Portrait,* 356.

27. "Experience," 34.

28. It was A. L. Coburn's "The English House." For the second volume, James used Coburn's "The Roman Bridge." These illustrations appear in *Henry James's New York Edition: The Construction of Authorship,* ed. David McWhirter (Palo Alto, Calif.: Stanford University Press, 1995).

29. "Revisions and Thematic Change in *The Portrait,*" 79–81.

30. *Portrait,* 87.

31. Ibid., 88.

32. Ibid., 55.

33. *A Backward Glance,* 147.

Form, "Selection," and Ideology in Edith Wharton's Antimodernist Aesthetic

Frederick Wegener

In 1928, as she looked back over the fluctuating critical reception of her work, Edith Wharton stoically acknowledged what she described as "the inevitable curve of condescension, praise, dithyrambic enthusiasm and gradual cooling off, which any novelist who has run a twenty-years' career should be prepared to meet. . . . Whoever offers his wares for sale in the open market should accept rose wreaths or rotten eggs with an equal heart."[1] In private, however, she was not always quite so philosophical or serenely resigned. Three years earlier, she had been especially irritated by a review that paired her novel *The Mother's Recompense* (1925) with *Mrs. Dalloway*—one of those juxtapositions so convenient to scholars tracing changes in critical taste and value. Declaring that "Mrs. Woolf is a brilliant experimentalist, while Mrs. Wharton . . . is now content to practise the craft of fiction without attempting to enlarge its technical scope," the reviewer concludes that "Mrs. Woolf's is an inversion of the ordinary method of narration, the method of which Mrs. Wharton offers us a very respectable example. In 'The Mother's Recompense' [readers] will be affronted neither by technical innovations nor by subtleties of thought or vision."[2] Although subtler in most respects than the other novels of her final period, *The Mother's Recompense* is not a novel in which one would look for technically innovative narration, and it was precisely this observation that Wharton addressed, with characteristic hauteur, in a letter to her friend John Hugh Smith: "It is, of course, what an English reviewer (I forget in what paper) reviewing it with Mrs. Woolf's latest, calls it: an old-fashioned novel. I was not trying to follow the new methods, . . . & my heroine belongs to the day when scruples existed."[3]

Wharton may be forgiven such a dry response, for this was not the only occasion on which she saw her work uncharitably compared with Woolf's, or used to bring out, by contrast, the artistic virtues of her technically adventurous successors.[4] Yet her remarks to Hugh Smith reveal a good deal more than an increasing frustration with imperceptive reviewers. Distinguishing her own "old-fashioned novel" from novels that "follow the new methods," the "scruples" attributed to its heroine and background "existed," Wharton clearly implies, before the age in which such "new methods" arose. In one of several familiar gestures of critical reaction in her later work, Wharton links the disappearance of "scruples" to the vogue of "the new methods" in fiction, considering those methods not only symptomatic of a larger moral crisis or decline but somehow morally defective themselves. Her scornful tone, however, suggests that Wharton's judgment in this regard, like so much of the action in her own novels, is less an assertion of "moral meaning" than a reflection of "social power," to borrow Nancy Bentley's recent formulation, and that Wharton's concern with "scruples" can just as easily invoke "a complex machinery of decorous force" as "any definitive set of moral imperatives."[5] Ultimately, it is a very different sort of crisis and decline that Wharton associates with the rise of "new methods" in fiction; and the intriguing connection that she tacitly establishes in her letter to Hugh Smith—between "method" and "morality," between a question of technique or aesthetic practice and one of "character"—becomes more a connection between "method" and "decorum," or between "method" and "manners," referring not to "inherited values of propriety" but to "local forms of human society" (Bentley, 107) now under siege in an unscrupulous world of chaotic change. In other words, a social rather than an ethical or aesthetic concern underlies what Irving Howe delicately calls Wharton's "coolness to modernist innovations,"[6] and it is a correlation of the social with the aesthetic—evoked in her letter to Hugh Smith, but developed more fully in her later essays and fiction—that fundamentally shapes not only Wharton's inhospitable response to modernism in literature and the arts but also her critical outlook as a whole.

Although Wharton continued to look askance at Woolf,[7] she had much harsher things to say, in fact, about various other new novelists of the day. A couple of years following her death, for example, Edward Marsh recalled her disgruntled reaction after he "made Edith Wharton read *Sons and Lovers*": "[H]ow *could* I have recommended such a botched and bungled piece of work?"[8] A year after she remarked, not without some justice, that "characters in modern fiction are often (as, for instance, in the novels of D. H. Lawrence) no more differentiated than a set of megaphones, through all of which the same voice interminably reiterates the same ideas" (*UCW,* 175), the publication of a new study of Lawrence in 1935 moved Wharton to exclaim, "If any one had told me I shd ever read another book on that fraud of a great man I shd have laughed the idea to scorn."[9] More familiar is the letter in which she informed Bernard Berenson, in 1923, "I . . . already tackled Ulysses & cast it from me. . . . It's a turgid welter of pornography (the rudest schoolboy kind) & unformed & unimportant drivel" (*L,* 461). Faulkner's *Sanctuary* prompted a similar response, along with an intriguing analogy: "All these books, so obviously written to make the hair of the elderly stand on end, seem to me to have such a schoolboyish side, such as Emily Brontë presents in comparison with Jane Austen."[10]

Moreover, Wharton's later fiction has much diabolical fun, of course, with the posturings and eccentricities of modernism. In "Writing a War Story" (1919), responding to the heroine's publication of a book of poems, "the editor of *Zigzag,* the new 'Weekly Journal of Defiance,'" assures her "that their esoteric significance showed that she was a *vers-librist* in thought as well as in technique" and "that they would 'gain incommensurably in meaning' when she abandoned the superannuated habit of beginning each line with a capital letter."[11] Featured in *The Gods Arrive* (1932) is "an advanced group of artists and writers" usually "presided over" by "[a] young woman with violently red hair and sharp cheek-bones . . . when she could spare the time from a mysterious bookshop in the Latin Quarter, which she and a girl friend managed,"[12] in what is presumably a gratuitous caricature of Sylvia Beach and Shakespeare & Company. As is well-known, Wharton had no contact—much less any affinity—with Gertrude Stein's Parisian coterie, while many of the references to modern art throughout her later novels are so entertaining that one wonders why they are not more frequently quoted: the description, for example, of "Factories," Lorry Spear's futurist extravaganza, "a great musical spectacle, to be expressed entirely in terms of modern industrialism, with racing motors, aeroplanes and sub-marines as the protagonists, prodigies of electric lighting, and stage effects of unprecedented complication" (*GA,* 88); or of the studio in *Hudson River Bracketed* (1929) in which Rebecca Stram displays "a gigantic Cubist conundrum which looked like a railway junction after a collision between excursion trains, but was cryptically labelled: 'Tea and Toast for One.'"[13]

Yet, as her biographers have amply noted, Wharton's response to younger writers and artists was more complex and varied, and her tastes in her later years—embracing Yeats and Colette, Rilke and Gide, Huxley and Cocteau, Evelyn Waugh and Anita Loos, Cézanne and Gauguin, Richard Strauss and Igor Stravinsky and Isadora Duncan—remained far more eclectic than one would guess from the asperity of her remarks on the writers and artists soon to be canonized as "modernist." She was capable of welcoming the debuts of novelists as different as William Gerhardie and Alberto Moravia, seems to have been at least aware of Céline, and was among the earliest and most astute of Proust's American admirers. Despite her skepticism, moreover, Wharton was not always purely dismissive, conceding to a friend that Faulkner "is certainly full of talent" and "certainly has a vivid and masterful style,"[14] while eventually softening her views of Joyce's earlier fiction. Even as she found *Prufrock* "not particularly striking," she declared to a friend, "I am glad to know what the American songsters are doing."[15] If nothing else, Wharton seems to have made at least a conscientious effort to come to terms with her younger contemporaries, recognizing in their work a force perhaps deplorable but impossible to ignore. In 1923, she told her editor at *Scribner's Magazine* that she needed more time on the articles that became *The Writing of Fiction* (1925) "chiefly because, having lately read a good many novels and tales by the rising generation in England and America, . . . I have come to the conclusion that the whole matter must be dealt with from a new point of view."[16] Throughout her final phase, she evidently felt the need to address the work of the newer novelists more directly; in 1928, she contemplated "writing an article on the modern European novel" for the *Yale Review,* while the publication of *Sanctuary* in 1931 left her "more than ever determined to write my article 'Wuthering Depths' on the new school of fiction," a determination that resulted, three years later, in Wharton's two principal statements on the subject, "Tendencies in Modern Fiction" and "Permanent Values in Fiction."[17]

Even at her most vituperative, Wharton seems to have been concerned at her own lack of enthusiasm about the work of her younger contemporaries. Her attack on *Ulysses* in her letter to Berenson is followed by the plaintive assurance, "I *know* it's not because I'm getting old that I'm unresponsive. The trouble with

all this new stuff is that it's à thèse: the theory comes first, &
dominates it" (*L*, 461).[18] It is hardly uncommon, of course, to
denounce an unsettling new method in the arts as "theoretically" rather than "creatively" or "imaginatively" driven, a conviction that underlies the argument of "Permanent Values in
Fiction," in which Wharton finds it "less dangerous for an artist
to sacrifice his artistic instincts to the pursuit of money or popularity than to immolate them to a theory" (*UCW*, 176). By "theory," Wharton seems to have had in mind the bent of "many
'radical' novelists" whose quirks she discussed with an inter-
viewer the year before her death: "Their preoccupation with new
methods and the details of technique is simply a sign of fa-
tigue. . . . Dropping out capital letters and punctuation is only a
symptom of poverty of imagination."[19] For Wharton, there is "no
theory more contrary to the free action of genius than the persuasion that a given formula—alphabet, language, or any generally accredited form of expression—is worn out because too
many people have used it" (*UCW*, 176). It is precisely this "persuasion" that Chris Churley, the indolent would-be essayist in
The Gods Arrive, expresses to Vance Weston in extenuating his
own failure to complete any piece of writing: "If only there was
a new language perhaps we'd have new thoughts; if there was a
new alphabet, even!" (*GA*, 186). When Vance demurs, and Churley replies, "Oh, I know what comes next. You're going to tell me
that all the big geniuses have managed to express themselves
in new ways with the old material," another central theme of
Wharton's later critical prose is sounded. Arguing in "Tendencies
in Modern Fiction" that "the initial mistake of most of the
younger novelists . . . has been the decision that the old forms
were incapable of producing new ones," and elsewhere attacking
"the belief that new 'forms' are recurringly necessary in all the
arts," Wharton stresses that "what critics of any of the arts
should surely remember," above all, "is the incessant renovation
of old types by new creative action" (*UCW*, 170, 176). Earlier, she
had offered, as an embodiment of this "new creative action," the
work of no less unimpeachably "modern" a writer than Proust,
who "is apparently still regarded as a great novelist by the inno-
vators, and yet is . . . that far more substantial thing in the world
of art, a renovator" (*WF*, 153–54).

Many will find this distinction between "innovation" and
"renovation" a specious one, calculated to "recuperate" the complexity and originality of such challenging new work, and to
rationalize a pervasive idolatry of "tradition." The distinction is

necessary to Wharton, however, because it helps to place her antimodernist polemic on what appears to be a squarely "formal" basis. Referring to "a generation nurtured on James Joyce and Virginia Woolf," she contends that "[t]he real preoccupations of some modern novelists seem so unrelated to the form they have chosen that one is almost driven to wonder if practical interests have not tempted them to expand the scope of the novel" (*UCW*, 175). Expanding the scope of any art form would ordinarily appear to be unobjectionable, but the new novelists had taken the effort to such an extreme that "one is almost tempted to say," as Wharton puts it elsewhere, "that in certain schools formlessness is now regarded as the first condition of form" (*WF*, 14). Nearly twenty years earlier, she had observed to a friend, "Personally, I think that a long apprenticeship should be given to form before it is thrown overboard" (*L*, 106). And it is precisely such an abandonment of form that marked, for Wharton (as for so many), the innovation of "the new methods" employed by younger contemporaries who seemed to have dispensed with an apprentice period altogether. As she insisted to Berenson, in commenting on *Ulysses*, "until the raw ingredients of a pudding *make* a pudding, I shall never believe that the raw material of sensation & thought can make a work of art without the cook's intervening. The same applies to Eliot" (*L*, 461).

Admittedly, Wharton's approach to such phenomena is not always quite so stodgy or reflexive. In "The Spark" (1924), which dates from the same period, Whitman is described, after all, as "an originator of new verse-forms," not a renovator of old ones. Already in "The Criticism of Fiction" (1914), furthermore, H. G. Wells's "brilliant plea for the greatest possible laxity in the interpretation of the term 'novel'" had elicited from Wharton both a concession and an essential qualification:

> It may well be that some new theory of form, as adequate to its new purpose as those preceding it, will be evolved from the present welter of experiment; but to imagine that form can ever be dispensed with is like saying that wine can be drunk without something to drink it from. (*UCW*, 125, 124)

Her younger contemporaries, in this indifference to "form," ignore at their peril a precept repeatedly expressed in Wharton's criticism, the precept that "art . . . is a compromise, a perpetual process of rejection and elision," and that "any theory of art . . . must begin by assuming the need of selection" (*UCW*, 112; *WF*,

8). As she once cautioned, "The novelist may plead as much as he pleases for the formless novel, the unemphasized notation of a certain stretch of a certain runnel of the stream of things." The essential point, for Wharton, is the fact that "that particular stretch of that particular runnel" has been "chosen," and that the "notation," or recording, of that stretch is, or should be, the result of a conscious artistic "selection" on the part of the novelist (*UCW,* 124).

As one can tell from her prescient image of "the stream of things," Wharton might almost be describing ahead of time the very method that would soon typify, more than any other, the "experimental" temper of modern fiction. How urgently, in her eyes, this particular form of experimentation needed to be contested may be gauged from a remark in 1928 to Desmond MacCarthy, who had solicited an article for *Life and Letters:* "I want to do one called 'Deep Sea Soundings' on this tiresome stream-of-consciousness theory which is deflecting so much real narrative talent out of its proper course."[20] Wharton's initial impulse, as in her treatment of Proust the "renovator," had already been to "familiarize" such an unorthodox and iconoclastic new "theory," this time by assimilating it to a supposedly discredited earlier method. In *The Writing of Fiction,* she declares that "the once-famous *tranche de vie*" of late-nineteenth-century French novelists "has lately reappeared, marked by certain unimportant differences, and re-labelled the stream of consciousness" (*WF,* 10–11), a formulation evidently so appealing that she returned to it more than once (*WF,* 144; *UCW,* 172). For Wharton, such a technique surpasses even its antecedent in failing to satisfy the primary requirement of "selection":

> The stream of consciousness method differs from the slice of life in noting mental as well as visual reactions, but resembles it in setting them down just as they come, with a deliberate disregard of their relevance in the particular case, or rather with the assumption that their very unsorted abundance constitutes in itself the author's subject. (*WF,* 12)

In a presumably deliberate irony on her part, a passage from an earlier version of "Tendencies in Modern Fiction" offers, as a counterexample, the very novel with which *The Mother's Recompense* had been so vexatiously contrasted. Rather than simply reproduce the "unsorted abundance" of a character's "mental . . . reactions," according to Wharton,

> the irrepressible creative intelligence [is] always selecting, rejecting, interfering with the flow of the gelatinous mass—as for instance, in

Virginia Woolf's "Mrs. Dalloway," hailed when it appeared as one of the text-books of the new school, where the author, apparently weary of noting the formless rush of sensation through her heroine's mind, abruptly abandons Mrs. Dalloway & inserts the reader's mind into that of a couple sitting on a bench in the Park through which Mrs. Dalloway happens to be passing.

As Woolf shifts the focus of her narrative to Septimus Smith and his wife, the faculty of "selection" has necessarily intervened, in Wharton's reading, and displaces the fatiguing randomness of a fashionably "unselective" method of narration.[21]

More cogent than her analogy of such a method to the "slice-of-life" aesthetic is Wharton's contention that the "attempt to note down every half-aware stirring of thought and sensation, the automatic reactions to every passing impression, is not as new as its present exponents think." The technique, as she goes on to observe, "has been used by most of the greatest novelists, not as an end in itself, but as it happened to serve their general design. . . . All the greatest of them, from Balzac and Thackeray onward, have made use of the stammerings and murmurings of the half-conscious mind whenever—but only when—such a state of mental flux fitted into the whole picture of the person portrayed" (*WF,* 12–13). The danger of a new method like "stream of consciousness" lay in its misplaced emphasis on rendering that "state of mental flux" throughout, in attempting to limit language and narrative to the operation of the mind's half-conscious processes. Quarreling with the insistence of Lorry and his Bohemian friends "that unless the arts were renewed they were doomed, and that in fiction the only hope of renewal was in the exploration of the subliminal," Vance Weston specifies one of the dangers that result from such a demand: "The new technique might be right, but their application of it substituted pathology for invention. . . . The fishers in the turbid stream-of-consciousness had reduced their fictitious characters to a bundle of loosely tied instincts and habits, borne along blindly on the current of existence" (*GA,* 115–16). At such moments, as so often in the Vance Weston diptych, its protagonist is rehearsing views soon expressed in similar terms in Wharton's own voice, as she will argue a couple of years later that the younger novelists "reduce to the vanishing point any will to action, and their personages are helpless puppets on a sluggish stream of fatality" (*UCW,* 172).

Strangely, such descriptions are more reminiscent of the "naturalism" of writers whom Wharton vastly preferred (like Norris, Lewis, and Dreiser) than of the overtly "experimental" novels of the modernists. From such an argument, however, Wharton is able to derive a certain comparative basis on which aesthetically "innovative" or disruptive methods of narration, along with their "pathological" overtones, may be judged. Part of what she finds so objectionable about the stream of consciousness is its departure from the assumption "that in the world of normal men, life is conducted, at least in its decisive moments, on fairly coherent and selective lines" (*WF*, 13). Ideally, experience is ruled no less than art by the necessity of "selection" and "rejection," a process of consciously and deliberately choosing. And Wharton seems almost to envision the celebrated experiments of a writer like Faulkner when she insists that the modern novel, in its refusal to abide by these guidelines, occupies "a pathological world where the action, taking place between people of abnormal psychology, and not keeping time with our normal human rhythms, becomes an idiot's tale, signifying nothing" (*WF*, 27–28). By 1934, the appearance of novels such as Faulkner's could only have strengthened her belief that "the greatest error of the younger novelists, of whatever school, has been to imagine that abnormal or highly specialized characters offer a richer field than the normal and current varieties" (*UCW*, 178).[22] Describing to Berenson the notorious middle volumes of Proust's sprawling novel, Wharton finds it "a pity he didn't devote himself to the abnormalities of the normal, which offer a wide enough & untilled enough field, heaven knows" (*L*, 441). As far as such "abnormal" characters are concerned, "their chief interest, for the reader, lies not in their own case," according to Wharton, "but in its tragic and destructive reactions on the normal" (*UCW*, 178). One notes here the way in which the formal has shaded into the "psychological" in her argument, as Wharton seems to imply that the "abnormal" are of aesthetic interest not intrinsically but only insofar as the normal are affected by their behavior. And the "psychological" slips, promptly and almost as insensibly, into yet another realm, as Wharton further contends that "[t]he novelists most in view reject form not only in the structure of their tales but in the drawing of character" (*UCW*, 172).

What does the absence of "form" in characterization turn out to mean in Wharton's critical vocabulary? Arguing that "their personages ... are as spectral as the fugitive apparitions of a

dream," she advances in "Tendencies in Modern Fiction" an observation far more revealing, or revealing in many more ways,
than she probably intended: "To counteract this evanescence,
the younger novelists . . . naturally incline to situate their tales
among the least developed classes; and in America, for instance,
our young novelists are frequently praised for choosing the 'real
America' as the scene of their fiction—as though the chief intellectual and moral resources of the country lay among the poor
whites of the Appalachians, or their counterparts in other regions" (*UCW,* 172–73). That its "chief intellectual and moral resources" necessarily constitute the finest source of a nation's
literary material, or that the whereabouts of those resources
goes without saying, is obviously an undemonstrated assumption, while one quickly notices how "abnormal or highly specialized characters" correspond to the "rudimentary characters"
hailing from "the least developed classes," as the psychological
gives way, in turn, to the social in the antimodernist rhetoric of
Wharton's later criticism. For Wharton, the chief mistake of her
younger contemporaries lies not only in the new methods that
they employ but in the characters to whom those methods are
applied; neglecting to exercise "selection" in devising techniques
like stream of consciousness, the new novelists have been insuf-
ficiently "selective" in another sense, favoring with imaginative
treatment certain areas of society and members of certain
classes instead of selecting them *out* as somehow inherently
unsuitable.

What becomes clear throughout her later essays is that Wharton objects not only to the form but also to the focus of the
newer fiction, both to its techniques and to its material. "New
methods," "rudimentary characters": In her analysis of the modernist emergence, the two are seen as interrelated and mutually
determining in a way that surreptitiously crosses the aesthetic
with the social as categories of value. The idea that "it is easier
to note the confused drift of subconscious sensation than to
single out the conscious thoughts and deliberate actions which
are the key to character" is debatable both psychologically and
as a matter of method. It is dubious on more than purely technical or strategic grounds, however, to say that such a method is
easier "[f]or the same reason" that "it is obviously much easier
to depict rudimentary characters, moved from the cradle to the
grave by the same unchanging handful of instincts and prejudices, than to follow the actions of persons in whom education
and opportunity have developed a more complex psychology"

(*UCW,* 173). Some years earlier in "The Great American Novel" (1927), Wharton had complained about what she regarded as the stipulation that the modern American novel "must tell of persons so limited in education and opportunity that they live cut off from all the varied sources of culture which used to be considered the common heritage of English-speaking people" (*UCW,* 152).[23] In her view, such persons—the "rudimentary characters" belonging to "the least developed classes"—are eligible for aesthetic transposition not if portrayed from within but only when screened or filtered through the consciousness of a very different presence, like the narrator of *Ethan Frome,* in which "it is natural enough," according to Wharton, "that he should act as the sympathizing intermediary between his rudimentary characters and the more complicated minds to whom he is trying to present them" (*UCW,* 260).

Loftily remarking that such a strategic choice "is ... self-evident, and needs explaining only to those who have never thought of fiction as an art of composition" (*UCW,* 260), Wharton seems far less alert in her critical prose than in her fiction to the ways in which the "natural" or "self-evident" can disguise the social or cultural. Such statements place in a perturbing light her understanding not only of "the new methods" of younger novelists but of literary method itself. A decade before asserting that "the trend of the new fiction, not only in America and England, but also on the continent, is chiefly toward the amorphous and the agglutinative" (thanks largely to its use of methods like stream of consciousness), Wharton told Gerhardie, in praising his first novel, "it is a joy to turn back ... above all to that amorphous agglutinated mass of helpless humanity that trails back & forth across your pages" (*UCW,* 172; *L,* 456). What appears joyous to Wharton in the depiction of "humanity" as a "mass" is unacceptable as a new formal "trend," disfiguring those novels that cultivate "the new methods" and "rudimentary characters" and thereby come to resemble in shape the "humanity" left commendably unindividuated in Gerhardie's novel.

Although these invidious distinctions are perhaps only to be expected from a writer of her background, such remarks are nonetheless surprising, for they openly depart, in fact, from some of Wharton's own wisest, long-cherished tenets as a critic. Maintaining in one of her earliest reviews, "the sincere critic's first business is to accept the author's postulate," and later castigating "the average critic," who "is too busy ... saying what subject he would have found more interesting than the one chosen"

(*UCW,* 107, 126) by the novelist under review, Wharton is even less ambiguous on the same point in her memoirs: "There could be no greater critical ineptitude than to judge a novel according to *what it ought to have been about.*"[24] By passing exactly this sort of judgment on the newer fiction, Wharton's criticism violates the "first" of its own "principles for the novelist," the principle "that he should write of any class of people who become instantly real to him as he thinks about them" (*UCW,* 162). One wishes that Wharton had adhered more consistently to this expansive and sensible position when approaching the work and methods of many emerging writers, particularly given the terms in which she disputed, as late as 1928, the similar rebuke often aimed at her own fiction: "But of late a far more serious charge has been brought against me. It is that I write only about the rich! . . . Supposing I *did* write only about the rich—what then? If I did, the chances would be that it was because they happened to be the material most 'to my hand'" (*UCW,* 161–62). Members of other classes, however, might be more "to the hand" of those novelists for whom Wharton elsewhere fails to make the same allowances. According to one of her earlier essays, "There seem to be but two primary questions to ask in estimating any work of art: what has the author tried to represent, and how far has he succeeded?—and a third, which is dependent on them: Was the subject chosen worth representing . . . ?" (*UCW,* 126–27). By the mid-1920s, Wharton seems to have inverted these priorities, as the representational worth of a chosen subject (to be determined on social rather than purely aesthetic grounds) soon becomes the "primary" question in her criticism. Only a year before observing, in 1928, that one of "the two chief weaknesses of modern reviewing" is "the idea that certain categories of human beings are of less intrinsic interest than others," Wharton had already declared that "the common mean of American life . . . stands for everything which does not rise above a very low average in culture, situation, or intrinsic human interest" (*UCW,* 162, 153) and which thus disqualifies itself for aesthetic representation. According to a distinction that turns out to be less reassuring than it sounds, "[s]ubjects differ from one another in scope and in plastic interest, but not categories of people" (*UCW,* 162). For Wharton, however, one must ultimately belong to a particular socially defined "category of people" to achieve the dignity of becoming a "subject" in fiction.

Clearly, it is in an effort to withstand the pressure of so many threatening new developments in the arts, and to make sense of the "welter of experiment" in the modern novel, that Wharton's criticism becomes decidedly prescriptive in this respect, contradicting itself even from one essay to the next on the question of subject as a determinant of form and aesthetic value. Such pressures certainly account for the indiscriminate, scattershot approach of her antimodernist writing. Only a writer "haunted by the demons of modernism as they encircled her both in life and literature" (Howe, 133) could toss together such different (and often mutually antagonistic) figures as Woolf, Joyce, Lawrence, and Wells, while bizarrely associating modern art with interior decoration and Jazz Age decadence, and experimental novelists and painters with the crassest sort of careerism, throughout the crudely antimodernist satire of Wharton's later fiction. Charging the younger novelists with a misguided effort "to note the confused drift of subconscious sensation" and "the stammerings and murmurings of the half-conscious mind," while paradoxically concluding in "A Reconsideration of Proust" (1934) that "nothing interests the modern novelist and his readers less than the inner life" (*UCW*, 183), Wharton's is an understandably confused, even incoherent, reaction to the disorienting variety and "newness" of modern writing. And the inconsistencies and confusions in her criticism reflect not only "a certain defensiveness of tone" (Lewis, 492) but also the fear, of course, that her own work has already been overlooked and forgotten, eclipsed by the flashier "new methods" that Wharton mentions in her letter to Hugh Smith. Note how the same language in which she will begin to formulate her position on "stream of consciousness" in *The Writing of Fiction* already appears, three years earlier, as Wharton expresses gratified surprise at Gerhardie's admiration: "I am so accustomed nowadays to being regarded as a deplorable example of what people used to read in the Dark Ages before the 'tranche de vie' had been rediscovered, that my very letter-paper blushes as I thank a novelist of your generation for his praise" (*L*, 457).

Most have followed Wharton's lead in tracing her anxieties along these lines to the effect of what she calls, in "Tendencies in Modern Fiction," "[t]he moral and intellectual destruction caused by the war" that "was shattering to traditional culture" (*UCW*, 170). In its aftermath, however, one of the gravest threats to the survival both of that culture and of her fiction became, for Wharton, the ascendancy of a critical environment in which "[t]he idea that genuineness is to be found only in the rudimentary, and that whatever is complex is unauthentic," had triumphed, and in which "the modern American novelist is told that the social and educated being is an unreality unworthy of his attention, and that only the man with the dinner-pail is human, and hence available for his purpose" (*UCW*, 155). In Wharton's rather reductive characterization of American critical dogma of the 1920s and 1930s, the emerging proletarian American novelists (such as Gratz Blemer in *Hudson River Bracketed*) are scarcely distinguishable from the "modernist" writers with whom they had so little in common, joining them in a bloc before which her own work risks dwindling into irrelevance.

What is striking, however, is that Wharton had already begun, in fact, to make such remarks over twenty years earlier, complaining to W. C. Brownell in 1904, for example, about "the assumption that the people I write about are not 'real' because they are not navvies & char-women" (*L*, 91). Nor is this the only respect in which her comments on the "newer novelists" form part of a more comprehensive antimodernist critique originating well before the First World War. Interestingly, that which makes the "new methods" of modern fiction "easier" in Wharton's eyes, correctly or not, also links them with other "innovations" of a different kind: "I have often wished ... that these facilities did not so temptingly concord with the short-cut in everything which is the ideal of the new generation, with the universal thirst to surpass the speed-record in every department of human activity" (*UCW*, 173). Written at a time when "[t]he whole world has become a vast escalator," a time marked by "[t]he universal infiltration of our American plumbing, dentistry, and vocabulary" (*UCW*, 156), such statements equate a host of disturbing "modern" technological developments to changes in all forms of expression, from the form and technique of the novel to language itself.[25] Wharton even holds such developments responsible for drastically narrowing (and cheapening) the material on which novelists may draw for their subjects. If "nothing can alter the fact that a 'great argument' will give a greater result than the perpetual chronicling of small beer," then it follows for Wharton that "the conditions of modern life in America, so far from being productive of great arguments, seem almost purposely contrived to eliminate them." And those conditions have had such an effect, as far as Wharton is concerned, for the simple reason that modern America "has chosen ... a dead level of prosperity and security" as its ideal and "reduced ... the whole of life to a small house with modern plumbing and heating, a garage, a motor, a telephone, and a lawn undivided from one's neighbor's" (*UCW*, 153, 154).

In her later novels, not surprisingly, fallen aristocrats or members of the nouveau riche tend to be the characters through whom Wharton conveys this rather odd parallel between the works of newer artists and writers and the amenities not only of modern America but of the postwar world. One of "the Bohemians among the crowned heads" whom Nick Lansing encounters in *The Glimpses of the Moon,* for example, "the Princess Mother adored prehistoric art, and Russian music, and the paintings of Gauguin and Matisse," while "she also, and with a beaming unconsciousness of perspective, adored . . . powerful motors . . . and modern plumbing," among other fashionable items.[26] Similarly "unconscious" is the response of Lorry Spear's chief patron, Mrs. Glaisher, to his call for someone with "the imagination," as he puts it, "to break the old moulds, to demolish the old landmarks" of art: "'Ah, that's it: we *must* have imagination,' Mrs. Glaisher announced in the same decisive tone in which, thirty years ago, she might have declared: 'We *must* have central heating'" (*GA,* 131).[27] Even more ludicrous, in *Twilight Sleep* the desperately up-to-the-minute Paulina Manford, who "flattered herself that few women had a wider range," is said to be "ready for anything, from Birth Control to neo-impressionism" (*TS,* 199).

Throughout Wharton's later essays and novels, the subjects and the technical experiments of modern writing become directly associated with the devices that so many members of her transitional generation, like her beloved Theodore Roosevelt, deprecated as signs of "overcivilization" and of excessive "material comfort and convenience" producing "bodily and spiritual enervation."[28] Most disquieting to Wharton about this proliferation of comforts, however, is what she sees as its aesthetically and socially deleterious consequences. America has thus "reduced . . . the whole of life" just "[a]s she has reduced the English language to a mere instrument of utility" (*UCW,* 154), in a correspondence similar to the one that she will later establish between "the conditions of modern life" and the technical "facilities" of the "newer novelists." Even as she acknowledges "the material advantage of these diffused conveniences," Wharton argues that "the safe and uniform life resulting from them offers to the artist's imagination a surface as flat and monotonous as our own prairies" (*UCW,* 154). The fact that more than one contemporary had already succeeded, by that time, in deriving rich material and effects from such a landscape would have done little to compromise this analogy in Wharton's eyes, for she offered as a leading symptom of this sort of "uniformity" the fact that "literary criticism in modern America," like "the conditions of modern America" itself, "is a perpetual incentive to standardization" (*UCW*, 155). The "standardization" of every-day life goes hand-in-hand, for Wharton, with the "standardiza-tion" of modern writing, as literary "short-cuts," such as a reliance on "rudimentary characters" or the use of stream of consciousness, accompany the widening availability of certain "conveniences," resulting in a deterioration of aesthetic along with social "standards" and in the dilution of possibilities open to the literary artist.

Looking upon "the new methods" of "the younger novelists" as literary counterparts to modern plumbing and heating is per-haps an unduly fanciful way of relating such developments in the arts to the larger cultural crises of the time. More trouble-some, however, is Wharton's related contention that a nation producing and "diffusing" so many new "conveniences" on such a scale "abounds in the unnecessary, but lacks the one thing needful." The wider "diffusion" of "conveniences" will doubtless seem "unnecessary" to those capable of taking less exalted "ne-cessities" for granted, as Wharton goes on to argue that "the one thing needful" is "an old social organization which provided for nicely shaded degrees of culture and conduct" and which also supplies the prerequisite without which art would be impossible:

> Leisure, itself the creation of wealth, is incessantly engaged in trans-muting wealth into beauty by secreting the surplus energy which flowers in great architecture, great painting, and great literature. Only in the atmosphere thus engendered floats that impalpable dust of ideas which is the real culture. (*UCW*, 156)

As described in such etherealizing terms (its preconditions openly announced and at the same time elided), this "real cul-ture" originates for Wharton in a "social organization" that has disappeared, for "modern America has simplified and Taylorized it out of existence, forgetting that in such matters the process is necessarily one of impoverishment" (*UCW*, 154).

To lament the "impoverishment" that occurs when "conven-iences" are widely "diffused" among a greater number of people is remarkable enough. More astonishing, however, is Wharton's

analogy between this sort of material and cultural "simplifica-
tion" and the methods of "scientific management" with which
Frederick Winslow Taylor had revolutionized the efficiency of
industrial production some years earlier. By its effects on "an
old social organization" associated with "nicely shaded degrees
of culture and conduct," the more equitable distribution of "conveniences" easing everyday life for so many (and linked, as
"short-cuts," to "the new methods" of modern writing) is thus
said to resemble the very processes that had fully mechanized
and routinized the anonymous labor on which such a "social
organization" and its culture ultimately rests.[29] And that "social
organization" is sanctified, in Wharton's antimodernist criticism,
with even greater frankness than "the real culture" for which it
is responsible: "Traditional society, with its old-established distinctions of class, its pass-words, exclusions, delicate shades of
language and behavior, is one of man's oldest works of art, the
least conscious and the most instinctive" (*UCW*, 155). Privileged
as the source of "beauty," "real culture," and genuine aesthetic
possibility, and transformed over time into a kind of second nature, the same "traditional society" nostalgically re-created in
works such as *The Age of Innocence* and *A Backward Glance* is
itself overtly aestheticized in Wharton's later criticism, as a certain firmly hierarchical social order is deemed necessary to the
achievement of a different kind of order—as if a certain set of
contingent social forms were innately linked to aesthetic form
itself.[30]

Associated not only with the literary representation of certain
classes but also with the "diffused conveniences" replacing the
"richly shaded degrees of culture and conduct" that distinguished an earlier society, the "new methods" of modern novelists brought about certain transformations of narrative directly
related, in Wharton's eyes, to a whole range of equally pernicious
social transformations. Novelists gravitate more and more toward "rudimentary characters" as the "diffusion" of more and
more "conveniences" makes an increasing number of people,
and the social order itself, more and more "rudimentary." And,
although a novel like *Twilight Sleep* makes short work of the
"therapeutic world view" through which "antimodern thinkers
played a key . . . role in revitalizing the cultural hegemony of
their class during a period of protracted crisis" (Lears, 57–58),
Wharton's later work needed no such indirect way of expressing
the same allegiances. Indeed, she is not above insinuating that
"mediocrity has achieved universal diffusion," both socially and

aesthetically speaking, as a result of the "universal facility of communication" (*UCW*, 155, 154), or of the other "diffused conveniences" that enhance the safety and prosperity of the populace as a whole. And she had already made even more apparent the political complexion of these antimodernist sentiments as early as 1903, in an essay that begins by treating the popularity of "reading" (and thus the spread of literacy) as a "vice" resulting from "[t]hat 'diffusion of knowledge' commonly classed with steam heat and universal suffrage in the category of modern improvements" (*UCW*, 99). Similarly reduced in value, the technical "facilities" of modern fiction join the extension of the franchise, the "diffusion of knowledge," and what one historian calls the "democratization of comfort" (Lears, 38) among the "modern improvements" vehemently attacked in Wharton's critical prose; these maligned advances mark what she later calls "a world in which facilities for divorce and re-marriage have kept pace with all the other modern devices for annihilating time and space" (*UCW*, 269). Significantly, it is in one of her antimodernist essays that this "priestess of the Life of Reason," as Wharton once called herself (*L*, 483), excoriates in similar language the Enlightenment ideology of "the eighteenth-century demagogues who were the first inventors of 'standardization'" (*UCW*, 155). In this respect, her enthusiastic reading of Nietzsche and Schopenhauer, like her increasing attraction to forms of "primitivism," far from "working strongly against her conservatism" (Lewis, 357), may be said to reflect and reinforce it, joining her impatience with "modern improvements" of all kinds (aesthetic, social, political, practical) in a wider antiliberal, indeed antidemocratic, critique not all that far from the positions of some of the very figures (Eliot, say, or Lawrence) whose work she so disliked. In its alarmism and anxieties, on the other hand, Wharton's antimodernist criticism discerned all too clearly the potentially liberating and destabilizing energies that lay in the new techniques even of otherwise authoritarian writers. Early on, Wharton seems to have intuitively realized that a method such as stream of consciousness was "[n]ot merely a technical innovation in storytelling or a reordering of aesthetic principles," as Shari Benstock has noted, but a "change" that "had far-reaching political and social implications."[31]

Yet the political and social implications of her response to modernism remain unexplored, for the most part, by Wharton's scholars and critics, for reasons that have little to do with any lingering pressures of a once-impregnable modernist orthodoxy

in Anglo-American criticism. It is perhaps no accident that
Wharton's later essays, which make discomfortingly visible the
social premises of her aesthetic, are rarely cited even in recent
studies that have done so much to restore the long-neglected
final period of her career, or that her often rancorous antimodernism—magnifying those social premises as it does—tends to
be either neutrally presented and illustrated, or awkwardly de-
fused, or reconceived on some more agreeable basis.[32] As her
later essays demonstrate, however, Wharton's regressive social
and political views—now more and more regretfully acknowledged, but still denied any vital connection to her imaginative
work—are closely intertwined with her convictions about the
writing of fiction and the making of art, just as her aesthetic
embodies so many of her most fervently avowed social and political beliefs. A consideration of her antimodernist essays, or of
her critical prose as a whole, will make it harder to quarantine
Wharton's extraliterary views in this way, or to isolate the fastidious, heroically self-created artist from the critic who once remarked upon "a sense in which the writing of fiction may be
compared to the administration of a fortune" and who issued,
less than five years before the Great Depression, a rather infelici-
tously phrased warning to aspiring writers: "Characters whose
tasks have not been provided for them in advance are likely to
present as embarrassing problems as other types of the unem-
ployed" (*WF,* 57, 84). Ultimately, her antimodernist writing not
only discloses, with unusual candor, the ideology of Wharton's
aesthetic (or of the formalism to which she officially subscribed)
but unmasks that formalism (and thus her aesthetic) as itself
fundamentally ideological in concept and effect.[33] Indeed, it
might be not so much the politics of Wharton's antimodernism
as its unabashedly political disposition that yields a valuable
corrective at a time of increasing critical and intellectual reaction and retrenchment, exemplifying the interdependence of
form and ideology—of aesthetic judgment and social value—
while also demonstrating that the two refuse to be separated
from each other quite as readily or antiseptically as so many
cultural guardians of the moment might wish.

Notes

    1. Edith Wharton, "A Cycle of Reviewing," in *Edith Wharton: The Uncol-
lected Critical Writings,* ed. Frederick Wegener (Princeton: Princeton University Press, 1996), 160 (hereafter *UCW*).

2. Gerald Bullett, "New Fiction," *Saturday Review* 139 (30 May 1925): 588.

3. *The Letters of Edith Wharton,* ed. R. W. B. Lewis and Nancy Lewis (New York: Scribner's, 1988), 480 (hereafter *L*).

4. Two years later, for example, a reviewer of her next novel, *Twilight Sleep* (1927), remarks that "anyone who ... is familiar with Virginia Woolf reads these pages with a certain lack of conviction" (Charles R. Walker, "Mrs. Wharton versus the Newer Novelists," *Independent* 118 [11 June 1927]: 615).

5. Nancy Bentley, *The Ethnography of Manners: Hawthorne, James, Wharton* (Cambridge: Cambridge University Press, 1995), 112, 107.

6. Irving Howe, "Edith Wharton: Convention and the Demons of Modernism," in *Decline of the New* (New York: Horizon, 1970), 124.

7. For a thorough and informative account of their literary relationship, see Susan Goodman, *Edith Wharton's Inner Circle* (Austin: University of Texas Press, 1994), 39–55.

8. Edward Marsh, *A Number of People: A Book of Remembrances* (New York: Harper & Bros., 1939), 228.

9. Edith Wharton (EW) to John Hugh Smith, 9 October 1935, Edith Wharton Collection, Beinecke Rare Book and Manuscript Library, Yale University (hereafter Beinecke). This and all subsequent excerpts from Wharton's unpublished correspondence and manuscripts are quoted with the permission of the Estate of Edith Wharton and the Watkins/Loomis Agency.

10. EW to Edward Sheldon, 8 June 1931 (Beinecke).

11. *The Collected Stories of Edith Wharton,* 2 vols. (New York: Scribner's, 1968), 2:359.

12. Edith Wharton, *The Gods Arrive* (New York: Appleton, 1932), 76–77, 88 (hereafter *GA*).

13. *Hudson River Bracketed* (New York: Appleton, 1929), 383. In an earlier example, "that disturbing Tommy Ardwin, the Cubist decorator" in *Twilight Sleep,* while "unbosoming himself to a devotee" at a Bohemian party, "held up a guttering church-candle to a canvas which simulated a window open on a geometrical representation of brick walls, fire escapes and back-yards" ([New York: Appleton, 1927], 71, 88–89 [hereafter *TS*]).

14. EW to Edward Sheldon, 8 June 1931 (Beinecke).

15. Quoted in R. W. B. Lewis, *Edith Wharton: A Biography* (New York: Harper & Row, 1975), 442.

16. As quoted in my "Edith Wharton and the Difficult Writing of *The Writing of Fiction,*" *Modern Language Studies* 25 (spring 1995): 63.

17. EW to *Yale Review,* 26 October 1927, and to Edward Sheldon, 8 June 1931 (Beinecke).

18. Wharton goes on to add, "Grau ist alle Theorie," the line that she would again quote from *Faust* two years later, as an illustration of "the argument against theorizing about one's art," in *The Writing of Fiction:* "Goethe declared that only the Tree of Life was green, and that all theories were gray" ([New York: Scribner's, 1925], 117, 116 [hereafter *WF*]). Although scarcely opposed to theoretical reflection on the part of novelists and poets, she seems to be contrasting "theory" to one of the properties she described to Gaillard Lapsley in praising A. E. Housman's verse, "that great gift of Experience, ... the gift that modern art affects to spurn but will have to get back to, to get effects like these. The famous 'continuous excitement' may have vanished; but that far rarer & greater thing, 'the depth & not the tumult of the soul,' has come

instead; & the gods & I approve"—the same Wordsworth allusion that later provides the epigraph to one of her most bitterly antimodernist novels (*L*, 459).

19. Loren Carroll, "Edith Wharton in Profile," *New York Herald Tribune*, Paris edition, November 16, 1936, p. 6.

20. EW to Desmond MacCarthy, October 17, 1928 (Beinecke).

21. Edith Wharton, "Documentation in Fiction," ms., Beinecke, 10. She made the same objections, while mentioning another favorite target among contemporary art forms, in some trenchant comments on Thomas Wolfe, who "certainly has talent, . . . but he is swamped in the stupid 'stream of consciousness' method which has been so disastrous to recent English fiction. Every work of art must be based on selection, and when one tries to ignore this and drag in everything that passes through the mind, it seems to me that one inevitably drops from art to the cinema—than which I can imagine no lower fall" (EW to Edward Sheldon, December 11, 1935 [Beinecke]).

22. Although "a woman of genius," Emily Brontë is again invoked as a predecessor of "the younger novelists" in this respect, for "if she had lived longer, and attained to a closer contact with reality," as Wharton rather impertinently observes, "she might have made, out of the daily stuff of life at Haworth Parsonage, a greater and more deeply moving book than by picturing a houseful of madmen" (*UCW*, 178). As in the working title ("Wuthering Depths") of her "article . . . on the new school of fiction," and in the contrast to Austen in her comments on *Sanctuary*, Wharton seems to have regarded Brontë as a reference point in her effort to make sense of the new novelists—an element of her antimodernism that would repay further exploration.

23. In one of the weaker arguments of her antimodernist criticism, Wharton suggests that the novelists themselves exhibit the same deficiencies, which explain their attraction to such "new methods" as stream of consciousness; for Wharton, it is in part "the lack of general culture . . . which makes so many of the younger novelists, in Europe as in America, attach undue importance to trifling innovations," whereas "only the cultivated intelligence escapes the danger of regarding as intrinsically new what may be a mere superficial change, or the reversion to a discarded trick of technique" (*WF*, 154). It is no coincidence, of course, that the "advanced" young artists and writers whom Vance Weston encounters throughout *Hudson River Bracketed* and *The Gods Arrive*—the critics meeting at the Cocoanut Tree, the habitués of Rebecca Stram's studio, the members of Lorry Spear's circle—are invariably uncultivated and déclassé, their appearance and demeanor as unsavory as their aesthetic views.

24. Edith Wharton, *A Backward Glance* (New York: Appleton, 1934), 206 (EW's emphasis).

25. According to one recent study, her later novels demonstrate "Wharton's discomfort with both high modernism, in writers like James Joyce and Virginia Woolf, and technological modernity, in advance men, advertising, and production-line culture" (Dale M. Bauer, *Edith Wharton's Brave New Politics* [Madison: University of Wisconsin Press, 1994], 114). More troubling to Wharton, however, among the effects of "technology" are the novelties described in her antimodernist essays, "conveniences" related to literary "facilities" such as "the new methods" through which these two aspects of "modernity" become specifically linked.

26. Edith Wharton, *The Glimpses of the Moon* (New York: Appleton, 1922), 234, 235.

27. Alternatively, modern art joins the newer "conveniences" in replacing those of an earlier social world, as when Mrs. Glaisher "had suddenly discovered that Grand Opera, *pâté de foie gras,* terrapin and Rolls-Royces were no longer the crowning attributes of her class" and "had begun to buy Picassos and Modiglianis, to invite her friends to hear Stravinsky and Darius Milhaud, to patronize exotic dancers, and labour privately (it was the hardest part of her task) over the pages of 'Ulysses'" (*GA,* 127–28).

28. T. J. Jackson Lears, *No Place of Grace: Antimodernism and the Transformation of American Culture, 1880–1920* (New York: Random House, 1981), 28.

29. Elsewhere, the process is used to signify the futility, say, of Paulina Manford's tyrannical hygienic regimen: "What was the use of all the months and years of patient Taylorized effort against the natural human fate: against anxiety, sorrow, old age—if their menace was to reappear whenever events slipped from her control?" (*TS,* 114). In Wharton's antimodernist vision, an industrial process that epitomized the triumph of organized capitalism is thus associated with a futile progressivism vainly resisting those forces ("the natural human fate") to which one should instead quiescently resign oneself. As long as sorrow and old age are inevitable, why attempt to alleviate the human lot? Similarly, the "spare Taylorized gestures" with which Kate Clephane is served by Aline, in *The Mother's Recompense* (1925), are registered as the mark not only of a servant's efficiency but of Kate's diminished social status as well. One study cites both of these passages as Wharton's illustrations "of the way in which business and technology have infiltrated the domestic realm" and of "a culture which turns selves into Taylorized subjects" (Bauer 58, 73), but it is hard to reconcile these inferences with the contexts in which Taylorization is invoked in, say, an essay like "The Great American Novel."

30. As Penelope Vita-Finzi observes, "Edith Wharton's aesthetic, moral and social values are based on an ideal of order," celebrating an "adherence to traditional principles of order, reason, discipline and harmony," as well as "the traditional civilizations that preserve and value them in social forms"; but a more dialectical sense of the interaction of social and aesthetic forms in her criticism is needed to explain why "she was unable to appreciate experiments with form in the novel or with the portrayal of character." See *Edith Wharton and the Art of Fiction* (New York: St. Martin's, 1990), 23, 17, 22.

31. Shari Benstock, "Landscape of Desire: Edith Wharton and Europe," in *Wretched Exotic: Essays on Edith Wharton in Europe,* ed. Katherine Joslin and Alan Price (New York: Peter Lang, 1993), 35.

32. The omission of her critical prose is particularly regrettable in the case of Bauer's ambitious and wide-ranging study, impressive in its grasp of the complexities of her later work, but highly acrobatic in its attempt to rehabilitate the conservative antimodernist Wharton. In another valuable reading, "The body of critical opinion that has characterized Wharton as a 'literary aristocrat' or antimodernist . . . cannot explain her popular following of 1905," but the commercial success of her early work would appear to have little relevance to the antimodernism of Wharton's later years. See Catherine Quoyeser, "The Antimodernist Unconscious: Genre and Ideology in *The House of Mirth,*" *Arizona Quarterly* 44 (winter 1989): 55. The audacious subjects of some of her later novels might indeed suggest that "the so-called repressed and proper 'Mrs. Wharton' was writing fiction that was as 'advanced' as anything Modernism produced," without necessarily altering, however, the social drift of her

own antimodernism (Robert A. Martin and Linda Wagner-Martin, "The Salons of Wharton's Fiction," in Joslin and Price, *Wretched Exotic*, 108). Its social and political dimensions are not especially mitigated when her antimodernism is reevaluated in terms of gender, as in the suggestion that Wharton's "savage satires of contemporary writing . . . miss their mark" primarily "because she recognized the aggressivity behind certain forms of Modernism" (Benstock 33); or in Judith L. Sensibar's more subtle treatment of what she called "Edith Wharton's revision, from a woman's view, of one of mainstream Modernism's central and most compelling tropes," in "Edith Wharton Reads the Bachelor Type: Her Critique of Modernism's Representative Man," in *Edith Wharton: New Critical Essays*, ed. Alfred Bendixen and Annette Zilversmit (New York: Garland, 1992), 159. Using her antimodernism to test any "linear and progressive model" of literary classification that "does not allow for writers who resist movement, who question progress, who refuse to innovate," Katherin Joslin points out that "feminist analysts have struggled to find room for Wharton's philosophical and aesthetic conservatism in the Modernist landscape by pronouncing her a transitional figure." These are not the only conservative elements of Wharton's antimodernism, however, and Joslin's admirably balanced conclusion that her "aesthetic and philosophical stance is not on the periphery of Modernism" but "place[s] her with her contemporaries in an intense and entangled debate over the form and content of fiction" does not really engage itself with the important social components of Wharton's contribution to such a debate. See "'Fleeing the Sewer': Edith Wharton, George Sand, and Literary Innovation," in Joslin and Price, *Wretched Exotic*, 349, 352.

33. Only by passing over her later essays, it seems to me, can one argue that Wharton's "approach to form, in all its manifestations, can be grasped through a non-ideological reading of her work" (see Lawrence Jay Dessner, "Edith Wharton and the Problem of Form," *Ball State University Forum* 24 [1983]: 55). Nor is this the only such example, for as Bauer observes, "Wharton critics have typically divorced her work from larger ideological issues implicit in the act of writing fiction" and "have denied her politics, in part because her views are often conflicting and in part because her work has not been read in light of the relevant intellectual debates of her day" (11). Although highly informative about those debates, and acutely aware of her ideological confusions, Bauer's own presentation of Wharton's later work seems itself ideologically strained, since the pattern thus discerned in Wharton studies has to do more with the nature of her politics, or of her views, and reflects a wider continuing reluctance to think ideologically about her work on a basis other than that of gender. For a refreshing and perceptive exception to this consensus, addressing Wharton's travel writing, see Brigitte Bailey, "Aesthetics and Ideology in *Italian Backgrounds*," in Joslin and Price, *Wretched Exotic*, 181–200. The critical and theoretical literature on the interrelations of these phenomena is of course voluminous; for a sampling of recent thought, see *Aesthetics and Ideology*, ed. George Levine (New Brunswick: Rutgers University Press, 1994), and the contents of the special issue published under the same title (ed. Judith Stoddart) by *Centennial Review* 39 (fall 1995). With regard specifically to American figures, well-known models of the sort of critical analysis attempted here may be found in *Ideology and Classic American Literature*, ed. Sacvan Bercovitch and Myra Jehlen (Cambridge: Cambridge University Press, 1986).

Fighting France: Travel Writing in the Grotesque

MARY SUZANNE SCHRIBER

> The war was over, and we thought we were returning to the world we had so abruptly passed out of four years earlier. Perhaps it was as well that, at first, we were sustained by that illusion.
>
> —Edith Wharton, *A Backward Glance*

AN ERA OF TRAVEL ABROAD THAT HAD BEGUN IN THE 1820S EFFECtively ended in the trenches of World War I. Between the 1820s and 1918, the people of the United States had crossed the oceans in steam-powered ships and eventually in luxury liners, and learned of an amazing new mode of transportation, the aeroplane, destined to shrink the globe. They had traveled on land in diligences and donkeys and jinrickshaws, later on trains and bicycles, and eventually in motorcars, the invention that, in Edith Wharton's judgment, "restored the romance of travel" stolen earlier by the railroad. These travelers had witnessed the birth of what was to become a massive tourist industry, with "Cookies," as the patrons of Thomas Cook were called, covering the face of the earth and paying their way with travelers' checks in place of letters of credit. Between 1820 and 1918, travel had been transformed.

Figures show the rise in sheer numbers of travelers. More than 300 Americans visited Rome in 1835. In 1866, 50,000 Americans crossed the Atlantic to Europe. According to Mrs. John Sherwood, by 1890 there were "more than eleven thousand virgins who semi-yearly migrate[d] from America to the shores of England and France."[1] More travelers meant, of course, more transformations of travel into narratives and essays, in books and in travel articles that were monthly features of many magazines in an era in which the magazine industry burgeoned. Between 1800 and 1900, the men and women of the United States published, in the United States, more than 2,000 books of travel abroad; 603 of these books appeared before the Civil War, and 1,162 appeared between 1860 and the turn of the century.[2] Travel writing was an old and conventional tradition in which rhetorical displays were made from the itineraries and accoutrements of travel, monuments and landscapes, tourists and indigenes, talk about travel talk, and comparative reflections on the homeland. Travel writers male and female had recorded, debated, and shaped in their accounts of travel the major and minor discourses about art, politics, manners, morals, technological advances, gender politics—the ideological and spiritual concerns of the nation as it came of age and entered maturity.

Edith Wharton's *Fighting France, from Dunkerque to Belfort* stands as the beneficiary, repository, and culmination of this epoch in travel and travel writing. Wharton had already published two books of travel, *Italian Backgrounds* (1905) and *A Motor-Flight Through France* (1908), when she put her hand to *Fighting France.* She used in *Fighting France,* as she had in her earlier books of travel, virtually all the conventions of the travel genre: attention to modes of transportation; visits to sacralized sites; construction of the people of foreign lands as the "other"; and all these were constructed into a narrative of adventure. Yet what is remarkable about *Fighting France* is the nature of its reliance on the history and traditions of travel writing to do its cultural work: to urge Americans to support the war effort. *Fighting France* uses the conventions of the genre to evoke the world of travel before World War I, the world whose end is marked by the war. Inserting the grotesqueries of war into a narrative frame, and inverting a tradition historically associated with the opposite of war, a world of peace and leisurely travel, *Fighting France* is a journey into a nightmare. It is travel writing in the grotesque.

Fighting France is part of the seemingly tireless Wharton's effort on behalf of the French during World War I. With Elisina Tyler, she formed the "Children of Flanders Rescue Committee" and "American Hostels for Refugees." Wharton organized an *ouvroir* where refugees were enabled to sustain themselves through work; and she sustained her own efforts financially by soliciting funds through various means, including the seeking of contributors for *The Book of the Homeless* (1916), a volume whose publication she oversaw. As Shari Benstock puts it, Wharton "cleverly joined philanthropy to propagandism, using all her social, diplomatic, and political connections to further the war relief effort."[3] The French recognized Wharton's work on behalf of France by making her a Chevalier of the Legion of Honor in 1916, and the Belgian government recognized her work with refugees with the Medaille Reine Elisabeth in 1918.[4]

Like Margaret Fuller, Edith Wharton became a war correspondent. She continued the war work, the political work, of foreign travel and writing about it begun by Fuller, who had sent dispatches from revolutionary Italy to the *New York Tribune* from 1846 through 1849. Again like Fuller in Italy, Wharton took remarkable risks, immersing herself in a world at war, skirting the front lines within sight of the Germans, parking her motor and proceeding by foot to reduce the danger of being shot. Wharton's adventures matched in their daring and perhaps outstripped in their generosity those of other intrepid, more theatrical travelers such as Annie Smith Peck, who scaled the Matterhorn in 1895 and the summit of "the apex of America," Mount Huascaran, in 1909; and Fanny Bullock Workman, who staked a claim to the peaks of the Karakoram in 1913. In her partisan focus, Wharton echoed Margaret Fuller again, identifying with the French as Fuller had identified with the Italians. The French were not "other" to Wharton; their cause was her cause.[5] As Fuller had sought to shape the attitudes of her compatriots toward an Italy in the throes of conflict, so Wharton undertook to publish her impressions of France at war so that "the description of what I saw might bring home to American readers some of the dreadful realities of war."[6] Immersed in war work, she made four trips to the front in 1915: to Verdun, Lorraine and the Vosges, western Belgium, and the Alsacian front. She agreed to write a series of articles for *Scribner's Magazine* that were subsequently collected in *Fighting France,* a "little book," as she called it in the best tradition of the disclaimer. "Wishing to lose no time in publishing my impressions," Wharton explains, "I managed to scribble the articles between my other tasks."[7]

Writing the articles for *Scribner's* that became *Fighting France,* she was, as Sarah Bird Wright observes, "an anguished beggar."[8] She was writing about the war for a recalcitrant America unwilling to bring France and the Allies in under what she called, in a poem sent to the *New York Times* in August 1915, "the great blue tent of rest" offered by the American flag. Faced with a daunting task in persuasion, how was she going to bring the war home to an America comitted to isolationism? By now an established professional writer, she chose a genre in which she was long since expert, travel writing and its conventions, as her vehicle. The very idea of travel and travel writing "sets free," as Edith Wharton wrote about Vezelay in *A Motor-Flight Through France,* a "rush of associations,"[9] and she knew that her target audience was susceptible to such a "rush." Wharton wished to tap those "rich and generous compatriots" of hers who might be persuaded to come to the aid of France.[10]

She could rely on this audience to associate travel with journeys into civilization, with echoes of leisure, adventure, and aesthetic satisfaction. Transatlantic travel was common among them, and armchair travel, aided and abetted by innumerable books of travel, was a staple of their class. Wharton knew this audience harbored generic expectations that, rendered in the grotesque, would provoke shock and horror, a response that might, in turn, prompt action. Turning the conventions of travel writing on end, she could emphasize and deliver in bold face, as it were, the destruction of the very civilization into which Wharton's contemporaries and their parents and grandparents had journeyed before the war. Her own travel books, *Italian Backgrounds* and *A Motor-Flight Through France,* had been immersed in the ambience that war transgressed. Dressing this war and its horrific new machinery in the old costumes, the conventions, of travel writing, she could amplify the grotesqueries of war, making them resonate against a backdrop that, having everything to do with the evolution of civilization, makes thunderous the grotesque devolution of civilization that was World War I.

Having selected the travel genre as her vehicle, Edith Wharton proceeded to amplify her purpose. In *A Motor-Flight Through France* (1908), she had transformed several "flights" in a Panhard to various places in France, including the northeast, with her husband Teddy. Wharton's travel to the front lines in 1915, this time accompanied by Walter Berry, Mildred Bliss, and Victor Berard, with the faithful Charles Cook at the wheel of Edith's Mercedes, repeated this earlier journey. Likewise, *Fighting France* repeats and revises *Motor-Flight,* which had also originally appeared in the pages of *Scribner's Magazine.*

Motor-Flight had evoked a sense of safe passage, an enlarged liberty, leisure, prosperity, pilgrimage, discovery, enchantment, and the preservation of historical and artistic treasures for the traveler's perusal. Wharton the traveler had been led to the grail, to knowledge of the past and the accumulated art and wisdom of the ages. This pre-war account records her excursion into civilization, an enabling immersion in history and culture. Like other travelers, she had come to see herself in perspective, to arrive at self-understanding, and at the end of the journey, to reflect in tranquillity on what she has seen in order to, in the words of Robert Frost's "Directive," "drink and be whole again beyond confusion."[11]

In contrast, *Fighting France* records a dangerous and frightening, rather than safe, passage to the war lines; the fatiguing work of war rather than leisure; hunger, cold, and poverty rather than warmth and prosperity; the devastation, rather than preservation, of buildings, the countryside, and, in Wharton's view, western culture. Although travel ordinarily serves to renew the traveler, in this case horror creates a species of perverse exhilaration. Tourist sites are here both the sights and sites of war, and the culture in which the traveler is immersed is hastily and clumsily built, made up of odd, impermanent architecture to house a temporary population. This is a nightmare journey. The travel frame enables the "unnatural" juxtapositions that place *Fighting France* as a book of travels in the tradition of the grotesque.

The dream of travel inscribed in *A Motor-Flight Through France* is immediately invoked and reversed in *Fighting France;* it is a dream which has been contorted into the nightmare of war. Whereas one of Wharton's "flights" in *Motor-Flight* takes Wharton and her companions from Paris to Poitiers, *Fighting France* opens on the road, going in the opposite direction, from Poitiers to Paris. *Motor-Flight* begins with the memorable opening line, "The motor-car has restored the romance of travel." *Fighting France,* too, begins with motoring, this time "north from Poitiers" on July 30, 1914. On this "flight," Wharton and her companions have picnicked "by the roadside" (FF, 3) as Wharton and her companions did in *Motor-Flight.* Despite ominous thunderclouds, they are en route to a sacralized tourist site, as they invariably were in *Motor-Flight* as well. They are about to visit a hoary object of the ritual and liturgy of travel, Chartres cathedral, whose incomparable windows, "steeped in a blaze of mid-summer sun," on this occasion prophetically "glittered and menaced like the shields of fighting angels" (FF, 4–5). As if to create a contrast with what is to come upon arrival in Paris, Wharton includes her stop at Chartres in the text. Establishing the magnificence of the history and civilization threatened with death in the Great War, Wharton writes this poetic and moving sentence: "All that a great cathedral can be, all the meanings it can express, all the tranquillizing power it can breathe upon the soul, all the richness of detail it can fuse into

a large utterance of strength and beauty, the cathedral of Chartres gave us in that perfect hour" (FF, 5)—perhaps the final "perfect hour" Wharton knew until the end of the war. Leaving
Chartres, the travelers approach Paris at, significantly, sunset,
to see "The Look of Paris," as the chapter is called, another evocation of the history of travel and the traveler as observer.

What they come to see, however, is a crazy-mirror image of
the world of travel, a realm of adventure which has become
defined by the grotesque. War has replaced "travel" as ordinarily
understood. Travel is now dictated and circumscribed by a war
that has effectively destroyed the larger liberty associated with
travel. Whereas the thrill of "travel" requires leisure and the
disturbance of routine,[12] it is now war, rather than travel, that
disturbs routine, that brings about "the abeyance of every small
and mean preoccupation" (FF, 15). Ordinarily, architecture and
the Old Masters are the artworks the traveler "reads," as in
Motor-Flight, Wharton reads "[t]he poetry of the descent to
Rouen" (MF, 18) and "the great hymn interrupted" (MF, 17), as
she calls the cathedral at Beauvais. Now, in Paris, it is "a great
poem on War" (FF, 15) that is read. The "army of midsummer
travel" has been "immobilized" and replaced by "the other army"
of soldiers who must now be mobilized. Refugees, "dazed and
slowly moving—men and women," carrying "sordid bundles on
their backs" (FF, 33), the luggage of refugees rather than of sight-
seers, are now the travelers Wharton sees in the streets of Paris.
Rather than carrying tourists, "[r]are taxi-cabs [are] impressed
to carry conscripts to the stations" (FF, 15). Whereas a ritual
of travel is letter writing to friends and family at home, now
correspondence is forbidden (FF, 19). In short, the energy the
"casual sight-seer" of *Motor-Flight* had given over to the study
of civilization is redirected in *Fighting France* and absorbed in
the study of war.

In *Fighting France,* that is, Wharton reverses the characteristics and rituals that resonate in the history of travel writing and
in her own previous texts of travel. The "sights" that Wharton,
leaving Paris en route to the front, goes out to see in the rest of
Fighting France are the sites of war, "sights that the pacific
stranger could forever gape at" (FF, 50–51) as she used to "gape"
at art and architecture. She travels through a "chartless wilderness" (FF, 83) that, in the absence of map and guidebook, would
have thrilled her on other journeys but is now frightening.
Wharton piles up details that, to the devotee of travel and travel
accounts, must be juxtaposed with the conventions of ordinary

and peaceful travel and travel writing to create this journey into the grotesque. Whereas in *Motor-Flight,* Wharton is the romantic traveler entranced by ruins, ruing the importunities of Viollet le Duc at Carcassonne and cherishing the "gashed walls and ivy-draped dungeons of the rival ruins" alongside the "curious church of Saint Pierre" in Chauvigny (MF 93), she now visits the ruins of the town of Thann, a "tormented region" where the "lamentable remains of the industrial quarter along the river" had been "the special target of the German guns" (FF, 190–91). Describing the towns of Lorraine, "blown up, burnt down, deliberately erased from the earth," Wharton uses the name of an iconic tourist site to suggest the dimensions of the destruction: "At worst they [the towns of Lorraine] are like stone-yards, at best like Pompeii" (FF, 152). The traveler to Belgium traditionally shops for lace. But on an afternoon in Poperinghe, and "bound on a quest for lace-cushions of a special kind required by our Flemish refugees," Wharton "roams from quarter to quarter" and finally comes upon an "orderly arrest of life": "rows and rows of lace-cushions" symbolizing "the senseless paralysis of a whole nation's activities" (FF, 155–57). Whereas an earlier Wharton, energized by the automobile, would have thrilled (as she later did) to the thought of air travel, in *Fighting France,* she hears "a whirr overhead, followed by a volley of mitrailleuse": "High up in the blue . . . flew a German aeroplane" (FF, 154), the symbol of a new era of travel harnessed to the destruction of the old.

On a larger scale, the movements of the traveler as she progresses through once-peaceful landscapes toward historic monuments, previously staged as thrilling and breathtaking and adventuresome in *Motor-Flight,* have become an exercise in the grotesque in *Fighting France.* A comparison between Wharton's ascent to Vezelay in *Motor-Flight*—her *Paradiso,* and her ascent to the German frontier in *Fighting France*—her *Inferno,* shows the deftness of Wharton's generic work not simply in the details but in the broad strokes of her travel prose, exercised in the interests of bringing home to her compatriots the horrors of war. The ascent to Vezelay in *Motor-Flight* is developed along the lines of a suspense narrative, heightening the adventure of travel by repeatedly and tantalizingly naming the object of desire, Vezelay, to italicize the delay of desire's gratification and the serial ordeal required of those who are worthy of the grail. The "hungry travellers" in "the final stage of their pilgrimage to Vezelay" must sacrifice the full enjoyment of a luncheon filet and "fragrant coffee" to get on the road in timely fashion. "Old villages perched high on ledges or lodged in narrow defiles" must be sacrificed on the altar of the greater glory of Vezelay because of "[t]he strain of our time-limit" (MF, 158). Wharton imposes obstacles to prolong the agony of desire, observing, for example, that Avallon brings them nearly to "defer Vezelay," but "the longing to see the great Benedictine abbey against such a sunset as the afternoon promised was even stronger" (MF, 159). Suspense is made to mount: "All day," Wharton writes, "the vision of the Benedictine church had hung before us beyond each bend of the road" until "at length we saw its mighty buttresses and towers clenched in the rock, above the roofs and walls of the abbatial town" (MF, 159–60). Having created a sizable ado and a serial ordeal from the ascent to Vezelay, Wharton finally allows herself to arrive. Wharton's narrative craft makes fresh and new, exciting and adventuresome, a ritual performance of travel to a sacralized site.

The pilgrimage to Vezelay is utterly transformed, to echo Yeats, in *Fighting France.* The adventure and suspense of arriving at Vezelay and the salvation promised to pilgrims to the cathedral church are grotesquely inverted. The renewal offered by travel, leisure, and a religious pilgrimage becomes the paradoxical renewal of war: "War is the greatest of paradoxes: the most senseless and disheartening of human retrogressions," Wharton writes, "and yet the stimulant of qualities of soul which, in every race, can seemingly find no other means of renewal" (FF, 53–54). The religious exercises to secure the salvation of the individual soul, at Vezelay, are now war exercises to secure the salvation of civilization or the soul of western culture. Wharton builds a suspenseful narrative to create and delay the fulfillment of desire, the gratification of seeing war at work, as she had delayed the gratification of seeing faith at work in the architectural splendor of Vezelay. This time, the front lines of the Germans are the travelers' destination, and the landscape leading there is "furrowed by a deep trench—a 'bowel,' rather—winding invisibly from one subterranean observation post to another" (FF, 117). The pilgrims en route to the front lines lurch from a "vigilant height" and "down the hillside to a village out of range of the guns" (FF, 118). "Below the village the road wound down to a forest that had formed a dark blue in our bird's-eye view of the plain" (FF, 119). The quaint town of Avallon that had threatened to detain the pilgrims on the way to Vezelay, in *Motor-Flight,* is replaced by the "'villages nègres' of the second line of trenches, the jolly little settlements to which the troops retire after doing their shift under fire" (FF, 119). The next day, "an intenser sense of adventure" comes about, not from the unknown of history and landscape but from the security precautions of war. "Hitherto we had always been told beforehand where we were going and how much we were to be allowed to see," Wharton writes, "but now we were being launched into the unknown" (FF, 122). "Up and up into the hills" they go, and "[h]igher still," until finally "we were within a hundred yards or so of the German lines," the "other" at the root of war (FF, 124, 125, 131). This is the end of the quest, and this is what Wharton finds: "I looked out and saw a strip of intensely green meadow just under me. . . . The wooded cliff swarmed with 'them,' . . . and here . . . one saw at last . . . a grey uniform huddled in a dead heap" (FF, 133–34). The sacralized site of the Vezelay of *Motor-Flight* has been replaced by a dead German soldier. The hallmarks of travel and pilgrimage, danger and suspense, and desire and adventure devolve into a dead body on the front lines.

This is travel writing in the grotesque. This is *Fighting France,* situating a France at war in the generic practice Wharton deliberately chose for it. Creating sympathy for war-wracked France, this is the cultural work and another form of war work to which Wharton turned her deft hand in the dark days of the Great War. Evoking the shades of a long tradition of travel and travel writing that lingered in the minds of travelers and readers, *Fighting France* transforms what were the dreams of a century into the nightmare of war. It drew down the curtain on a period in western history and on an epoch in women's practice in travel writing.

Notes

This essay appeared as the coda to Mary Suzanne Schriber, *Writing Home: American Women Abroad, 1830–1920* (Charlottesville: University Press of Virginia, 1997): 201–9.

New York: Scribner's, 1934, 362.

1. Paul R. Baker, *The Fortunate Pilgrims: Americans in Italy, 1800–1860* (Cambridge: Harvard University Press, 1964), 20; Allison Lockwood, *Passionate Pilgrims: The American Traveller in Great Britain, 1800–1914* (Rutherford, N.J.: Fairleigh Dickinson University Press, 1981), 283; "American Girls in Europe," *North American Review* 150 (1890): 681.

2. Figures compiled from Harold Smith, *American Travellers Abroad: A Bibliography of Accounts Published before 1900* (Carbondale: Southern Illinois University Press, 1969).

3. *No Gifts from Chance: A Biography of Edith Wharton* (New York: Macmillan, 1994), 311.

4. For full biographical information on Wharton's war efforts, see R. W. B. Lewis, *Edith Wharton: A Biography* (New York: Harper & Row, 1975), 363–403; Sheri Benstock, *No Gifts from Chance: A Biography of Edith Wharton* (New York: Macmillan, 1994), 301–49; and Alan Price, *The End of the Age of Innocence: Edith Wharton and the First World War* (New York: St. Martin's, 1996).

5. See Radhika Mohanram, "Narrative Practices and Construction of Identity: Edith Wharton," in *Commonwealth and American Women's Discourse: Essays in Criticism,* ed. A. L. McLeod (Columbia, MO: South Asia Books, 1996), 278–91). Mohanram argues that because Wharton was "other" in America because she was a writer, and "other" in Europe because she was a colonial, she constructed in her letters and her autobiography, as well as in her fiction, a spiral of identities. She was always the *sujet-en-procès.*

6. *Backward Glance,* 352.

7. *Fighting France, from Dunkerque to Belfort* (New York: Scribner's, 1915). Subsequently cited in the text as FF. The articles that became *Fighting France* appeared as "In Argonne," *Scribner's Magazine,* 57 (June 1915): 651–60; "In Lorraine and the Vosges," *Scribner's Magazine,* 58 (October 1915): 430–42; and "In the North," *Scribner's Magazine,* 58 (November 1915): 600–610. Wharton also fashioned a novel out of the war: *A Son at the Front* (1923). Wharton calls *Fighting France* a "little book" and refers to it as "scribbles" in *A Backward Glance* (New York: Scribner's, 1934), 339, 352–53.

8. *Edith Wharton Abroad: Selected Travel Writings, 1888–1920* (New York: St. Martin's, 1995), 36.

9. New York: Scribner's, 1908, 160. Subsequently cited in the text as MF.

10. For Wharton's own account of this, see *A Backward Glance,* 345–57.

11. For a full discussion of the characteristics and evocations of *Motor-Flight,* see my "Edith Wharton and Travel Writing as Self-Discovery," *American Literature* 59 (May 1987): 257–67.

12. See Dean MacCannell, *The Tourist: A New Theory of the Leisure Class* (New York: Schocken, 1989), x.

Edith Wharton As Propagandist and Novelist: Competing Visions of "The Great War"

Judith L. Sensibar

THROUGHOUT THE FIRST WORLD WAR, EDITH WHARTON WORKED UN-
ceasingly for the French war effort, raising money to care for
allied refugees, and initiating and supervising various war relief
operations in Paris and its suburbs. In spring 1916, the French
government awarded her its highest decoration "for her devotion
to humanitarian relief"—the French Legion of Honor.[1]

Besides such traditional women's war work, she also served
the French government as an unofficial propagandist and
"spokesman" for the French war effort and for France's imperialist policies in North Africa, particularly in Morocco, where Ger-
many, too, had made significant inroads. Her travel book *In
Morocco* (1920), which she researched in September 1917, en-
thusiastically endorsed those policies.[2] Between 1914 and 1923,
she also pursued her art. She was inventive and prolific—moving easily between different genres as she wrote and rewrote
the Great War and its fall-out.[3] Almost all her writing during
this period consciously identifies with and supports hegemonic
and Western attitudes toward race and class, particularly the
imperialist project of the war itself, which she explicitly ties
to France's ongoing colonization of North Africa. However, her
constantly shifting and often subversive constructions of state,
family, and sexual ideologies destabilize these very same biases.
Even her explicit war propaganda, such as *Fighting France* and
The Book of the Homeless, illustrate what Lillian Robinson calls
"the continuities and contradictions between the gender tensions and the other historical forces that make up the post-
traumatic stress of modernism: war, imperialism, race, class, and
national identities."[4]

Between 1914 and 1923, as Wharton became committed to an
expatriate life, she also shifted from writing almost exclusively

about upper-class urban American women—like Lily Bart, who is colonized by the patriarchal gaze in *The House of Mirth*—to more politically and psychologically complex and inclusive renderings of colonizing processes. This change is registered most clearly in her later fiction and prose. It occurred, in part, because Wharton was keenly responsive to the specific historical events, people, and cultural contexts. This essay examines passages from her letters, her book *In Morocco,* and her postwar novel, *A Son at the Front,* which she began planning in 1919 and published four years later. Her 1923 novel both destabilizes many of the imperialist assumptions about race and gender that dominate *In Morocco*'s narrative and explores the attendant psychological tensions her travel book describes but then ignores. Read together, these works raise central questions about the social construction of gender and sexuality in Wharton's writing. Of particular interest are the vacillations of the feminine between male and female, and between subject and object, as these are reflected in Wharton's self-constructions, in her authorial masks, and in her portrayals of the colonialist and imperialist forces motivating and shaping the lives of her fictional characters.

Colonized and Colonizing Bodies in Wharton's Wartime Propaganda and Her Fiction

Between February and November 1915, Wharton was one of the first women war correspondents to visit the "forbidden zone," making five trips to the French front "travel[ing] from end to end" with Walter Berry, who would also accompany her in 1917 to Morocco.[5] Like her British and American counterparts May Sinclair and Mildred Aldrich, Wharton spoke as the voice of the French government. Her purpose was to enlist America's aid. Her terms, as one would expect in these dispatches, are racialist and essentialist as she writes of the "intellectual audacity" of the "French race," "the innate "moral courage" of French women, their "instinctive ... devotion and self-denial," "the French hate" for "militarism," and France's disdain for "the savage forms of sport which stimulate the blood of more apathetic or more brutal races" like the Germans and the Spanish (*Fighting France,* 221, 222, 235, 234).

In Paris, however, as her letters, some short stories, and parts of her two war novels reveal, she was seeing the war from a different and more critical angle. *A Son at the Front* offers "a picture," as she later described it, of "that strange war-world of the rear" (*ABG*, 369). Embedded in *A Son at the Front* (and, to a lesser extent, her earlier war novel, *The Marne*) are searing critiques of all heads of government as well as of the rich international community in wartime Paris.[6] Wharton fills her opulent and overstuffed drawing rooms with wealthy British, French, and American speculators who expect the war to improve their profits both in the art market and war relief organizations (*Son*, 333, 371). The French State rewards the most dishonest speculator with the Legion of Honor (256). Wartime Paris is "a hideous world" in which the rich are "dancing and flirting and money-making on the great red mounds of dead" (334).

Wharton wrote from experience. Daily she confronted the devastation war wreaks on civilian populations, especially poor women and children, and old people—and in that process, she witnessed the human costs resulting from the venality of war profiteers. Alan Price provides a detailed account of her involvement in the turf wars waged between various Paris-based relief organizations and the internal tensions that complicated Wharton's own relief efforts.[7]

Wharton, as an international writer, but also as a privileged American woman, is highly conscious of the limits and possibilities of her own political power as an internationally recognized "woman of letters." Whether as novelist, as correspondent of Henry James (*L*, 348–53, 354–56), as war-reporter crossed with Lady Bountiful motoring with her chauffeur and Walter Berry to Verdun with hospital supplies and crates "of fresh eggs and bags of oranges" for the French troops (*L*, 351–53), or as exhausted war-relief worker taking a three-week respite by touring (again with Berry) French Morocco, Wharton constantly probes the social construction of gender and imperialism in her representations of the French war effort (*L*, 348–53, 354–56, 351–53). In Edward Said's and Donna Haraway's terms, Wharton's writing reveals the means by which those in control use language and technology to colonize the bodies of their subjects. Her narratives also reveal the ways in which those stories and technologies of domination can be disrupted or subverted.[8]

In Morocco as Imperial Travelogue
and Homoerotic Fantasy

In Morocco and *A Son at the Front,* when read together, present one of Wharton's most serious challenges to French imperialism, in particular the type of imperialism favored by the
controversial first French resident general of Morocco, Hubert
Lyautey. The disjunctions, ambiguities, and ambivalences in *In
Morocco* and her other earlier propaganda pieces work on the
reader in many of the same ways as realistic fiction.[9] Attention
to these works reveals an organic relationship between the confusion registered by her own earlier voices and the increasing
intensity, range, and depth with which she probes the relation
of cultural contexts to the dynamics of human relationships in
her postwar fiction.

In many ways, Wharton's travel book on Morocco is similar to
those written beginning in the 1830s by travelers to the Americas. These writers, who were often commissioned by their gov-
ernments or by private companies with large colonial interests,
were part of what Mary Louise Pratt calls "the capitalist van-
guard."[10] In the midst of the war, General Lyautey, whom Wharton had met in Paris, invited Wharton to Morocco to report on
his success in transforming the French protectorate into a
model colonial venture and a highly effective war machine. The
ambitious colonial general received the publicity he desired as
Wharton's essays appeared first in the widely circulated
Scribner's magazine. When *Scribner's* published *In Morocco,* it
was dedicated to Lyautey and his wife. Wharton's chapter praising the general's colonizing skills and her glowing descriptions
of his "enlightened" social, political, and economic policies echo
what Pratt identifies as the "goal oriented rhetoric of conquest
and achievement" typical of mid nineteenth-century travel
books on the Americas.[11]

Both the personal and political contexts of Wharton's visit bear
directly on the sexual/textual politics of *In Morocco.* Writing to
André Gide prior to her trip, she explains that "the [French]
government is organizing an 'official tour' to visit the annual
Trade Fair at Rabat, and I have been invited to join it" (*L,* 397).
From his own acquaintance with her in Paris and from mutual
friends such as Gide, Lyautey knew that among Wharton's closest friends were politically and intellectually powerful men
whose sexual lives, like his own, did not conform to the meagre

binarisms of a heterosexual imperative. He also knew she had
a public political voice—something unusual—even for an
American woman. She published in major international journals, and she dined and corresponded with men on both sides
of the Atlantic who set international policy, including Teddy
Roosevelt and John Pershing, the commander of the American
Expeditionary Force in France. Modeling his fair on international trade expositions such as the World's Fairs in the industri-
alized countries, Lyautey organized an impressive "trade fair" to
showcase Morocco's economic potential and demonstrate that
France's economy was thriving in wartime. The economic importance of Wharton's mission is underscored by the business
credentials of her travel companion. Besides being her closest
friend, Walter Berry was a well-known international lawyer and
president of the American Chamber of Commerce in Paris.

But Wharton as propagandist is also a novelist. Thus, her personal interest is in presenting the human drama of Morocco. Her
definitions of what *is* human are, of course, socially constructed.
However, her definitions—in general, so colored by colonialist
desire in this travel book—are problematized by knowledge
gained from her friendships (of varying degrees of intimacy)
with men whose sexual orientations were not heterosexually
fixed and who were all friends, with each other as well. They
included her travel companion, Walter Berry, André Gide, and
Hubert Lyautey. Lyautey's original exile into France's colonial
army was precipitated both by his public critiques of the French
military and his openness about his homosexuality.[12] The narrative voice of *Fighting France, French Ways and Their Meaning,*
and *In Morocco* is deeply identified with French nationalism
and imperialism. But *In Morocco* clearly demonstrates that
Wharton's attitudes about military interventions in colonial territories are aligned with Lyautey's. Further complicating her
gaze and equally important to the cast of her colonial eye regarding sexual politics and gender issues were her relationships with
Lyautey and with the other (mostly American) "bachelor types"
who formed what she called her "inner circle." Susan Goodman
details the nature of these and Wharton's other close male
friends' polymorphous or irresolute sexualities and observes
that "For people who were asexual, homosexual, or otherwise
inclined not to wed . . . [e]xpatriation provided an artificial country because it conferred more freedom than either the native or
adopted land. For those who did not conform (socially, sexually,
politically), a foreign theater . . . gave them more latitude."[13]

When Wharton had first visited North Africa in 1914, she also traveled with friends from her inner circle. In a sense, this circle permitted her to escape some of the constructions of compulsory heterosexuality.[14] But just as her male companions may have served—to borrow Eve Sedgwick's terminology—as Wharton's closet, so she served as theirs—perhaps nowhere more so than on these two North African trips.[15] On both excursions, as her letters and *In Morocco* confirm, her vision was informed by what Goodman describes as their veiled and complex "sexually dissident . . . identities" and attendant fears and desires—identities captured so memorably in the friendship between Michel and Ménalque in André Gide's *The Immoralist*. (Gide, perhaps wishing to provide her with an "inside" guide, gave her a newly published edition of his novel just before she left for Morocco in 1917.[16]) Wharton's representations of Morocco are then further complicated by the fact that her gaze seems at times simultaneously phallocratic and homoerotic even though it issues from a woman whose public persona, as presented in her memoir, *A Backward Glance,* is firmly anchored in the heterosexual imperative. I suggest that what Joseph Boone calls "the complex undercurrents" that link "the homoerotics of an orientalizing discourse with phallocentri[sm]"[17] color Wharton's representations of Morocco in her travel book and go far to explain its paradoxes and dissonances. Gide had anatomized this "orientalizing discourse" in *The Immoralist.*[18] Wharton would enact it in her travel book. *In Morocco* is propaganda; it is also, at moments, an imaginative representation of the psychosexual dynamics that inform her own Orientalism and her host's idiosyncratic colonial policies. Both were shaped, in part, by what Boone calls "orientalist homoerotics."[19]

Wharton and Walter Berry were ardent supporters of the controversial self-described "[m]onarchist, aristocrat, religious"[20] who had been resident general of the French protectorate since 1912. Lyautey, a veteran foreign officer, was both famous and infamous. Like the maverick foreign service officer Ménalque in Gide's *The Immoralist* (for whom he was the reputed model), Lyautey's career smoked of political and sexual scandal.[21] Furthermore, his hostility to French assimilationist colonial policy in Morocco involved excluding French colonials from his government and ignoring orders from the Home Office. His own policy, honed in Indo-China and Algeria and known as "la indigence," was built upon paradox. Like Ménalque, he was a scholar/soldier and an informed Orientalist. He was also a royalist and antimilitarist who disclaimed all traditional authority but his own. Theoretically adhering to a policy of indirect rule, his highly centralized and almost absolutist administration depended on the loyalty of the native elites, a loyalty built on expanding and strengthening Morocco's economy and preserving its religious and cultural infrastructure.[22] André Maurois, who calls Lyautey an enlightened despot, writes that when Lyautey was a child, his friends named him "Emperor." His colonial policies were driven by a "dream" of exercising "absolute and beneficent power . . . under cover of a Sultan of his own creation." Under Lyautey's rule, Morocco became "the image of the man."[23] As Wharton conveys this in *In Morocco,* she appears to identify with Lyautey. With rare exceptions, she describes herself as viewing Morocco from his perspective: his motor, his dais, his balcony, his residences.

Wharton's 1914 North African Holiday: A Prelude to *In Morocco*

Wharton's letters make clear that when she drove across Algeria and Tunisia, one of the anticipated subtexts of her party's excursion (as it is for Michel, the narrator of Gide's novel) was what Boone characterizes as "a vacation agenda" that included "exposure" to "what has come to be known within Western sexual discourse as male homosexual practice."[24] This agenda, as Boone writes, "remains unspoken in most commentaries on colonial narrative." He explains as follows:

For over a century, numerous gay men have journeyed to North Africa to discover . . . a colonized Third World in which the availability of casual sex is based on an economics of boys. Seized by the French in 1834, Algeria became a popular cruising site for Gide, Wilde, . . . and many other homosexual men of means by the century's end. During the first two decades of the twentieth century, Algeria's reputation for gay tourism was superseded by that of . . . Morocco.[25]

This was the same North Africa where Wharton, accompanied by Percy Lubbock, another member of the inner circle, took a four-week motor trip in 1914 (*L,* 317–18, 320).[26] They toured the cities, deserts, and mountains of "this magic land," feasting, as Western travelers have since at least the eighteenth century,

on its exotica and erotica. The latter is well represented in Wharton's letters to Morton Fullerton, Gaillard Lapsley, and Bernard
Berenson. Unfortunately, the postcards (probably pornographic)
that Wharton sent Berenson, who collected pornography, are not
in the voluminous collection of Wharton letters at Berenson's
villa, I Tatti,[27] but the Lewises' selection of Wharton's letters
gives a clear sense of how Wharton situates, eroticizes, and ob-
jectifies North African male bodies to evoke, as Boone describes
it, "the attractive yet dangerous lure of polymorphous eastern
sexuality"[28] (90). For example, she writes Berenson that Tunis
is "a cauldron of 'louxoure' . . . and one can't take two steps in
the native quarter . . . without feeling one's self in an unexpur-
gated page of the Arabian Nights!"[29] Producing an Orientalizing
spectacle that encodes homoerotic fear and desire, she portrays
these male bodies as simultaneously effeminate, penetrable, and
in need of Western/white male civilizing force: "[I]t's all effemi-
nacy, obesity, obscenity or black savageness. But, oh, the dresses,
the types, the ways of walking, sprawling, squatting—."[30] En-
grossed in narrating a "poetic" scene of "blacks carrying baskets
of rosebuds on their heads, & the little solemn pale children in
the booths holding skeins of silk and scraps of leather, & slippery
fig-colored babies in bangles and rags," she almost "forget[s]" to
"tell . . . of a horrid adventure I had at Timgad." To Berenson,
and, later, to Fullerton and others,[31] she then writes of her defining moment with Algeria's "blackness," that is, her narrative
of the dark rapist, whom she describes euphemistically as a robber. (He steals nothing.) She characterizes it as a "horrid mid-
night adventure" on "the wild African campagna" with a
bedroom intruder whom she touches but never sees. She writes
that she "was waked by a noise in my room, put out my hand
for the matches (no electric light), & touched a man who was
bending over me." Somehow, even though she is only "half conscious," she knows just by "touch" what the intruder is and is
not: "I was half conscious of a very brief struggle in the blackness, of his being rather small, and I think *not* an Arab." If not
Arab, then what? Racially and sexually he is other, a part of the
impenetrable blackness of the wild African night. To Fullerton
she would write, "It was the inability to get a light, even the
gleam of a match, that was so horrible—& seemed to last *so*
long! I should be very glad to die, but it's no fun struggling with
you don't know what in the dark—" (*L*, 324). Although Wharton
claims the incident as fact, her narrative suggests it might have
been a nightmare. When her cries for help bring "people with

candles and without trousers," they find "no one in my room." Nor can they find any trace of the "robber." The only verification Wharton offers is that there had been other recent robberies adding, as if to assure herself and Berenson that she has not been violated, "*I* lost nothing but my voice," and "I would rather have given him my checkbook than gone through that minute when I touched him" (*L*, 318–19; italics mine).[32] For a writer, loss of voice spells impotence and the narrative confusion registered in this letter feels like impotence. Furthermore, the hint at transracial erotics of the scene she narrates for her two sexually polymorphous white male correspondents, Berenson and Fullerton, invites them to appropriate (vicariously) both bodies.

In her public writing on North Africa, Wharton never directly resorts to circulating this experience. Her intent was to promote the French war effort, please her host, and encourage tourism. To this end, *In Morocco* includes much looking at black male bodies, voyeurism which feels those bodies as violent, sado-masochistic, and homoerotic. However, in Marrakech, "a city of Berbers and blacks, the last outpost against the fierce black world beyond the Atlas" (*M*, 129), Wharton relates another experience which, read in the context of her Algerian letters, suggests a repetition, but one that represents a more managed, if compromised, reliving of that earlier event. At Marrakech, she stays at the Bahia, "one of the loveliest and most fantastic" of Moroccan palaces. Now a home of the resident general, it was built by "Ba-Ahmed, a nineteenth century all-powerful black Vizier." She sees nothing ironic about her being ensconced in the Apartment of the Grand Vizier's favorite concubine, "a lovely prison."[33] Lying on her cushioned divan in this "fabulous place," she gazes through the frame created by her "secret sanctuary['s] . . . vermilion doors" to the atrium beyond. One morning she is awakened by the "dream-like" scene of "negro" intruders: "silhouetted against the cream-colored walls, a procession of eight tall negroes in linen tunics who filed noiselessly across the atrium like a moving frieze of bronze." For the racializing eye, white cannot exist without black. Thus, white or light generally both distances and frames, contains and illuminates blackness as it does here in what Wharton calls her "vision, like some fragment of a Delacroix or Decamps floating up into the drowsy brain" (*M*, 132–33). Still, these black men seem vaguely threatening: "I almost fancied I had seen the ghosts of Ba-Ahmed's executioners revisiting with dagger and bowstring the scene of an unavenged crime" (*M*, 133). Why this fantasy and what is the crime? Wharton does not say. Could it be the resident general's appropriation of the black vizier's palace? In her 1914 experience, she failed to contain blackness/the other. Unable to find a match to light up the darkness, she violated the invisible boundary that separates East from West and darkness from light when she touched the intruder. But now, when she asks what the "tall negroes" had "been doing in my room at that hour," the response that they are just France's servants performing a daily duty permits her to domesticate them further. Although she paints this scene in erotic and sensuous language, only her eyes make contact with these silent black bodies. Furthermore, *she* is looking at them, not *they* at her. Neither touch nor speech occur to break the illusion of containment that Wharton's language creates to mask fear *of* (masquerading here as threat) and desire *for* the body of the dark other. After all, it is she who is sleeping in the apartment of the black vizier's favorite.

Yet, Wharton's discourse of attempted rape/robbery differs from the typical colonial narrative in one important way. Although it narrates "the violent reproduction of gender roles that positions white women as innocent victims," it does not depict white men as their avengers and restorers of moral order.[34] Neither her 1914 account nor its veiled repetition in *In Morocco* make any mention of her white male travel companions or her host. Instead of an external rescuer, Wharton alone regains control of both situations by taking charge of the narrative. In the first instance, she adopts a self-mocking tone that minimizes the incident—"I lost nothing but my voice, which was reduced for several days to a faint squeak" (*L*, 319), and in the second, she aesthetisizes "the eight tall negroes in linen tunics" and then domesticates them—they are only the resident general's municipal lamplighters (*M*, 132–33). Perhaps the absence of the image of the white heterosexual male as civilizing force in these emblematic moments represents the moment when Edith Wharton refuses to provide the closet of compulsory heterosexuality for her Prufrockian companions.[35] Perhaps it shows her understanding, so clearly articulated in much of her later fiction, of the ways in which that closet at best ignores her female characters' erotic desires and at worst, as Gide depicts it in *The Immoralist,* destroys them. However, both her narratives of the specter of the dark rapist also bar white men from being joined with black men through or over the body of a white woman. Neither provides the sexual promise such narrative scenes offer when viewed from the perspective of the male homoerotic gaze. There are other ruptures in *In Morocco,* particularly in her obligatory harem chapter as she attempts to rationalize France's collusion in, what to her, is an abhorrent concept of family.

With these exceptions, Wharton's commentary in letters to members of her "inner circle" and in *In Morocco* is typical of other nineteenth-and twentieth-century white Westerners' accounts of travel in North Africa. As one reviewer observed when *In Morocco* was first published, its author was very much in favor of "the general theory of imperialism."[36] Wharton unintentionally reveals the homosocial and homoerotic subtext of the colonial rape narrative by assuming the phallic role as she makes herself her own savior in these two thinly disguised, racialized sexual fantasies. Yet, for the most part, her consciously stated attitude toward the discourse of rape and other "barbarous narratives of native culture . . . that [either] position colonial women as the innocent victims,"[37] or make them invisible, answers to the political and psychological needs of France's appropriation of Morocco.

In Morocco's Dioramas of Western Imperialism

Wharton's *In Morocco,* published one year before Carl Akeley began constructing his African Hall (which was partly financed by Wharton's good friend, Teddy Roosevelt, Akeley's fellow game hunter and "preservationist"), functions as a series of dioramas created to explain French imperialism. Like the dioramas in the Museum of Natural History, which Zora Neale Hurston saw as a form of "simian orientalism,"[38] *In Morocco* is consciously constructed as imperialist propaganda. The myths of the origins of culture that form its superstructure are also Orientalist and masculinist. They privilege West over East, white over black, Christian over Muslim or Jew, and male over female, assigning Western culturally defined feminine characteristics to what Kipling called "the lesser breeds throughout the world." Wharton describes how the protectorate's French rulers have surveyed, dualized, classified, and categorized every aspect of Morocco so as to, in Said's words, "speak for it" on the assumption that the colonized body cannot speak for itself.

In her descriptions of the Moroccan scenery, architecture, gardens, and people, she constructs for her reader a series of dioramas—in fact she often calls them friezes, spectacles, or stage sets—that reveal the "truth" about this culture. She also de-

scribes actual dioramas that French Orientalists have built to
colonize and contain Morocco as she applauds the "skill and
discretion" with which the French government has "restored
and transformed" a mosque into a museum of Moroccan art (*M*,
21, 26). Like Akeley's, Wharton's dioramas are what Haraway
calls "meaning-machines," which produce "narratives of race,
class, and culture" that are informed by imperialist and colonialist notions of what Morocco is.[39] These narratives are first and
foremost Orientalist. By this I mean they appropriate what
Boone calls "the so-called East in order to project onto it an
otherness that mirrors Western . . . needs."[40]

Travel books also serve a similar purpose as "meaning machines." Said points out that they, like other literary texts, function as "a kind of intellectual *authority* over the Orient within
Western culture" and thus are an important product and tool
of "academic as well as literary Orientalism that bear on the
connection between British and French Orientalism on the one
hand and the rise of an explicitly colonial-minded imperialism
on the other." Like other imperialist technologies, they "serve
to contain the Orient and speak on its behalf." Their narrator is
always the external spectator who assumes that because the Orient cannot "represent" or speak for itself, the Orientalist's representation "does the job." Orientalists don't recognize that what
they put forward as "truth" is, in fact, "representation."[41]

In like fashion, Wharton's travel book "represents" Orientalist
"truth." With maps, photographs, and descriptive language (all
"objective" evidence), it charts, displays, and so reveals the essential meaning it constructs for the land, the people, and the
culture the French have colonized. Its claim to truth is that it
is mapping the real, the actual, and the scientific. But despite her
enthusiasm for the French achievements, Wharton's imperial
narrative periodically ruptures itself. While praising the transformed mosque, she also observes that native life has "been
replaced by the lifeless hush of a museum." This is the same
adjective she will apply to the Caïd's wives in a later chapter
on Moroccan harems. She then adds that "while the medursa's
physical perfection will be revived," it will "never again be more
than a show-medursa, standing empty and unused" and that
therefore it will "die" like the country's "learning and her commerce" (*M*, 26). Passages like this, which are strategically placed,
covertly question the aims and the costs of the French colonial enterprise.

Viewing Morocco literally from the seat of the French colonial presence, her "military motor," Wharton invents a land of romance: If one loses one's way, "civilization vanishes as though it were a magic carpet rolled up by a Djinn" (*M*, 14). All is spectacle and theater, which gives Morocco "a blessed air of unreality" (*M*, 52). Like her profiles of the French and Germans in *Fighting France,* her constructions of the French and the Moroccans are racialist and essentialist. Morocco is a place of secrets, an "inimitable Eastern scene" (*M*, 29) where, to her colonialist eye, her first encounter with a veiled woman represents "all the mystery that awaits us." Yet in another one of those ambivalent turns that seems simultaneously to empower and silence the Moroccan woman's gaze, Wharton observes that she (unlike the black lamplighters) also "*looks out* through the eye-slits in the grave clothes muffling her" (*M*, 10; italics mine).

Throughout *In Morocco,* in her dioramas of market scenes, family groupings, and religious rites, Wharton privileges the French, "the new thriving French Morocco" (*M*, 28), over its subjects. All Moroccans are "indolent merchants" (*M*, 24) who in a moment can be transformed into a violent "army of hucksters . . . shrieking, bargaining, fist-shaking . . . and then, struck with the mysterious Eastern apathy," sink down "in languid heaps of muslin among black figs, purple onions, and rosy melons" (*M*, 27). All Arabs are lazy: "[T]he Moroccan Arab . . . has, like all Orientals, an invincible repugnance to repairing and restoring." Thus, through "oriental neglect," ancient Moslem buildings now lie in ruins (*M*, 198). Even Western ruins are better than their Oriental counterparts. Oriental buildings "do not 'die in beauty' like the firm stones of Rome" (*M*, 22). Wharton privileges Roman ruins over Muslim ruins for the same reason she privileges those "firm French roads." In her value system, the Roman represents "a system, an order, a social conception that still runs through all our modern ways; the other, the Moslem . . . , [is] more dead and sucked back into an unintelligible past than any broken architrave of Greece or Rome" (*M*, 45). The colonialist must also claim that even Moroccan ruins speak only nonsense. Fortunately, though, the French are repairing this rubble and transforming it from student lodging houses, where Muslims are subjects, into French-controlled museums, where they are objects.

Among the natives she establishes a pecking order. Because she privileges white over black and Christian over Muslim or Jew, some of her most racist observations are her portraits of blacks and Jews. Some blacks are "big friendly creatures" whom she photographs with "their womenkind [who] were washing the variegated family rags. They were handsome blue-bronze creatures, bare to the waist . . . with firmly sculptured legs and ankles; and all around them, like a swarm of gnats, danced countless jolly pickaninnies, naked as lizards" (*M*, 43). Later she portrays a harem guard, "the chief eunuch," as "a towering black with the enameled eyes of a basalt bust" (*M*, 171). Like the taxi-dermists who literally made live animals into sculptured repre-sentations for the Museum of Natural History dioramas Haraway critiques, Wharton uses sculptural metaphors to transform these living people into statues, to empty and contain them. Only the children move—as gnats or lizards. Moroccan Jews are transformed under Wharton's gaze to filthy, drunken rabbits. A "typical Jewish quarter" becomes a "sort of subterranean rabbit warren" of "demoralizing promiscuity" and "black and reeking staircases," where sacks of gold are hidden in the walls while their owners dress in rags and "dirty curtain muslin" and drug themselves and their infants with drink: "[T]he babies of the Moroccan ghettos are nursed on date brandy, and their elders doze away to death under its consoling spell" (*M*, 113–16, passim).

Friezes, paintings, and stage-sets are metaphors for many of the dioramas of Moroccan life she represents in her narrative. As Joseph Boone observes, imagining another country's "curi-osities as panoramas and tableaux depends, of course, on the illusion of some ineffable but inviolate boundary dividing spec-tator and spectacle, subject and object, self and other."[42] The unflinching, voyeuristic, and schizophrenic gaze that reports a violent ritual blood-letting ceremony is that of the colonizer. As Wharton implies here, viewing "sanguinary rites" is normally included in a Western tourist's vacation agenda, and other nineteenth- and twentieth-century travel accounts bear her out. Indeed, she had seen a similar display during her 1914 North African trip. Yet, oddly, she insists on her disgust and repulsion both at the related spectacles and at the rite she is about to describe: "Any normal person who has seen the dance of the Aïssaouas and watched them swallow thorns and hot coals, slash themselves with knives, and roll on the floor in epilepsy must have privately longed, after the first excitement was over, to fly from the repulsive scene" (M, 52). This said, she launches into a fascinated narrative of what she, a "normal" person, has just named a disgusting perversion. The scene is "like a setting for some extravagantly staged ballet." As in "a bas-relief," the musicians are "flattened side by side against a wall." Despite the dancers' "convulsions" and "contortions," "the pools of blood" forming from "the great gashes which the dancers hacked in their own skulls and breasts," Wharton insists that "the beauty of the setting redeemed the bestial horror. In that unreal golden light the scene became merely symbolical" (*M*, 52–55, passim).

But her description suggests that for the western voyeur, the rite's beauty and erotic attraction *is* its so-called bestial horror. For the politics of the ritual Lyautey has arranged for Walter Berry and her to observe, a ritual during which black male slaves mutilate themselves to demonstrate their love for their white male masters, seems to be a spectacle of racialized sadomasochism. In the midst of the dancing, Wharton realizes that although the dancers comprise both slaves and freemen, "most of the bleeding skulls and breasts belonged to negroes" (*M*, 55). She then explains that the "dance of the Hamadchas," a hierarchical "confraternity" devoted to worship of Saint Hamadch, celebrates the suicide of the white saint's faithful black slave "who, when his master died, killed himself in despair." Thus "the self-inflicted wounds of the so-called brotherhood are supposed to symbolize the slave's suicide" (*M*, 56). This is why the fraternity "divides its ritual duties into two classes, the devotions of the free men being addressed to the saint" while the black devotees must "simulate" the slave's "horrid end." The cult's leader, a "sinister" and "passionless figure ... stimulating the frenzy" of the dancers, is white and wears the white caftan that marks him as a free man (*M*, 54). Wharton does not wonder why Lyautey would choose to display such a spectacle nor does she question her reproduction of it for Western consumption. But her reading of the scene suggests that the resident general has appropriated and invited his guests to watch a spectacle that they are to experience voyeuristically as an enactment of their own erotic and imperial desires. White males' long practice of viewing and cataloging such sexually and racially charged scenes "often explains the historical appeal of orientalism as an occidental mode of male perception, appropriation, and control." Wharton's description of the ritual suggests that she is seeing it through her host's eyes.[43] However, the only conscious disjunctions in *In Morocco* appear when Wharton tours a series of harems. And even here, where she observes the sexual and racial exploitation of women and children present in this slave culture, she is apparently blind to her host's or her own complicity (*M*,

56). She does not recognize that the "fat oriental" keeps his harem at the pleasure of her host, General Lyautey.

When her narrative dioramas of the harems reveal the most blatant disjunctions—as with the harem of European women owned by "the magnificent eagle-beaked" Caïd of Fez, who is one of the general's strongest native supporters, Wharton's rhetorical move is a conventional one—she blames these women's enslavement on another "other," in this instance Jews. She imagines that "fate (probably in the shape of an opulent Hebrew couple . . .) carried [the women] from the Bosphorus to the Atlas" and sold them to the Caïd (M, 198, 203). Although she recognizes that Lyautey's greatest achievement has been his "successful employment of native ability," she seems unaware that the Caïd's harem is part of this employment (M, 214). She uses Orientalist rhetoric to rationalize colonialism.[44]

In Morocco, like Akeley's dioramas in the Museum of Natural History, claims status as a text based on scientific, observable fact. Although there may be chinks in Wharton's friezes, the overall impression is of a white patriarchy firmly in control of the display of the culture it has subdued. Now that Lyautey has rid Morocco of the German invaders and is ruling the country indirectly through its own elite, he will preserve its artifacts and represent its reality through the "meaning-machines" of Western technology—museums, trade fairs, and travel books. Ironically, Lyautey, the architect of French imperialist policy in North Africa, whose rule one contemporary Moroccan sociologist characterizes as unrelievedly "bloodthirsty and repressive," has himself been enshrined in a small diorama in Paris's Musée de L'Armée.[45]

A Son at the Front: Fictionalizing the Unspoken of *In Morocco*

In many ways, Wharton's last novel about the war years, *A Son at the Front* (1923), destabilizes the colonialist biases of state, family, and sexual ideologies that *In Morocco* supports. Its dioramas fail miserably and their crass purpose is exposed.[46] In this novel, the dioramas are the portraits and sculpture that the long-divorced, expatriate American artist John Campton creates to re-present and contain his soldier-son George, and thereby control George's identity and commodification. The abuses of harem children that Wharton blamed on the other in her travel book are practiced in this novel by both a biological father and the French state. And the dominant sexual ideologies Wharton interrogates as she details Campton's rivalries with the French government, with George's mistress, but most importantly, his fantasied rivalry with George's stepfather for "possession" of the son's body, undermine hegemonic attitudes toward state, family, and compulsory heterosexuality. Campton's obsession with his grown son is the ruling passion of his life. In his final diorama, where he begins to sculpt a war memorial in the image of his son whom the state has killed, Campton assumes the feminine position in a partnership with George's stepfather, his hated rival. Campton needs the stepfather's money to pay for the memorial. The object of his art is to re-create, immortalize, and appropriate George, and the fertilizing agent—the semen, as it were—is George's stepfather's money. Thus, in this novel, Wharton both anticipates and extends Eve Sedgwick's theorizing on male homosexual panic as she portrays one man triangulating his desire for another man, *not through the body of a dead woman,* but through the dead body of another man who is also his own son. As she probes her fictional artist's appropriation of his dead son, Wharton reveals the sexual politics underlying both imperialism and the development of mainstream modernist aesthetics. I suspect that her 1914 introduction to North Africa in the company of her bachelor traveling companions and her later Moroccan trip, combined with her other war experiences, were part of the impetus that led her to explore the sexual fantasies and practices of what I have argued elsewhere was canonical modernism's representative man, the persona whom Sedgwick first identified as "the bachelor type."[47] Wharton chose the genre of the war novel to invoke and then question a major trope of the fiction and poetry that, until recently, has been identified as "The Literature of the Great War." The "sexually irresolute" bachelor figure plays a constant role in her ongoing dialogue with canonical modernism—the subject of many of her late and often maligned "lesser" novels. In *A Son at the Front,* she introduced subjects to which she would return in *The Children* (1928): the complicated psychology of male homosexual panic and the ways in which social disruptions caused by World War I exposed and affected socially constructed notions of state, family, and masculinity and femininity. Particularly in the fiction Wharton wrote during and after the war, she portrays masculinity as mutable and fluid.[48]

The disjunctions Wharton records but ignores or rationalizes in *In Morocco* and other war propaganda—her "factual" and thus hegemonic constructions of colonial realities—become a central concern of much of her late fiction. That is, fiction allows her a larger realm of play for her subversive, questioning voice, the same playful and ironic voice that invents those multiple and contradictory and subversive selves at the beginning of her 1934 memoir, *A Backward Glance.*

As her epigraph for *A Son at the Front,* Wharton used a sentence from Walt Whitman's *Specimen Days,* one in which he describes the war-torn soldiers he has been nursing, "Something veil'd and abstracted is often a part of the manners of these beings." Their experience with battlefield atrocities has made them irretrievably other, masked, hidden behind a veil. But here Wharton chooses Whitman as much, if not more, for the other otherness he writes, "the love that dare not speak its name," to signal her own novel's thinly masked subject. As her letters to Morton Fullerton reveal, Wharton's interest in Whitman was personal and aesthetic.[49] Her close friendships with a bachelor circle that included Henry James, Berry, and Fullerton, and her fiction on the subject all indicate that Wharton was well versed in what Sedgwick calls "the broad field of forces within which masculinity—and thus *at least* for men, humanity itself—could (can) . . . construct itself."[50] Wharton saw that broad field as well as the effects of those constructions on all manner of relationships. Her window on this subculture—a subculture lived by white males in positions of political and economic power such as Morocco's Resident General Lyautey and Walter Berry, as well as by artists such as Proust, Gide, and James—her unique position of being, in a sense, *their* May Bartram—placed her where she could interrogate the politics of sexuality in a homosocial but homophobic and gynophobic world. By Wharton's own logical extension in her novels of this period, these become the politics of the family and the state and thus give her an indirect means by which to interrogate the politics of imperialism. She does so in *A Son at the Front, The Age of Innocence,* and *The Children,* to take only three examples. However, when writing in "factual" genres (travel books and more explicit war propaganda), Wharton tries and generally succeeds in seeing with a male colonizer's eye, and her best dioramas are the equal of any in Carl Akeley's wing of the New York Museum of Natural History. But when she tries and fails, producing instead the kinds of gaps, narrative fractures, and contradictions that I have discussed here, her war propaganda is of greatest interest. From these "failures" slip questions to which her later fiction speaks.[51]

Notes

1. Alan Price, *The End of the Age of Innocence: Edith Wharton and the First World War* (New York: St. Martin's Press, 1996), 87.

2. Quotations from Edith Wharton's works are cited in the text with the abbreviations listed as follows: *M: In Morocco*. (New York: Charles Scribner's Sons, 1920); *ABG: A Backward Glance* (New York: Charles Scribner's Sons, 1934); *L: The Letters of Edith Wharton*, ed. R. W. B. Lewis and Nancy Lewis (New York: Charles Scribner's Sons, 1988); *Son: A Son at the Front* (New York: Charles Scribner's Sons, 1923); *FF: Fighting France, from Dunkerque to Belfort* (New York: Charles Scribner's Sons, 1915).

3. Wharton's war publications include outright propaganda, such as dispatches from the French Front, which appeared in *Scribner's* magazine during the first six months of 1915 (published in book form as *Fighting France*), and *The Book of the Homeless* (1916). She also wrote a subtler form of propaganda—two travel books, *French Ways and Their Meaning* (1919) and *In Morocco* (1920). And she continued to write novels and short stories. Among her five novels published during these years were *Summer* (1917), *The Age of Innocence* (1920), and her second and last war novel, *A Son at the Front* (1923). She supplemented these with numerous reviews and articles which appeared in French, British, and American magazines and newspapers as well as hundreds of personal letters.

4. Lillian Robinson, "Critical Mass," *Women's Review of Books* (May 1991): 11.

5. Walter Berry, whose ancestors, the Van Rensselaers, were among New York's oldest families, was an important member of Wharton's inner circle, one of the three expatriate American "bachelor types," which included himself, Morton Fullerton, and Henry James. Of the three, as the highly respected international lawyer and judge, friend, like Wharton, of Teddy Roosevelt, and president of the American Chamber of Commerce in France, Berry was most directly connected to international centers of money and power. See R. W. B. Lewis, *Edith Wharton: A Biography* (New York: Harper and Row, 1975), 366 and *passim*. Susan Goodman's *Edith Wharton's Inner Circle* (Austin: University of Texas Press, 1994) offers a fascinating reading of how Wharton's relations with these and other members of the inner circle enlarged and empowered her imaginative vision.

6. See my "'Behind the Lines' in Edith Wharton's *A Son at the Front*: Rewriting a Masculinist Tradition," *Journal of American Studies* 24, no. 2 (1990): 187–98; revised in *Wretched Exotic: Essays on Edith Wharton in Europe*, ed. Katherine Joslin and Alan Price (New York: Peter Lang, 1993), 241–58.

7. Price, *The End of the Age of Innocence*, chap. 4, "At War with the American Red Cross: 1917," 107–40, especially.

8. See Donna Haraway, "Teddy Bear Patriarchy: Taxidermy in the Garden of Eden, New York City, 1908–36," in *Primate Visions: Gender, Race, and Nature in the World of Modern Science* (New York and London: Routledge, 1989); and Edward Said, *Orientalism* (New York: Vintage Books, 1978).

9. See Amy Kaplan, *The Social Construction of American Realism* (Chicago: University of Chicago Press, 1988), 10.

10. Mary Louise Pratt, *Imperial Eyes: Travel Writing and Transculturation* (London and New York: Routledge, 1992), 148. See also her essay, "Arts of the Contact Zone," *Profession '91*: 33–40.

11. Pratt, *Imperial Eyes*, 148.

12. Douglas Porch, *The Conquest of Morocco* (New York: Alfred A. Knopf, 1983), 85. In 1891, Lyautey published a blistering attack on the military establishment in the influential *Revue des Deux Mondes* which "firmly established [him] as one of the French army's renegade officers, as Pétain and de Gaulle were later to be. Disgrace, however, was not immediate" (Porch, 84). See André Maurois, *Lyautey* (New York: D. Appleton & Co., 1931), 53, for a somewhat more circumspect reading. With the exception of Porch, references to Lyautey's homosexuality are hidden in footnotes. See, for example, William A. Hoisington, Jr., *Lyautey and the French Conquest of Morocco* (New York: St. Martin's Press, 1995), 4; and Daniel Rivet, *Lyautey et l'institution du protectorate français au Maroc*, 3 vols. (Paris: L'Harmattan, 1988), 3:300.

13. *Edith Wharton's Inner Circle*, 12–13.

14. See ibid. for a detailed and insightful treatment of Wharton's relationships with Fullerton, Berry, James, Lubbock, and others, and also see Sensibar, "Behind the Lines."

15. See Eve Kosofsky Sedgwick, "The Beast in the Closet: James and the Writing of Homosexual Panic," in *Sex, Politics, and Science in the Nineteenth-Century Novel, Selected Papers from the English Institute, 1983–84*, ed. Ruth Bernard Yeazell (Baltimore/London: Johns Hopkins University Press, 1986), 148–86.

16. See Goodman's *Edith Wharton's Inner Circle*; and Sensibar, "Edith Wharton Reads the Bachelor Type: Her Critique of Modernism's Representative Man," *American Literature* 60 no. 4 (December 1988): 575–90.

17. Joseph Boone, "Vacation Cruises; or the Homoerotics of Orientalism," *PMLA* 10, no. 1 (January 1995): 89–108.

18. Gide and Lyautey frequented some of the same social and literary circles in Paris, and Gide visited Lyautey at least once in Morocco. See *Cahiers André Gide*, ed. Jean Lambert, 9 vols. (France: Gallimard, 1979), 9:413. It has been suggested that Gide modeled his French foreign service officer, Ménalque, to whom Michel feels "attracted by a secret influence," on the French resident general of Morocco. *The Immoralist* (New York: Vintage, 1958), 80–81. See Peggy Friedman, "*L'immoraliste* and French Imperialism," unpublished MLA paper, December 1992.

19. Boone, "Vacation Cruises," 90.

20. Quoted in Robin Bidwell, secretary of the Middle East Centre, University of Cambridge, *Morocco under Colonial Rule: French Administration of Tribal Areas, 1912–1956* (London: Frank Cass and Co., 1973). Lyautey also claimed that "Les trois titres qui sont le secret de ma réussite au Maroc" (Bidwell, 26).

21. For a sympathetic account of Lyautey, see Bidwell. Lyautey's refusal to permit the colons (resident French colonials) any part in governing Morocco infuriated them to such a degree that colonial-owned newspapers "passed all the bounds of decency in their attacks upon him. Scarcely veiled accusations ranging from graft to homosexuality were hurled at him and produced an atmosphere so poisonous that he was more than once tempted to resign." Although Bidwell acknowledges Lyautey's "tolerance for corruption," noting

both that "he himself said: 'On ne fait pas une colonie avec des pucelles,'" and
that he allowed "dishonesty" to become "entrenched," Bidwell himself makes
no comment on charges concerning Lyautey's sexual orientation (27, 28). In
a brief allusion concerning the relationship of Lyautey's personal and political
life, Hoisington notes that Lyautey sought "total independence from bourgeois
social conventions which he hoped, acceptance by a socially prominent (Parisian) upper crust would assure" (4). In a note, he adds that "perhaps Lyautey's
alleged homosexuality pushed him in this socially independent direction"
(n. 24, 210). Lyautey's imperialism was similar to Richard Burton's in that he,
too, was a serious Orientalist who learned Arabic, steeped himself in Morocco's
cultures, and made a point of living among and like the Moroccan elite. He
also rebelled against the authority of his own government and French moral
codes. But as an imperialist (albeit an anti-assimilationist), Lyautey saw himself as the chief agent of authority in France's colonies, and he used his knowledge of Moroccan culture to control and subjugate it. For Burton, see Said,
Orientalism, 194–97; and Joseph Boone, "Vacation Cruises, 91–94.

22. Bidwell, *Morocco under Colonial Rule,* 12–13.

23. André Maurois, *Lyautey,* trans. Hamish Miles (New York: Appleton and
Co., 1931), 216, 225.

24. See Boone, "Vacation Cruises," 90.

25. Ibid., 99.

26. Originally the party included Gaillard Lapsley, Lubbock's closest friend
and confidant (Goodman, *Edith Wharton's Inner Circle,* 27), but he became
ill and returned home. EW to BB, April 16 [1914], *L,* 317.

27. Edith Wharton wrote to Bernard Berenson that she would "deluge" him
with "picture post-cards" (September 13, 1917). Edith Wharton Collection, Villa
I Tatti, Florence. She also sent "a shower of provocative post-cards" to "the
Hermit of Carlyle Mansions." EW to GL, Tunis, April 23, 1914. *L,* 321. For a
description and analysis of one genre of these postcards, see Malek Alloula,
The Colonial Harem, Theory and History of Literature Series, vol. 21, trans.
Myrna Godzich and Wlad Godzich, intro., Barbara Harlow (Minneapolis: Uni-
versity of Minnesota Press, 1986).

28. Ibid., 90.

29. *L,* 318. In a 1920 letter to Mary Berenson, Wharton refers to *In Morocco*
as "Aladdin's first literary effort." EW to MB, October 15, 1920, Wharton Collection, Villa I Tatti.

30. Further encoding, and perhaps even teasingly, she writes to the now
returned Lapsley, "I have acquired for you in the bazaars here a phial of essence
of sandalwood & sycamore, which, diluted with the purest alcohol, is said to—
mais ne précisons pas! Vous m'en donnerez des nouvelles—or your victims
will" and "a so-called ambergris necklace from a 'coloured' prostitute," adding
that "it appears that to be seen with one of these fragrant baubles is to lose
one's reputation forever." Continuing to confuse and scramble Lapsley's sexual
and racial identity, she explains that their purpose is "to make the negresses
irresistible to the Arabs" (*L,* 316, 318, 320).

31. Edith Wharton to Morton Fullerton, Tunis, April 23, [1914], *L,* 320.

32. Edith Wharton to Bernard Berenson, Tunis, April 16, [1914], *L,* 318–19;
and to Morton Fullerton, Orvieto, May 11, [1914], *L,* 324.

33. *L,* 318 and *M,* 131. Wharton's Harem chapter makes no reference to this
earlier event.

34. Jenny Sharpe, *Allegories of Empire: The Figure of the Woman in the Colonial Text* (Minneapolis: University of Minnesota Press, 1993), 6.

35. For an analysis of Wharton's critique of this icon of high modernism, see Sensibar, "Edith Wharton Reads the Bachelor Type," *American Literature* 60 no. 4 (December 1988): 575–90.

36. Irita Van Doren, "A Country Without a Guide Book," *Nation* 111 (27 October 1920): 479–80.

37. Sharpe, *Allegories of Empire*, 6.

38. Haraway, *Primate Visions*, 29 and 11.

39. Ibid., 54.

40. See Boone, "Vacation Cruises," 89 and 104, n. 1.

41. Said, *Orientalism*, 18, 19, 20–21.

42. Boone, "Vacation Cruises," 93.

43. Ibid., 90.

44. This is a tricky question as is obvious from reading colonial and postcolonial critiques, because women are exploited by both cultures. Barbara Harlow, the Occidental woman who introduces Alloula's book, states diplomatically, "The question whether Islam and its social organization of men and women represented a significant improvement over previous family patterns and customary law in nomadic Arabia at the time of Muhammad (seventh century A.D.) continues to be debated by scholars, feminists and theologians, Muslim and non-Muslim alike." But she also points out that "Possession of Arab women came to serve as a surrogate for and a means to the political and military conquest of the Arab world." See her introduction in Malek Alloula, *The Colonial Harem,* xv. Often such acts were rationalized as liberating Arab women from their men. The question is: Is this what Wharton has in mind when she criticizes the institution of the harem? Or does she have another agenda that only reveals itself when she translates her response to the harems into the fictions she then writes about various colonizing practices of Occidental families in such novels as those which follow her Moroccan trip, *A Son at the Front* and *The Children?*

45. Although Lyautey's policies in Morocco were ultimately a failure (Porch, *The Conquest of Morocco,* 297–98), he is honored by the French. His tomb is in Les Invalides very near Napoleon Bonaparte's. See Hoisington, Jr., *Lyautey,* 205. Moroccans are less enthusiastic. After independence, the Place Lyautey was renamed, and Lyautey's statue carted off to the French consulate. Only a garage in Rabat bears his name (Hoisington, 207). Aicha Belarbi, a professor at the Ecole Normal Supérieure, writes that until 1934, "the prevailing [French] policy was the bloodthirsty and repressive one derived from that of General Lyautey, which denied direct rule and refused to respect Islam . . . or the native Moroccan administration." See *Social Science Research and Women in the Arab World, UNESCO, Paris, 1984* (London: Francis Pinter Publishers, 1984), 62.

46. See Sensibar, "Behind the Lines."

47. Sedgwick, "The Beast in the Closet," 155; and Sensibar, "Edith Wharton Reads the Bachelor Type," 575–76.

48. Sensibar, "Edith Wharton Reads the Bachelor Type," 575–76.

49. See Clare Colquitt, "Unpacking Her Treasures: Edith Wharton's 'Mysterious Correspondence' with Morton Fullerton," *Library Chronicle of the University of Texas at Austin* 31 (1985): 73–107; and the Wharton/Fullerton letters at the Harry Ransom Humanities Research Center, University of Texas-Austin.

50. Sedgwick, "The Beast in the Closet," 154.

51. Research for parts of this essay was made possible by the support of an NEH Travel Grant. I am grateful to the Harvard University Center for Italian Renaissance Studies for giving me access to Edith Wharton papers at Villa I Tatti. For their detailed critical readings and many good discussions, I want to thank my editors, Clare Colquitt, Susan Goodman, and Candace Waid.

A "Fairy tale every minute": The Autobiographical Journey and Edith Wharton's *In Morocco*

STEPHANIE BATCOS

IN THE AUTUMN OF 1917, EDITH WHARTON TRAVELED TO MOROCCO with Walter Berry, the comrade whose "deepest personality" seemed inseparable from her own.[1] She saw the trip as an escape from the death and destruction associated with World War I. Within the last year, Wharton's world had sadly shrunk. Both Henry James and Egerton Winthrop, her last links to the Old New York of her youth, had died. She filled her days with bureaucratic details, organizing and administering charities for the relief of Belgian refugees and the care of French casualties. The journey to Morocco promised to be a necessary respite from what she called "drudge work."[2] Life might be, as Wharton wrote in *A Backward Glance* (1934), "the saddest thing there is, next to death; yet there [were] always new countries to see, new books to read (and ... to write), a thousand little daily wonders to marvel at and rejoice in" (379). Morocco, a place she had "so long dreamed of,"[3] offered a new country, new wonders, and an escape from the "long horror" of war.[4]

While in Morocco, Wharton traveled as an official guest of the much admired French Resident General Hubert Lyautey and his wife. This meant that she enjoyed elegant accommodations in Moroccan palaces, a military escort throughout the country, and sightseeing privileges reserved only for the elite. Although Wharton had been invited to attend an annual artisan exhibition in Rabat, a venue that highlighted Lyautey's preservation of Moroccan culture, her attention moved well beyond it. Of more interest to Wharton, as R. W. B. Lewis notes, were the land, the rituals, and the everyday lives of the Moroccan people she encountered. The book that grew out of her experiences, *In Morocco* (1920), provides a glimpse into Wharton's ideas about culture, civilization, and self.

172

In Morocco marks a transition in Wharton's approach to the genre of travel writing. Her previous travel books, *Italian Backgrounds* (1905) and *A Motor-Flight Through France* (1908), function more like sophisticated tour guides. In those books, Wharton adopts the role of an experienced traveler. She shows readers how to avoid the crowds flocking to the starred sights found in guidebooks such as *Baedeker's*. By extolling the delights of visiting remote and obscure places, Wharton distinguishes herself and her books from the typical guides. Yet she did not have to worry about these issues while writing *In Morocco*. Because of the war, Wharton had Morocco to herself: There were no throngs of Western tourists to encounter nor were there previous guidebook writers with whom she had to compete. Hers was to be the first modern, English-language travel book on Morocco. For these reasons perhaps, *In Morocco* is something of an anomaly. Wharton writes the story of *her* experience, and the re-creation of that experience ties *In Morocco* more directly to another tradition of self-writing, that of autobiography.

In Morocco remains a difficult book to categorize because the boundaries between travel literature and autobiography have always been obscure. Although both genres occasionally overlap, the extent to which *In Morocco* becomes autobiographical depends upon how we define those terms. When Wharton labeled *In Morocco* a "travel book," she was probably thinking about presenting herself in a different way from the self we find in her formal autobiography, *A Backward Glance*. At what point, we must ask, does the subject of travel literature no longer become the place being visited, but the writer him or herself?

As its title suggests, *A Backward Glance* is a retrospective meditation on the past. *In Morocco* concerns itself with the lived moment. Wharton's perspective in her travel book does not allow time to filter her experiences. She positions herself in the present, a distinction that makes the events she describes seem both immediate and less mediated. Upon visiting the street bazaar in Marrakech, for example, the reader relives Wharton's sense of confusion and excitement when she encounters "the ancient traffic in flesh and blood" (*In Morocco,* 136). By its very nature, *A Backward Glance* looks back upon the moment of experience, adding a level of remove for Wharton as a subject and as a writer. Even in the book's opening episode—of "a girl, who bore my name, . . . going for a walk with her father" (*A Backward Glance,* 1)—Wharton detaches herself from the event being narrated.

This distance allows a degree of self-irony because it transforms Edith Wharton the person into "Edith Wharton" or more precisely "Edith Jones" the character. Because she did not have to contend with the burdens of the past in her Morocco book— such as the creation of a fully realized persona or the rendering of different life stages, for example—Wharton produced a more personal, if not more autobiographical, text.[5]

Paul Fussell has pointed out the dualistic nature of travel. On the one hand, the traveler defines such tangible experiences as staying at hotels, riding on trains, and eating strange foods as markers of "travel." On the other hand, the traveler also seeks intangible experiences inspired by the art, religion, or political mood of a place.[6] A writer must make meaning of information in a way that tells readers something about the place and something about the person experiencing the place. Other critics of travel literature view it as a means of self-definition. Terry Caesar has argued that in its attempt to define the other, travel literature defines the self. "Home" and "abroad" become symbolically interchangeable.[7] In Morocco exemplifies both of these tendencies. Following the standard conventions of the genre, Wharton describes the Moroccan landscape, relates part of the country's history, art, and architecture, and exoticizes its people. She remakes her own version of Morocco: By describing what Morocco is, Wharton defines what she is not.

Just as In Morocco enables Wharton to inscribe her cultural difference, it also places her in the role of the "female" travel writer.[8] For Wharton, travel writing became a forum in which her private voice could become more public. Without shedding her upper-class female persona, she could write about political and social issues. In this regard, Wharton was like many other American female travel writers, stemming from the tradition of Harriet Beecher Stowe in Sunny Memories of Foreign Lands (1854) and Margaret Fuller in At Home and Abroad (1856). Even if Wharton liked to think of herself as a "self-made man," travel writing was an area where she found herself participating in tradition already "made" by other women writers.

In addition to the political and social voice Wharton found in travel writing, the genre also provided her with a comfortable way to write about the self. Although she seemed to define her roles as "autobiographer" and "travel writer" differently, she faced, in both genres, the same problem of creating a narrative persona. To contemporary readers, Wharton appeared to be a literary grande dame, a woman who wrote in the mornings and dined with celebrities in the evenings. Ultimately this image liberated and imprisoned her. It allowed her to maintain a private self distinct from her public persona, but it also trapped her within a stereotype. Wharton's autobiography solidified, rather than altered, the public's image of her as a literary grande dame. In the preface to *A Backward Glance,* Wharton airs her concern about revealing more about herself than she felt willing to expose. Almost antagonistically, she warns her readers: If the public wants an autobiography in which "the memorialist 'spared no one,' set down in detail every defect and absurdity in others, and every resentment in the writer" (*A Backward Glance,* xx), they will not find it in her account. Wharton's remark here sets the tone for the imagined relationship she has chosen to share with the "public" who will read her life story.

Unlike autobiography, most travel literature presumes an amicable writer-audience relationship, and Wharton may have found comfort in that presumption. Her perceptions about the audiences of *A Backward Glance* and *In Morocco* bear out this difference in attitude. For *A Backward Glance,* Wharton imagined readers who subscribed to "illustrated magazines."[9] For *In Morocco,* she envisioned cosmopolitan people like herself. If she felt that some of the audience of *A Backward Glance* were reading to find out intimate details about *her* life, Wharton could assume that those who were reading *In Morocco* primarily did so to find out about the country, not her. As a travel writer, Wharton had a natural authority because readers wanted to learn from and enjoy what she experienced. As an autobiographer, she found herself at times "hopelessly stuck,"[10] a sentiment probably exacerbated by the feeling that any public exposure of her private life made her vulnerable.

The structures of both books elaborate the differences in how Wharton portrayed herself. *A Backward Glance* presents a coherent, chronologically evolving self; in contrast, *In Morocco* presents a more fractured, modernist self. With Wharton moving from cities to ceremonies to histories, the narrative reads as if it, too, is fractured. In using this shifting focus, Wharton discovered a way to veil herself behind her subject. Such an approach enabled her to emerge as a series of personalities, not as a unified persona. Wharton found she could represent herself in a fragmented, episodic, and therefore inconsistent manner without compromising the unity of her travel narrative. What makes this episodic and disjointed self of *In Morocco* significant, however, lies not in its formal adherence to the genre of travel writing, but in its closer ties to the conventions of female autobiography.

Feminist critics have argued that female autobiographers construct the self differently from their male counterparts. The chronological, linear, and coherent narratives of male autobiography, and the theories derived from such works, frequently have little relevance to most life writing done by women. Instead, theorists such as Mary Mason and Estelle Jelinek have argued that women's autobiographies tend to emphasize fragmented identities, framed by the individual woman's relationships with others, and personal, as opposed to public, matters of the self.[11] Whether such distinctions are universal is finally impossible to prove, but the importance of these claims has forced a reevaluation of what can adequately be termed "autobiographical" writing. In many female autobiographies, including Wharton's *In Morocco,* the constructed narrative self shares closer ties to the techniques of modernist fiction than to the type of unified self found in most male autobiography.

Fitting a book like *In Morocco* into the genre of autobiography becomes difficult when many of the genre's most prominent critical works omit discussion of women writers. The criteria set forth in Georges Gusdorf's early essay, "Conditions and Limits of Autobiography," are derived from a tradition of male autobiographies stemming from Augustine and Rousseau, and exclude the kind of life writing traditionally done by women. The majority of female autobiographers find themselves confined to a marginal existence in Gusdorf's terms, where the autobiographer must "take a distance with regard to himself in order to reconstitute himself in the focus of his special unity and identity across time."[12] A definition more fitting for a female autobiographer would be Gusdorf's description of the writer of private journals. Such a writer, Gusdorf explains, notes "his impressions and mental states from day to day [and] fixes the portrait of his daily reality without any concern for continuity" ("Conditions," 35). From this perspective, *In Morocco* easily fits into the category of female autobiography. With its discontinuous narrative style, its concentration on Wharton's personal experiences, and its fragmented presentation of self, *In Morocco* records Wharton's "female" self, a self she tried to keep veiled and concealed in *A Backward Glance.*

Before beginning her Moroccan journey, Wharton immersed herself in earlier French books on Morocco, including Vicomte de Foucauld's *La Reconnaissance au Maroc* (1888) and Marquis de Segonzac's *Voyage au Maroc* (1903). She also read John Windus's *A Journey to Mequinez* (1721), an English travel narrative describing Windus's encounter with Moulay-Ismael, the powerful sultan who ruled Meknez from 1673–1727. Although these previous representations of Morocco may have "exoticized" the way Wharton saw the country in 1917, they also prepared her to shed the literal world for a more imaginary one. Although Wharton, too, orientalizes many aspects of Morocco—from the "timelessness" of its architecture to the "obscurity" of its people—in some ways she transcends the limitations of the East/West binary which Edward Said and other anti-Orientalists have criticized, by turning them inward. Arguably, Wharton uses Orientalist imagery to alter her own outward condition, not that of others. For example, in her *A Motor-Flight Through France,* the car merely gives her access to the world of romance. Years later, in her Moroccan book, the car *becomes* the magic carpet upon which Wharton literally escapes from the real world. Her journey is not "*toward*" but . . . *away from*" the real world.[13] Once in that imaginative space, Wharton positions herself to see her surroundings from a variety of perspectives.

The view of Morocco that probably had the most influence upon Wharton was that of her friend, the modernist writer André Gide. Gide eventually wrote his own African memoir, *Travels in the Congo* (1925), but years before that, he sent Wharton a copy of his 1902 novel *The Immoralist.* A nihilistic book of travel and escape revolving around the Mediterranean Sea, *The Immoralist* prepared Wharton for her journey to Morocco. After reading it, she wrote Gide that its "beautiful evocation of the desert" would give her an "advance-taste" of what awaited her there.[14] What she read and what she saw helped to shape an informed reality, a reality that Wharton herself defined as "fabulous." From the city of Rabat, for example, Wharton told Mary Cadwalader Jones: "I write from a fairy world, where a motor from the 'Residence' stands always at the door to carry us to new wonders, & where every experience takes one straight into Harun-al Rashid land" (*Letters,* 399). Although Wharton was prepared to look at Morocco through Gide's lens, when she got there she began to resee it for—and through—herself.

Just as Gide helps frame Wharton's vision of Morocco, she, in turn, revises his. In the fictional world of *The Immoralist,* Gide relies heavily upon the sensual imaginations of his characters to create the atmosphere of North Africa. In the world of *In Morocco,* Wharton uses extensive details of Moroccan people and places to locate and shape her own place of sensuality. When Gide later wrote about Africa in the nonfictional *Travels in the Congo* (1925), his questions echo those which Wharton raised obliquely. Gide worries whether he can ever really know what he sees well enough to describe it accurately. Early into his Congo journey, he realizes that "it is impossible to get into contact with anything real" because "civilization interposes its film, so that everything is veiled and softened."[15] He acknowledges that the traveler may never succeed in truly representing a foreign culture. Unlike Gide, Wharton has less concern with accuracy. Rather, she seems to have faith in her movement between the real and imagined Morocco. To her mind, the boundary separating these two worlds has always remained obscure.

Whereas Gide seems anxious as a cultural documenter, Wharton uses that position to highlight the limitations of a singular vision. First, Wharton tells her readers that "authoritative utterances on Morocco are not wanting for those who can read them in French." She then lists some of these works in her preface and states that they invariably leave out "art and archaeology" or "the visual and picturesque side." Next Wharton creates a new space for *her* book. She claims that *In Morocco* will be "for the use ... of happy wanderers" and that it will combine personal impressions with "a slight sketch of the history and art of the country" (*In Morocco,* x–xii). Unconcerned with accurately describing what she sees, Wharton carves out an imaginative place for the world reflected inside the pages of *In Morocco.* She finds freedom in not confining herself to a singular vision. Instead she variously borrows, observes, and creates her own multifarious version of Morocco—Wharton's citizenship in the "Land of Letters" (*A Backward Glance,* 119), perhaps enabling her to paint Morocco in simultaneously real and fictional shades.

Wharton's imaginative movement between the tangible and intangible worlds of Morocco becomes evident when she recounts the brutality of a feast day's ritual dance. So transfixed by the dance of the Hamadchas, she wonders how long she would be able to stand the sight of what she sees (*In Morocco,* 52). She allays the anxiety the scene generates by assuming the stance of a historian:

> The beauty of the setting redeemed the bestial horror. In that unreal golden light the scene became merely symbolical: it was like one of those strange animal masks which the Middle Ages brought down from antiquity. (*In Morocco,* 53)

Wharton witnesses the dance as a detached spectator. Having stated that her primary obligation is to describe, she substitutes the "factual" for the "merely symbolical." Like Gide, Wharton unmasks a self whose fractured memory cannot be trusted. With the "bestial horrors" of trench warfare in her memory, Wharton transforms the violence of the dance from something meaningless into something meaningful. Art provides her with an instrument for change by turning the dance into a symbolic depiction. It allows her to preserve what is for her Morocco's imaginative timelessness while connecting this scene to an immediate experience. Because she elides the dance's historic specificity, at once tying it to ancient art and twentieth-century Morocco, Wharton creates a living monument that rationalizes, then replaces, her initial horror.

Gide's *Travels in the Congo* helps to illuminate the nature of Wharton's struggle to define the past. Exploring the distinction between always imagined memory and never fully remembered experience, Gide writes:

> I mean that I had imagined it so vividly that I wonder whether . . . this false image will not be stronger than my memory of the reality and whether I shall see [it] in my mind's eye as it is really, or as I first . . . imagined it would be. (*Travels in the Congo,* 60)

Throughout *In Morocco,* Wharton integrates the images she already has in mind with what she actually sees. This close association between reality and imagination enables her to perpetuate the mythical Morocco she prefers. It allows her both to lose and to reveal herself in the experience. When Wharton initially enters Fez, for example, her vision of the city gate conjures the memory of a painting, *The Preaching of St. Stephen,* by the Venetian artist Carpaccio. Here Wharton familiarizes the exotic. She exemplifies the claim that "every step of the way in North Africa corroborates the close observation of the early travelers." Her investment in preserving "the unchanged character of Oriental life" (*In Morocco,* 78) denotes the introspective rather than instructive purpose of her journey. Although Wharton distrusted psychoanalysis, travel writing gave her a way to work through the types of deeper issues psychoanalysis was being designed to address. In this way, her travel book marks Wharton's movement toward modernism. She saw herself traveling between disparate and contradictory worlds where everything, even her sense of a definite past and her vision of an uncertain future, became less tangible.

If Wharton's sense of self vacillates between past and present, so does her ability to experience Morocco. Her description of the cities of Volubilis and Moulay Idriss illustrates the way in which Wharton feels torn between two worlds. The Edith Wharton of *In Morocco* transcends the possibility of knowable history and establishes a sense of self unfettered by ties to family, friends, or even previous guidebooks. Initially intrigued by Morocco's "timelessness," she revises her views on what the "past" means in Morocco. Her longing for temporary refuge within an imaginary past emerges in her descriptions of Moroccan architecture. She paints a scene of hopeless dissolution when she arrives at the valley separating Volubilis, the ruins of a Roman colony, and Moulay Idriss, a Moslem town virtually closed to Westerners. Emphasizing the visible chasm between the two cities, Wharton describes Volubilis as "the lifeless Roman ruin, representing a system, an order, a social conception that still run[s] through all our modern ways" (*In Morocco,* 45). For all its symbolic grandeur, Volubilis stands as a monument to the past; Wharton likely saw this ruin's connection to the degenerative state of the Western world in the wake of World War I. She describes Moulay Idriss, which sits at the other end of the valley, as an "untouched Moslem city, more dead and sucked back into an unintelligible past than any broken architrave of Greece or Rome" (*In Morocco,* 45). Existing apart from any Western influence, Moulay Idriss survives as a place of "piled-up terraces and towers" without reference to a specific era. The "dead" city of the East still exists while the ruins of once "civilized" Volubilis remain inert. Wharton looked at these two worlds of the past—one abandoned, the other thriving—as a challenge to her sense of self and her sense of historic order. If a civilization's success depends upon its continued existence, then Wharton saw in this Moroccan valley an unexpected living monument.

As Wharton's Moroccan travels brought her closer to an "unknown" East, she began to examine her own place within that world—a process that was often dis*orient*ing. To her, the scenic "dominations" of the valley surrounding Volubilis and Moulay Idriss had become emblems of a region little affected by outside events. But instead of ordering what she saw, Wharton extended her sense of Morocco's rootlessness by drawing further attention to its anachronistic qualities. For example, while riding mules into Fez Eldjid, the newer part of the city, Wharton states that these creatures "carried us at once out of the bounds of time. How associate anything so precise and Occidental as years or centuries with these visions of frail splendor . . . ?" (*In Morocco,* 84). No longer a Western traveler, tied to either an itinerary or a definite history, Wharton abandons herself to Fez. Her desire to lose herself in time and place prompts a similar reaction to this ancient city's landscape. "Gradually," she writes,

> One falls under the spell of another influence—the influence of the Atlas and the desert. Unknown Africa seems much nearer to Morocco than to the white towns of Tunis. . . . One feels the nearness . . . of Timbuctoo. (*In Morocco,* 92)

Wharton's encounter with Africa recalls Toni Morrison's observations about the literary representation of whiteness, the very nature of which can only be defined by its opposite, "darkness." The unknown becomes a way for Wharton to articulate what Morrison calls the "self-contradictory features of the self."[16] Wharton uses racial imagery to draw attention to the idea that the deeper she penetrates into the "spell of another influence," the closer she comes to the heart of self-knowledge— Conrad's metaphoric "Africa." The awkwardness of Wharton's use of the impersonal "one" points to her discomfort with personal revelation. In feeling the nearness of Timbuctoo, she exposes the layers of identity her inward journey into Morocco has helped her to shed. The journey becomes a catalyst for Wharton's transformation from recording the process of foreign travel in her book to her nuanced movement toward self-discovery.[17]

Wharton's voice in the text changes as she herself changes. Sliding between intimate "I" and the generalized sense suggested by the word "one," she manipulates her status as an "outsider" with "insider" privileges. When she wants to distance herself from an experience, as she does in the bazaars of Marrakech, she uses the pronoun "one." Stating that "one's feet seem literally to stumble" over the "many threads of native life" (*In Morocco,* 136), Wharton pulls her readers through bazaars populated by an "exotic" variety of people and wares. Leaving this "[stifling] atmosphere of mystery and menace," "one" comes to a "quiet corner" (*In Morocco,* 137) that opens out to a maze of quarters for skilled craftsmen, eventually ending with a street of metal workers and mud huts. The whirlwind tour of public Marrakech leaves Wharton out of the frenzied action, her authoritative voice sounding from a safe, but knowing, distance.

In contrast, Wharton uses the first person when she wants to assert herself as a presence. Her earlier description of the Palace of the Bahia stands out because of its abundant use of the pronoun "I." To a certain degree, Wharton's self-presentation seems tied to her sense of class. Her use of the "I" in the palace section draws attention to her elite status in Morocco. Describing the apartment of the "Grand Vizier's Favorite" by detailing its architectural beauty and isolation from the outer world, Wharton lets readers know that "it was my good luck to be lodged [there] while I was at Marrakech" (*In Morocco,* 131). She chooses to remain anonymous in the "dark, fierce, and fanatical" (*In Morocco,* 135) public world of the bazaar, but within the private confines of the Palace walls, Wharton finds comfort in her isolation. Yet both in the bazaar and the Palace of the Bahia, Wharton evokes labyrinthine imagery that cuts her off from the outside world. The favorite's apartment offered Wharton a "sense of plunging into a deep sea-pool" (*In Morocco,* 132), an environment in which she could lose herself entirely. This sensual image of silence and tranquillity prepares readers for Wharton's next positioning of herself: inside Morocco's harems. Although the erotic notions of confinement that enabled Wharton to lose herself imaginatively in the Palace foreshadow her account of the harems, the actual spaces, in turn, become the means by which she later returns to a more traditional sense of identity.

Wharton is most clearly aligned with the narrator of *In Morocco* when she is most "Western." Her status as a wealthy American woman undoubtedly affected her impressions of the lives of Moroccan women. Many of her observations in the harems, however, came through the filters of others. Cultural critics such as Christopher Herbert have argued that any outsider's observation of a foreign culture must be questioned.[18] Although Wharton's views remained distant from a "Moroccan" perspective, the Morocco that Wharton saw had already been shaped by numerous influences. Rarely were translators provided during these visits, and when they were, the gulf between Wharton and the other women remained as wide as the valley separating Volubilis from Moulay Idriss. Often most of her experiences came to her through "cultivated and cordial French officials, military and civilian" (*In Morocco,* xii), who interpreted the customs and manners of a land that was foreign to them as well. Although Wharton herself translated her experience into writing, the tenor and quality of the resulting book depended upon these external factors. Her representation of Moroccan women seems an attempt to expose what she termed a society whose structure "hangs on the whim of one man" (*In Morocco,* 163). Wharton's gender becomes the means by which she re*orients* herself through "unknown" Africa and journeys back to the "known."

The "Harems and Ceremonies" chapter emerges as the climax of *In Morocco* because Wharton self-consciously draws attention to herself as a woman. No longer relying on the veiled "one" who travels through the landscape and bazaars, Wharton lets her readers know that,

> The Sultan would allow Madame Lyautey, with the three ladies of her party, to be present at the great religious rite of the Aid-el-Kebir. . . . The honor was an unprecedented one . . . as a rule no women are admitted to these ceremonies. (*In Morocco,* 163–64)

Shifting once again from "one" to "I," Wharton begins to identify herself with the category of "women" to set up the chapter's main comparison. Permitted to watch a forbidden ceremony, Wharton states that "I had lain awake wondering if I should be ready early enough" (*In Morocco,* 164). Her unconcealed excitement, coupled with her status as a "lady," marks a departure from the more reserved narrative voice found in earlier sections of *In Morocco.* This openness about her identity as a woman also distinguishes *In Morocco* from Wharton's earlier travel writings on Italy and France, where the narrator primarily remains part of a nameless group of travelers referred to as "we." No longer a faceless, gender-neutral narrator, Wharton politicizes her voice to illuminate the "sad" lives of the Moroccan women she meets.

Wharton accentuates the differences between herself and the Moroccan women by juxtaposing their material riches with hers. When she identified herself as a woman, Wharton had a particular kind of "woman" in mind: one of a certain class and privilege who possessed both knowledge and experience. The Moroccan women Wharton met were of a similar class, but she found their material riches no compensation for the circumscribed lives they led. The art of conversation, always one of her great pleasures in life, had no place in the harems. Having "exhausted the limited small talk" available to these women (*In Morocco,* 180), Wharton describes their restless existence as punctuated by watching dancers and receiving an occasional official visitor. Speaking through the Sultan's brother-in-law at a Rabat harem, Wharton asks the group of women whether they "never [have] any desire to travel, or to visit the Bazaars?" (*In Morocco,* 186), activities which Wharton herself enjoyed. Without relaying her question to the women, the brother-in-law responds, "No indeed. They are too busy to give such matters a thought" (*In Morocco,* 186). Wharton pities these women; they seem to her lost souls controlled by inconsequential, sometimes comical, men called "sultans." She wonders, "What thoughts, what speculations go on under the narrow veiled brows of the little creatures?" (*In Morocco,* 187), and concludes that the women who led the most limited lives before entering the harem would best survive: "It is well that no one from the outer world should come to remind these listless creatures that somewhere the gulls dance on the Atlantic and the wind murmurs through olive yards" (*In Morocco,* 189). Through her descriptions, Wharton debunks Westerners' "images of sensual seduction" (*In Morocco,* 192), replacing them with her eyewitness accounts of "pale women in their moldering prison" (*In Morocco,* 189).

Having dismantled the harems from the "inside," Wharton moves "outside" to condemn Morocco's entire social system. Although she offers her own life for comparison, Wharton begins to see that not much more than a veil separates her from the lives of the women she patronizes and pities. Another disappointing harem visit finds Wharton with her "lips stiffening into the resigned smile of the harem" (*In Morocco,* 187). But unlike the "pale flock," Wharton feels relief when "at last . . . the handsome old gentleman who owned them reappeared on the scene, bringing back my friends, [a return] followed by slaves and tea" (*In Morocco,* 187). Wharton does not suffer the encumbrances of the system that imprisons the harem women; she enjoys the sultan's company for a "civilized" tea. Yet she finds herself caught among Morocco's multiple worlds. "Inside" she feels too paralyzed to speak, but "outside" she unstiffens her lips to engage in livelier conversation. Wharton's movement between these worlds becomes more complicated as she recognizes her precarious position in Moroccan society. Her Western identity allows her to travel as a woman—albeit, a woman granted the privileges and freedom of a man. Without these privileges, Wharton's differences from the harem women become less evident. In the "Harems and Ceremonies" chapter of *In Morocco,* then, Wharton highlights the contrasting identities of Eastern and Western women only to uncover the degree to which identity itself must be an ephemeral masquerade.

Wharton's presence in the harems, hovering between the regions of private and public, self and other, confinement and exposure, parallels her own journey into "Morocco." Like many explorations into identity, Wharton's journey takes her back to an earlier state of being. Perhaps because this experience has reduced her to speechlessness, she ends her account of the harems with the image of a silent child. Although the image itself contains a Western comment on the "evolving" East, for Wharton, acutely aware of her own childlessness, it also seems to hold something more. As a writer, she could create her own child—whether symbol or book. As Wharton's Moroccan hosts pity her childlessness, Wharton makes clear to her readers that they do so while surrou nding themselves with child slaves. At a tea ceremony, Wharton shifts positions. Rather than being pitied, she pities a small, black slave, "not more than six or seven years old" (*In Morocco*, 199): "With preternatural vigilance she [the child] watched each movement of the Caid, who never spoke to her, looked at her, or made her the slightest perceptible sign, but whose least wish she instantly divined" (199–200). Using the slave girl as a symbol of the Moroccan social system's "shadowy evils," Wharton bares the discrepancy that "the abyss [of] slavery and the seraglio put between the most Europeanized Mahometan and the Western conception of life" (201). To the others in the scene, the child does not exist. As the creator of this girl's image, Wharton gives the child presence and uses her to make an artistic and political statement. In combining childhood innocence with a disdain for childless women, Wharton exposes two fundamental similarities between the East and the West. She uses these issues to reveal the complicity of her position as a woman inside and outside Moroccan society: she fashions herself both as the privileged guest of the Caid and as the maternal, empathetic observer of the invisible slave girl. At its most foreign and alienating, Morocco elicits from Wharton her most personal, self-defining, and contradictory response.

Like most journeys, *In Morocco* concludes with a return home. Running away from the death and suffering of 1917 Europe, Wharton's Moroccan trip ironically discovered a different kind of death and suffering. The "bestial" rituals, the "unintelligible" Moroccan architecture, the "lifeless" Roman ruins, and the "vacant" existences of the harems mimicked the cycle of life and death she saw in the Great War and echoed the impressions of other modernist writers. Her attempt to "cheat death" in Morocco results in the realization that it was impossible to escape it.

Never forgetting this lesson, Wharton significantly reiterates it in *A Backward Glance,* through an Arabic tale told to her by Jean Cocteau. In it, a young man goes to the sultan asking for "his Majesty's swiftest horse" so that he might go to Baghdad. The story continues:

> The Sultan asked why he was in such haste to go to Baghdad. "Because," the youth answered, "as I passed through the garden of the Palace just now, Death was standing there, and when he saw me he stretched out his arms as if to threaten me, and I must lose no time in escaping from him.
> The young man was given leave to take the Sultan's horse and fly; and when he was gone the Sultan went down indignantly into the garden, and found Death still there. "How dare you make threatening gestures at my favourite?" he cried; but Death, astonished, answered: "I assure your Majesty I did not threaten him. I only threw up my arms in surprise at seeing him here, because I have a tryst with him tonight in Baghdad." (*A Backward Glance,* 285, 286)

Wharton found this story "strangely beautiful" (*A Backward Glance,* 285). To her mind, the inevitability of death could restore a sense of order amidst the world's chaos.

Cocteau's story also suggests the inevitability inherent in Wharton's trip to Morocco. A record of her autobiographical journey, *In Morocco* retells the story of her encounter with an unknown country that initially seemed part of a fairy tale. That "unknown country" soon becomes a metaphor for Wharton's exploration of her own identity in relation to her surroundings. The "Edith Wharton" of *In Morocco* successively loses, fragments, and recovers her self. She comes face-to-face with its limits and presents her "selves" not running away from death, but continuing toward it in an endless search through life.

Notes

1. Edith Wharton, *A Backward Glance* (New York: D. Appleton, 1934), 116.
2. R. W. B. Lewis, *Edith Wharton: A Biography* (New York: Harper and Row, 1975), 389.
3. Edith Wharton, *In Morocco* (New York: Charles Scribner's Sons, 1920), v.
4. Wharton to Bernard Berenson, October 15, 1915, *The Letters of Edith Wharton,* ed. R. W. B. Lewis and Nancy Lewis (New York: Scribners, 1988), 361.
5. Judith E. Funston, in her article "*In Morocco:* Edith Wharton's Heart of Darkness" (*Edith Wharton Newsletter* 5 no. 1 [1988]: 1–3, 12), has argued that *In Morocco* might be considered Wharton's feminist autobiography.
6. Paul Fussell, *Abroad* (New York: Oxford University Press, 1980).

7. Terry Caesar, *Forgiving the Boundaries* (Athens, GA.: University of Georgia Press, 1995).

8. Mary Suzanne Schriber, *Telling Travels* (DeKalb; Northern Illinois University Press, 1995). Schriber claims that the elasticity of the genre provided late nineteenth- and early twentieth-century women with a public voice. She also discusses, among several other issues, the lucrative aspects of travel writing for women.

9. Wharton to Rutger B. Jewett, April 29, 1933, *The Letters of Edith Wharton*, ed. R. W. B. Lewis and Nancy Lewis (New York: Scribners, 1988), 558–59. Parts of *A Backward Glance* first appeared in an abbreviated, serialized version in *Ladies' Home Journal*.

10. Wharton to Mary Berenson, June 4, 1932, in *The Letters of Edith Wharton*, ed. R. W. B. Lewis and Nancy Lewis (New York: Scribners, 1988), 553.

11. Some of the recent books exploring theories of women's autobiography include Estelle C. Jelinek, ed., *Women's Autobiography: Essays in Criticism* (Bloomington: Indiana University Press, 1980); Domna C. Stanton, ed., *The Female Autograph: Theory and Practice of Autobiography from the Tenth to the Twentieth Century* (Chicago: University of Chicago Press, 1984); Shari Benstock, ed., *The Private Self: Theory and Practice of Women's Autobiographical Writings* (Chapel Hill: University of North Carolina Press, 1988); and Bella Brodzki and Celeste Schenck, eds., *Life/Lines: Theorizing Women's Autobiography* (Ithaca: Cornell University Press, 1988).

12. Georges Gusdorf, "Conditions and Limits of Autobiography," in *Autobiography: Essays Theoretical and Critical*, ed. James Olney (Princeton: Princeton University Press, 1980), 35.

13. Janis Stout, in *The Journey Narrative in American Literature* (Westport, Conn.: Greenwood Press, 1983), observes this of American plots in general (30).

14. Wharton to André Gide, August 10, 1917, in *The Letters of Edith Wharton*, ed. R. W. B. Lewis and Nancy Lewis (New York: Scribners, 1988), 397.

15. André Gide, *Travels in the Congo* (Berkeley: University of California Press, 1957), 16.

16. Toni Morrison, *Playing in the Dark: Whiteness and the Literary Imagination* (Cambridge: Harvard University Press, 1992), 59.

17. As Mary Mason and Carol Green have observed in their preface to *Journeys: Autobiographical Writings by Women* (Boston: G. K. Hall, 1979), the self-documentation of a woman's journey "leads not to obliteration but to self-discovery and self-realization" (vii).

18. Christopher Herbert, *Culture and Anomie* (Chicago: University of Chicago Press, 1991), 8.

Wharton, Race, and *The Age of Innocence:*
Three Historical Contexts

ANNE MacMASTER

THE AGE OF INNOCENCE, MANIFESTLY ABOUT A NARROW SLICE OF American society at a particular moment in history, the swan song of that would-be aristocracy called Old New York, actually registers the central crux of American identity. Wharton's novel maps a paradox located at the intersection of several ironies: the history of slavery in the land of the free, the fear of the foreign in a nation of immigrants, the drive toward conformity behind the creed of individualism. Racial difference is a latent topic in *The Age of Innocence,* a topic at first invisible beside the obvious topic of Old New York, but—once discovered—never far from the narrative's central concerns. At work in this novel we find what Toni Morrison in *Playing in the Dark* identifies as "American Africanism" or the "Africanist presence" in American literature.[1] With the phrase "Africanist presence," Morrison refers to those black characters created by white writers who thus embody the "blackness that African peoples have come to signify" in the European-American imagination (*Dark,* 6). Rather than presenting the views of African-Americans, such characters "enable white writers to think about themselves" (*Dark,* 51). Through the use of such characters of color, Wharton expresses her main characters' rebellions, fantasies, and displays of power. Her use of dark characters both records and questions the construction of whiteness at her own cultural moment.[2]

Before turning to the Africanist presence in *The Age of Innocence,* however, I want to set the novel within the contexts in which it was produced: the intersection, that is, between Wharton's life and the history of race relations in America and France between 1870 and 1920. Three historical moments matter to *The Age of Innocence,* two in which its action occurs and another in which the novel was written. In the first of these three periods, which Wharton calls "the age of innocence," the body of the story takes place; in the mid 1870s, the young Newland Archer attempts to choose between his duty to May Welland and his desire for Ellen Olenska. In Wharton's life, the 1870s constitute the decade in which Edith Newbold Jones moved through childhood and adolescence to come of age in the style of Old New York. But while the young Edith lived in New York, Newport, and Europe, her view remained limited. Exposed to various national cultures in Europe, Wharton knew only the uppermost strata of her native New York. While in New York, Wharton's associations were only with "that tiny fraction of the city" that "extended along Fifth Avenue from Washington Square to 'the' Central Park";[3] meanwhile, in other parts of the city, waves of immigrants from abroad and blacks from the South arrived to change the city's racial dynamics. It is unlikely that these changes registered much on young Edith's consciousness, even though her family employed a black cook and coachman and a number of Irish servants, and even though her friend Emmeline Washburn explored various portions of the city, observing street life and speaking to all kinds of people.[4] According to R. W. B. Lewis, of the other New Yorks beyond Wharton's narrow strip, the sheltered debutante caught no more than "a fleeting glimpse" (22).

Such "innocence" was no longer possible a quarter-century later in the period of increased immigration that constitutes the second of the novel's three contexts. The novel's coda is set around the turn of the century: Newland Archer, now fifty-seven years old, looks back on his renunciation of Ellen and its consequences for his life, only to renounce her again. In Wharton's own life at the same time, the society matron broke out of her inherited role to transform herself into a professional novelist. Circulating between New York, her country home in the Berkshires, and Europe, Wharton gradually established France as her permanent home yet maintained her American identity. While Wharton came into her powers as a woman and a novelist, New York City's immigrant and African-American populations burgeoned, and across the nation white insecurities flared up in race riots, lynchings, and eugenics societies. At the end of "the age of innocence," a shift also occurred in the origin of the immigrants from abroad; around 1880, immigrants from Southern and Eastern (rather than Northern) Europe began to arrive in New York. A sharp increase in immigration since the 1870s and an economic downturn in the 1890s fueled a growing anti-immigrant sentiment among white native-born Americans.

By the close of the century, American notions of race were reconstructed to reflect new hostilities. According to Susan S. Lanser, "the common nineteenth-century belief in three races— black, white, yellow—each linked to a specific continent, was reconstituted so that 'white' came to mean only 'Nordic' or Northern European, while 'yellow' applied not only to the Chinese, Japanese, and light-skinned African Americans but also to Jews, Poles, Hungarians, Italians, and even the Irish. Crusaders warned of 'yellow inundation.'"[5] In this climate, in the first decade of the new century, Wharton's career took off just as her social acquaintance with Theodore Roosevelt deepened into friendship. Roosevelt not only was Wharton's friend, but also a fellow member of her "set" and a distant relative by marriage.[6] As president, Roosevelt urged women of the "proper sort" to abjure birth control lest America lose its national identity. In 1905, the same year that Wharton lunched at the White House with Roosevelt (Lewis, 6), her distinguished lunch companion ended one public speech by intoning, "race purity must be maintained." The following year, in his State of the Union Address, Roosevelt warned against "willful sterility"—the practice of birth control by middle-class whites—"the one sin for which the penalty is national death, race suicide."[7] When Wharton has Newland Archer, at the age of fifty-seven, weigh his gains against his losses, she throws into the balance her characater's friendship with Roosevelt: Although Newland is grateful to have had "one great man's friendship to be his strength and pride," he also perceives, "[s]omething he knew he had missed: the flower of life" (*Age*, 346, 347). Set in the era of Roosevelt's presidency, the coda of *The Age of Innocence* both condemns and mourns the loss of a vanished social order.

The third historical moment relevant to *The Age of Innocence* consists of those years during and right after World War I when the novel was conceived, written, and published. During the war, Wharton was mostly in Paris, witnessing the general upheaval, organizing relief for refugees, and at long last welcoming American troops. Soon after the war's end, she began to write *The Age of Innocence,* and within a year, the novel was complete. In the United States during the same years, race relations changed forever. In New York City, the war years created plentiful employment for black men and marked the start of the African-American move uptown to Harlem.[8] At the same time, African-American men in the military received decent treatment from the French and encountered from the U.S. military a variety of official and unofficial forms of discrimination based on race. African-American veterans, on their return from France, confronted heightened discrimination that they met with a new spirit of resistance. During the summer of 1919, while Wharton was at work in France on a novel about a more innocent age in an American city, "race riots transformed twenty-six U.S. cities into war zones, where black citizens, many still in uniform, were lynched with impunity and their homes were burned because they dared to organize to demand job opportunities."[9]

In New York City itself, African-American troops were initially welcomed home by large crowds, but their situation rapidly worsened as many whites blamed rising unemployment on the city's expanding black population. Even without major riots, New York City itself arguably underwent greater changes in race relations than any other U.S. city during 1919 and 1920. According to historians Moss and Franklin, it was the new prosperity of Harlem that made New York the site from which African-Americans voiced "their most eloquent demands for equality during and after World War I."[10]

By 1919, it must have been harder than it was at the turn of the century, even for someone of Wharton's class living abroad, to see New York and its dramas as contained within the area along Fifth Avenue from Washington Square to Central Park. In 1919, it would have been difficult to avoid the American implications of race, even in a novel set in earlier ages, even for a writer who could assume the "Americanness" of her own ethnicity. To view *The Age of Innocence* as a novel about race in the United States is not to diminish its focus on the disillusion with European civilization brought on by the Great War; it is rather to set the national context within the international one. Wharton's novel captures the inseparability for Americans of the social changes brought about by the Great War which led to the stirrings of a civil rights movement.

In *The Age of Innocence,* Wharton addresses her class's anxieties about race after World War I not only by contrasting two earlier time periods—the 1870s and the century's turn—but also by making racial doubling into a narrative strategy. Race enters the novel through Ellen Olenska's status as the novel's dark heroine. In her characteristic style, Wharton subverts the convention of paired heroines by making May Welland, the fair heroine, turn out again and again to be more knowing than Newland realizes, and Ellen, the dark heroine, to be more naive, vulnerable, and moral than Newland expects. Still, May remains

the fair heroine and Ellen the dark, each according to her respec-
tive devotion to or defiance of convention, and Wharton emphasizes this polarity through the heroines' contrasting colorings.
Repeatedly, Wharton poses Ellen's tight brown curls and dusky
cheeks against May's fair hair, blue eyes, and skin as white as
marble. Ellen, true to her nature as a dark heroine, rebels from
her social role and sees through its conventions. Her vision sets
her apart from all the other Society women except her grand-
mother, Catherine Mingott. And it is here, in this connection
between Ellen and Catherine, that the Africanist presence enters the novel.

Ellen and Catherine, the only two unconventional women in
this society, are the only New Yorkers who eagerly employ dark-
skinned servants. Ellen, who is herself described as a "dark
lady,"[11] travels with an Italian maid named Nastasia who is
"swarthy," "foreign-looking," and, for Newland, "vaguely . . . Sicilian" (*Age,* 68); Catherine relies upon "the mulatto maid," a character who, although not even honored with a name, asserts a
conspicuous presence in Catherine's house and Newland's consciousness (*Age,* 271). Other members of Society, by contrast,
employ dark-skinned servants only with the greatest displeasure. May's parents, wintering in Florida, view the hiring of
black servants as one of the "insuperable difficulties" of
"rough[ing] it" in a fashionable Southern resort (*Age,* 142). In
the houses of Catherine and Ellen, on the other hand, swarthy
maids not only serve, but seem to preside, embodying the spirits
of these unconventional households. Each servant, as gate-
keeper to her mistress's private rooms and uncanny abettor of
her designs, braces her mistress's stand against convention.

Ellen, Catherine, and their servants fit into a configuration of
characters that associates the dark heroine with women of color
and aligns darkness (or color) with resistance to conformity, with
passion, courage, and vitality. In the darker toned minor characters of this novel—the mulatto maid, the swarthy Nastasia, the
anonymous black man for whom the intellectual Sillertons
throw a party (*Age,* 220)—we have instances of what Morrison
calls "the strategic use of black characters to define the goals
and enhance the qualities of white characters" (*Dark,* 52–53).
In *The Age of Innocence,* the presence of the darker servants
not only marks the defiance of the central female characters,
but also reveals the desires and fears of the major male characters and, by extension, of the dominant culture. Newland Archer, Julius Beaufort, Larry Lefferts, and the rest of "masculine

New York" find the dark Ellen more desirable (and less marriage-able) than the fair May (*Age*, 11). In the context of Ellen's asso-ciations with Nastasia and the mulatto maid, this sexual preference for Ellen is implicated in certain American myths of race and realities of privilege and oppression. In the myths, white male culture projects its own lusts onto the black woman's body, exaggerating the black woman's sexuality while downplay-ing that of the white woman in some misguided pursuit of racial or sexual purity.[12]

In such a scheme, white women become associated with mar-riage, with legitimate offspring, with Theodore Roosevelt's cry that "race purity must be maintained." Making an appropriate match assures one's position in the tribe and fortifies the tribe's position in America. Engaged to May, Newland desires Ellen. He oscillates between wanting to escape his ties to May and "thank[ing] heaven that he was ... to ally himself with one of his own kind" (*Age*, 31). In its immediate context, "his own kind" means someone of the same social "set" (*Age*, 31); in the context of the chapter that it concludes, however, the phrase might just as well mean someone of the same skin tone. In this chapter, which places repeated emphasis on the whiteness of skin, Cathe-rine tellingly albeit inadvertently links marriage with color (as well as with class) when, admiring May's engagement ring, she comments: "Her hand is large ... but the skin is white.—And when's the wedding to be?" (*Age*, 29). Ellen Olenska, whom New-land is glad not to be marrying even though he desires her more than he desires May, has "foreign" ways, "dusky" skin, and calls to mind "the bold brown Ellen Mingott of his boyhood" (*Age*, 59, 64, 31). Ellen's darkness aligns her with Nastasia, the mulatto, and a series of dark-skinned and colorfully dressed women who seem to constitute, from the perspective of "masculine New York," a fantasy of extramarital sex. In this scheme, the class difference between the women men marry and the women men enjoy sexually outside of marriage is highlighted by a difference in pigmentation.

The tones of Ellen's skin and hair and the shades of her cloth-ing thus connect her with an array of vividly garbed and darkly hued women. Recalling the mulatto in her "bright turban" and Nastasia in her "gay neckerchief," Ellen is associated with gyp-sies, Neapolitans, and the "beautiful Spanish dancer" with whom her great grandfather disappeared to Cuba (*Age*, 214, 68, 10). These associations have their origins in Ellen's first appearance in New York as an orphan with "an air of gaiety that seemed

unsuitable in a child who should still have been in black for her
parents. . . . [Instead of mourning], Ellen was in crimson merino
and amber beads, like a gipsy foundling . . . and possessed out-
landish arts, such as dancing a Spanish shawl dance and singing
Neapolitan love songs to a guitar" (*Age,* 59). The references here
to the groups whom Wharton later calls "the southern races"
(*Age,* 69), in the context of Ellen's "gaudy clothes[,] . . . high color
and high spirits," show that she has been unfit for the monotony
of Old New York; at the same time, these references exaggerate
the erotic in Ellen's portrait. Any allusion to skin darker than
May's works as what Morrison calls a "metaphorical shortcut" to
suggest the erotic (*Dark,* x).

Drawing on a related series of race-based myths, Newland
heightens the erotic aspects of Ellen's character by projecting
the mystique of the "Orient" onto her drawing room. To Newland,
the room's "vague pervading perfume" calls to mind "some far-
off bazaar, a smell made up of Turkish coffee and ambergris and
dried roses" (*Age,* 70). Nourished by Western myths of the Orient
as a romantic, timeless realm, Newland's imagination transforms Ellen's room and his own desire into the elements of high
Romance. Newland finds "the atmosphere of the room . . . so
different from any he had ever breathed" that it arouses in him
"the sense of adventure" (70). Like the young narrator of James
Joyce's "Araby," Newland projects onto the object of his desire
and the prosaic settings associated with her a sense of the Orient
as a world elsewhere. Newland endows Ellen with the exotic
qualities of a Westerner's fantasy of "Oriental woman."[13] Such
links between Ellen and women of various "colors" imbue the
Countess with the primitive sexuality that Western culture, in
the late nineteenth century and on into the 1920s, projected
onto dark bodies.[14]

To heighten the polarity between Ellen and May, Wharton uses
what Morrison calls "the Africanist character as surrogate"
(*Dark,* 51). At the moments in the novel when Newland seeks
out Ellen, the dark-toned servants make their appearances.
Again and again in scenes of subtle replacement, Newland encounters a dark servant at times and in places where he expects
to find Ellen. When the Archers, recently returned from their
honeymoon, visit Catherine's house at Newport, both are discon-
certed to learn that Ellen is staying there; yet when Catherine
calls Ellen, the mulatto maid appears in Ellen's stead, entering
the novel just as Nastasia has done before her to explain Ellen's
absence. In the most telling of these instances of the dark ser-

vant's standing in for the dark heroine, Newland counts on find-ing Ellen at Catherine's house when he answers the sick woman's summons. Anticipating a private interview with Ellen, Newland arrives expecting a climactic encounter: "Archer's heart was beating violently when he rang old Mrs. Mingott's bell. . . . here he was on the doorstep. Behind the door, behind the curtains of the yellow damask room . . . , [Ellen] was surely awaiting him; in another moment he would see her, and be able to speak to her before she led him to the sick-room" (*Age,* 297–98). Wharton builds these expectations only to dash them: New-land expects Ellen, "but in the yellow sitting-room it was the mulatto maid who waited. Her white teeth shining like a key-board" (*Age,* 298). This image recalls Nastasia's "welcom[ing] him with all her white teeth" (*Age,* 68) on Newland's first visit to Ellen's house, and the image—in all of its "economy of stereo-type" (*Dark,* 58)—registers white America's simultaneous desire for and fear of a racial Other. Here American Africanism appears in what Morrison calls "its lush and fully blossomed existence in the rhetoric of dread and desire" (*Dark,* 64). The dark-skinned servants, in marking Ellen's difference from the other Society women, indicate that Newland desires not a particular person, but an Other, a romanticized or demonized version of his self.

Wharton's linking of Ellen and the mulatto maid in this way also clarifies Newland's later suggestion that Ellen become his mistress. The novel's association between dark heroine and dark servant points to an actual connection between mistresses and mulattas—a legacy from America's antebellum past. Under the American institution of slavery, sexual abuse of female slaves by their owners tended to take different forms according to the shade of the slave woman's skin. Whereas darker skinned slaves were often forced to have sex and children against their wills, mulatta women such as Linda Brent in Harriet Jacobs's *Inci-dents in the Life of a Slave Girl* were often compelled to submit to what Lauren Berlant describes as "white men's parodic and perverse fantasies";[15] owners could pretend that these light-skinned women were not their slaves but their mistresses. Mask-ing the reality that the mulatta lacks the power to resist her master's sexual advances, such fantasies transformed her into a mistress: one who comes to a man not because she is forced like a slave or legally obligated (and protected) like a wife, but out of her own desire for him and/or financial dependence on him. Such a mistress can be "kept on the side," in addition to a wife. With these fantasies, Berlant points out, slave owners "set up a

parallel universe" that "involved dressing up the beautiful mulatta and playing white-lady-of-the-house with her."[16] Viewed
against this historical role of the mulatta, Ellen's association
with the mulatto maid unmasks the insult behind Newland's
desire to make Ellen his lover after he has married May. In this
light, his earlier casting of Ellen's drawing room as "something
intimate, . . . suggestive of old romantic scenes and sentiments,"
already envisions Ellen as the kept woman. Against Newland's
perception of "what May's drawing-room would look like" (Age,
70), Ellen's house, with its boudoirlike drawing room, "parodie[s]
the big one."[17] Juxtaposed with Ellen's connections to the mulatta, Newland's vision of Ellen's bordellolike house anticipates
Faulkner's depiction of the house where Charles Bon's octoroon
mistress/wife in Absalom, Absalom! is kept.

The Africanist presence in The Age of Innocence, by serving as
a marker of both white male privilege and white female defiance,
seems to express two meanings that might cancel each other
out. Such a paradoxical use of darkness conforms to its function
in American fiction in general. As Morrison observes, darkness
can carry two contradictory meanings at the same time: "Images
of blackness can be evil and protective, rebellious and forgiving,
fearful and desirable—all of the self-contradictory features of
the self" (Dark, 59; author's emphasis). Darkness, color, difference, variety: All these, in the collective psyche of masculine
New York, threaten the integrity of the old order even as they
embody its "darkest" desires.

While Ellen's status as dark heroine points in different direc-
tions at once, May's status as fair heroine leads, through a string
of associations, nowhere at all. Whereas blackness has double
meanings in this scheme, whiteness is drained of meaning.
Among images in American literature, Morrison writes, "Whiteness, alone, is mute, meaningless, unfathomable, pointless, frozen, veiled, curtained, dreaded, senseless, implacable" (Dark,
59). The whitest characters in The Age of Innocence, both metaphorically and literally, exemplify these qualities and are associated with images of ice, snow, shrouds, and a living death. Henry
and Louisa van der Luyden, in their fair coloring and identi-
calness to each other, resemble "bodies caught in glaciers [that]
keep for years a rosy life-in-death" (Age, 52). With the van der
Luydens, Wharton creates a sense of fin-de-race exhaustion, of
the inbred lines collapsing in on themselves as in Poe's "The
Fall of the House of Usher." Whiteness or blue blood, taken to
an extreme, is revealed here as self-annihilating. The blue blood

of the van der Luydens, in all the imagery that characterizes the couple—from the snowscape of their estate on the frozen Hudson to the sheet-draped furniture of their house in town, from their faded coloring and unaging features to their own chilly response to human contact—connects their racial purity to May's sexual purity and suggests that their whiteness is no more an innate essence than May's innocence.

When Newland acknowledges that May's "abysmal purity" is a carefully cultivated artifice, he pictures her innocence in images that recall the whiteness of the glacial van der Luydens: "[H]e returned discouraged [from his fantasy of initiating May sexually] by the thought that all this frankness and innocence were only an artificial product[,] . . . so cunningly manufactured . . . because it was supposed to be what he wanted, what he had a right to, in order that he might exercise his lordly pleasure in smashing it like an image made of snow" (*Age*, 7, 45). More disturbing to Newland than May's "snow-like" artifice is his suspicion that May's innocence conceals nothing. Predictably, then, during the archery match, Beaufort's derisive comment about May's purity sends "a shiver through [Newland's] heart": "What if 'niceness' carried to that supreme degree were only a negation, the curtain dropped before an emptiness?" (*Age*, 212). Through curtains, veils, ice, and snow, the novel's imagery connects this possibility that nothingness lies behind the façade of May's innocence with the likelihood that emptiness underlies the van der Luydens' "whiteness."

However we define "whiteness"—as an historically changing variable;[18] as a curtain/veil to mask one's own color and privilege;[19] or a racist "artifice" that promotes "racial cleansing"— whiteness, with its claims to blankness, is often harder to see than darkness. Darkness or "color" is often defined as ethnicity itself; whiteness, in turn, is assumed to be the norm and signifies an absence of ethnicity. Like female innocence, whiteness in this novel is a curtain before an emptiness. Old New York's strategy for preserving whiteness, the practice of marrying "one's own kind," "carried to a supreme degree" may result in "a negation." That Old New York may be headed down an evolutionary cul-de-sac is implied when Newland draws an analogy between May's culturally inherited blindness and the biological blindness of "the Kentucky cave-fish, which had ceased to develop eyes because they had no use for them" (*Age*, 82). Whether the struggle for existence here is cast in Darwinian or Spencerian terms, the analogy can portend no good for Old New York.

But this self-selective and selected group does not die out.[20] Instead, the New York society represented in *The Age of Innocence* gets a transfusion of "new blood and new money," and this change registers significantly on the color imagery of the novel (*Age*, 30). Of the characters trying to "lay siege to" Society's "tight little citadel" in the beginning, one (Mrs. Lemuel Struthers) is associated with darkness and another (Fanny Ring of the canary yellow carriage) with bright color. Initially, these colors brand these characters as outsiders (*Age*, 30). Early in the novel, Mrs. Struthers's tainted sexual past and lower class origins make Ellen's attendance at one of her gatherings a damning social move. Mrs. Struthers's disreputable status is emphasized by her "intensely black" hair, the cut of which, in "the Egyptian style," links her (through racist etymology) to the "gypsy" Ellen (*Age*, 36). Over the time traversed in the novel, however, eventually even the decorous May can attend Mrs. Struthers's entertainments without a qualm. Mrs. Struthers's entry into New York Society represents the beginning of a real but relatively small demographic change that occurs between "the age of innocence" and the turn of the century: the infiltration of Old New York by new money. Her conquest calls to mind larger demographic changes and, more importantly, changes of thought occurring at the same time. Wharton figures Mrs. Struthers's entree into Society as the conversion of a darker element into a lighter one: "Once people had tasted of Mrs. Struthers's easy Sunday hospitality they were not likely to sit at home remembering that her champagne was transmuted Shoe-Polish" (*Age*, 260). Viewed against Progressive-era fear of "race suicide," this image betrays a nativist fantasy of averting "national death" by absorption of the ethnic Other. Mrs. Struthers's champagne anticipates Ralph Ellison's symbol of the paint factory in *Invisible Man* ("Keep America Pure with Liberty Paints"): When ten black drops are stirred into each can of Optic White paint, they simply disappear, not diluting but intensifying the paint's whiteness.[21] Aside from the obvious economic alchemy, Wharton's image of "transmuted Shoe-Polish" points to a process of ethnic alchemy similar to the one Ellison satirizes. In Wharton's trope for the move from "the age of innocence" to the twentieth century, the Africanist presence, already necessary to the definition of "whiteness," revitalizes an aged and dying "race" by being absorbed into it and thereby disappearing itself. Wharton emphasizes the vampirishness of Society here by referring to Catherine as "the carnivorous old lady" when she calls for "new blood" (*Age*, 30).

Wharton's image of shoe-polish-into-champagne also points to a change in thinking about race that began around the time this novel was written and published. After the Great War, according to Ruth Frankenberg, thinking about race was gradually moving away from the old "essentialist racism" to a view that Frankenberg labels "color evasiveness" and "power evasiveness."[22] This change complemented a shift toward "an 'assimilationist' analysis of what would and should happen to people of color in the United States."[23] Wharton's image of something dark transmuted into something light stands thus poised at an ideological shift that would ultimately lead to assimilationist racism. The failure of the dark and light elements to blend implies that they are essentially different; the tendency of Society to absorb newcomers by blanching them suggests assimilation.

The change set in motion by Mrs. Struthers's invitation to the Beauforts' ball and carried forward when her shoe polish turns to champagne culminates in another "assimilationist" event: the fulfillment of Lawrence Lefferts's prophecy that "If things go on at this pace . . . we shall see our children . . . marrying Beaufort's bastards" (*Age,* 338). In the approaching marriage of Newland's son Dallas to Fanny Beaufort, daughter of Julius Beaufort and his mistress Fanny Ring, the Archer family accepts the child of both the colorful (or sexual) woman and the Jew.[24] Because Beaufort himself, who "passed for an Englishman," was not fully accepted into "the clan" a generation before in spite of his marriage to Regina Dallas (Regina, in fact, had jeopardized her own standing in Society by marrying him), his daughter's marriage to Newland's son amounts to an act of assimilation (*Age,* 19). Everything objectionable to Society in the Jew Beaufort and his mistress Fanny Ring is dissociated from their daughter who, like a second-generation immigrant, assimilates into "the tribe" by leaving her parents' identities behind. Indeed, Dallas does not marry a "dark lady." By the time Fanny is engaged to Dallas, her identity has already been detached from her father's status as "a 'foreigner' of doubtful origin" and from her mother's place among "[s]uch 'women' (as they were called)" (*Age,* 44, 84). Although Newland's family welcomes Fanny, in her it admits neither Jew nor "dark lady." Her acceptance by Newland's family shows not that America embraces difference, but rather that admission to the ruling class requires the surrender of "ethnicity."[25] The upcoming name change from Fanny Beaufort to Mrs. Dallas Archer suggests how the new concept of assimilation could itself, like the old Progressive Era concept of essential difference between the races, constitute a form of racism.

But even as *The Age of Innocence* registers multiple theories of race, it disrupts racist "logic" as well. Much in the novel works against both essentialist and assimilationist concepts of race. Wharton, who could analyze so astutely how culture constructs gender, seems sometimes to be on the verge of a similar historicizing of race. The novel embodies a tension between viewing the absorption of difference as desirable and seeing such dilution as a loss. Although the images of absorbed others reveal the racist anxieties and fantasies of Wharton's class, gaps in the text uncover the illogic of such fantasies for Americans.

In a novel in which there is much talk of America and "Americanness," America is ostensibly contrasted with Europe, but Wharton repeatedly subverts the international theme to question American claims to freedom, individualism, and originality. As Ellen points out to Newland, New York parrots European forms. Far from encouraging individuality and freedom, "America" in this novel enforces conformity to convention, and this way of life at times constitutes Newland's main antagonist. One day during his engagement to May, Newland decides not to stop at his club on the way home from work because "a haunting horror of doing the same thing every day at the same hour besieged his brain" (*Age*, 83). As he looks in on the "familiar tall-hatted figures" inside his club, Newland voices what seems to be his argument with America: "'Sameness—sameness!' he muttered, the word running through his head like a persecuting tune" (*Age*, 83). Later, married to May, Newland "wonder[s] if the deadly monotony of their lives had laid its weight on her also" (*Age*, 293). Wharton connects the monotony of Newland's life, this deadly dullness of "see[ing] the same people every day" (*Age*, 106), with his people's all being the same. Their sameness, given the novel's color coding, takes on ethnic/racial significance.

Wharton, moreover, exposes New York's fear of difference as the nation's problem. Washington, D.C., "where one was supposed to meet more varieties of people and of opinion" (*Age*, 240) than elsewhere in America, fails to stimulate Ellen. In Boston, a city associated with American individualism, Newland is struck by the lack of variety among Americans. Strangely, Newland deplores the sameness of American faces immediately after noticing ethnic diversity in the features of people on the streets. These juxtaposed moments unveil a contradiction: the paradox that everyone looks alike in a land of immigrants. While Newland waits for Ellen outside her hotel, "A Sicilian youth with eyes like Nastasia's offer[s] to shine his boots, and an Irish matron to sell him peaches" (*Age,* 236). The next moment, Newland watches the people coming out of the hotel and "marvel[s] . . . that all the people . . . should look so like each other, and so like all the other hot men who, at that hour, through the length and breadth of the land, were passing continuously in and out of the swinging doors of hotels" (*Age,* 236). For whatever reason these hotel patrons resemble one another, the other Bostonians who might provide some relief from this uniformity—the Irish matron, the Sicilian youth—are excluded from the image of Americans moving across the length and breadth of the land. Newland is conveniently colorblind.

On a less-conscious level, however, Newland is not colorblind, because it is his encounter with the excluded immigrants that triggers his exasperation with the sameness of "American" faces. His exasperation, in turn, heightens the contrast between the one European face he sees in Boston, that of M. Rivière, and all the identical American faces. The moment after Newland notices the immigrants, he notes the similarity of "American" faces; the next moment, his glimpse of M. Rivière's face conveys to him all that America lacks: "And then, suddenly, came a face that . . . was so many more things at once, and things so different[,] . . . somehow, quicker, vivider, more conscious; or perhaps seeming so because he was so different" (*Age,* 236–37). Here, clearly, difference is good, and lack of difference is an American failing. To all America, then, Wharton extends Catherine's complaint about "the tribe": "Ah, these Mingotts—all alike! . . . No, no; not one of them wants to be different; they're as scared of it as the small pox" (*Age,* 152). Newland, too, perceives fear of difference as a national failing (and seems to equate the valuing of difference with national integrity) when, staring at a "row of stark white village houses" outside of Boston, he concedes to Ellen: "We're damnably dull. We've no character, no colour, no variety" (*Age,* 241).

While the racial difference of M. Rivière—his "sallow skin" is repeatedly contrasted with Newland's skin (especially when both men blush)—and that of other middle-class Europeans comes to stand in the conscious minds of Newland and the narrator for the variety that America lacks, the racial difference of the immigrants lacks this saving power (*Age,* 201, 250). These characters impinge upon Newland's senses, but not on his colorblind consciousness. They are not, in his view, candidates for inclusion in America. Similarly ironic is Newland's juxtaposition of "heat-prostrated and *deserted* Boston" with his perception that "a shirt-sleeved populace . . . moved through the streets near the station" (*Age,* 229; 228 emphasis added). Although typically the narrator is more perceptive than Newland, the irony of this description is left unremarked.

But while Bostonians like the Irish matron and the Sicilian youth are, in some ways, invisible to Newland and to the narrator, they nevertheless are connected to the differently colored and cultured characters associated with Ellen and to alternatives to America's deadening lack of "colour." The novel's logic of image and character, which aligns courage with color and vitality with variety, undermines Newland's narrow definition of what "American" means.

True to the contradictions of Newland's time and class, he can be dying of sameness in one of the world's most diverse cities. This paradox captures one important aspect of "whiteness" characteristic of his time and place (though not exclusive to either). Whiteness includes unexamined acceptances of the system of advantage that maintains one's privilege. Added up, these acts of acceptance constitute a "cunningly manufactured" ignorance of how one's own identity is "raced." To borrow a phrase from another of Wharton's novels, Newland's people possess "a force of negation which eliminated everything beyond their own range of perception."[26] One of Wharton's gifts as a novelist is her ability to depict such a force of negation from its own point of view, even as she indicates the extent of what it negates, wastes, destroys. *The Age of Innocence,* which is so incisive about social constructions of gender, also apprehends some of the ways society constructs racial categories. It is a short step from realizing the artificiality of May's sexual innocence to realizing the limitations of "whiteness" as a point of view. Between her fine sense of irony and her good eye for the cultural construction of identity, Wharton is able to record some of the complexities of American identity where race, gender, and class intersect. *The Age of Innocence,* written during an upwelling of anti-immigrant sentiment and during a nascent movement for racial equality, depicts whiteness as an active, artificial "innocence." However attractive this ignorance may appear against the alternative of facing the nation's racial problems, Wharton's novel marks the cultural moment at which this "age of innocence" must begin to give way.

Notes

1. Toni Morrison, *Playing in the Dark: Whiteness and the Literary Imagination* (Cambridge: Harvard University Press, 1992). References to this work are hereafter cited in the text with the abbreviation *Dark* and the page number in parentheses.
2. For a different but not opposing approach to ethnicity in Wharton's works, see Nancy Bentley's *The Ethnography of Manners: Hawthorne, James, Wharton* (New York: Cambridge University Press, 1995). In addition to the sections on Wharton, Bentley's second chapter, "Nathaniel Hawthorne and the Fetish of Race," is relevant to my approach to *The Age of Innocence* (24–67).
3. R. W. B. Lewis, *Edith Wharton: A Biography* (1975; New York: Harper Colophon Books, 1987), 21. References to Lewis's work are hereafter cited in the text with the author's last name and page number in parentheses.
4. Shari Benstock, *No Gifts from Chance: A Biography of Edith Wharton* (New York: Scribner's, 1994), 3, 34.
5. Susan S. Lanser, "Feminist Criticism, 'The Yellow Wallpaper,' and the Politics of Color in America," *Feminist Studies* 15, no. 3 (fall 1989): 415–41. For connections between African peoples and the Irish "race," whom British imperialists labeled "white Negroes," see Vincent J. Cheng, *Joyce, Race, and Empire* (Cambridge: Cambridge University Press, 1995). Cheng refers the reader to several historians and theorists of "race."
6. On Wharton's relation to Roosevelt, R. W. B. Lewis reports, "Within the community of cousins to which she belonged, Edith was distantly related to the second Mrs. Roosevelt, the former Edith Carow" (112).
7. Quoted in Angela Y. Davis, *Women, Race, and Class* (New York: Vintage Books, 1983), 209. All the phrases I quote from Roosevelt's speeches are cited by Davis except the phrase "the proper sort," which appears in Jane Sherron DeHart and Linda K. Kerber, *Women's America: Refocusing the Past* (New York: Oxford University Press, 1991), 340. Davis cites Melvin Steinfeld, *Our Racist Presidents* (San Ramon, Calif.: Consensus Publishers, 1972), 212; and Bonnie Mass, *Population Target: The Political Economy of Population Control in Latin America* (Toronto, Canada: Women's Educational Press, 1977), 20. De Hart and Kerber do not cite the sources of their quotations from Roosevelt.
8. See John Hope Franklin and Alfred A. Moss, *From Slavery to Freedom: A History of African Americans,* 7th ed. (New York: McGraw Hill, 1994), 323–60.
9. Blanche Wiesen Cook, *Eleanor Roosevelt: 1884–1933,* vol. 1 (New York: Penguin, 1992), 251.
10. Moss and Franklin, *From Slavery to Freedom,* 364.
11. Edith Wharton, *The Age of Innocence* (New York: Macmillan, 1986), 121 and 361. All further references to this work are cited in the text with the abbreviation *Age* in parentheses.
12. For a discussion of this trend, see Ann DuCille, *The Coupling Convention: Sex, Text, and Tradition in Black Women's Fiction* (New York: Oxford University Press, 1993), 72–74, 85.
13. See Shari Benstock, *No Gifts from Chance,* on how Wharton's view of non-Western cultures grew more realistic between 1888 and 1917 (the year before she wrote *The Age of Innocence*). In 1888, "Edith Wharton revels in the otherness and exoticism" of "Africa, Asia Minor, and the Aegean islands

[whereas] . . . thirty years later, visiting Morocco, . . . her perspective was still Western, Christian, and colonialistic, but her attitudes had changed toward the circumstances in which Arab women and children lived" (65–66).

14. See Sander L. Gilman, "Black Bodies, White Bodies: Toward an Iconography of Female Sexuality in Late Nineteenth Century Art, Medicine, and Literature," *Critical Inquiry* 12, no. 1 (autumn 1985): 204–42. Gilman shows that, by the end of the nineteenth century, the black woman had become—in art, literature, and medicine—an icon for sexuality. Most relevant to Wharton's novel is Gilman's tracing of the use of the black servant to mark the sexuality of white characters in European art and music from the eighteenth to the twentieth century. Works probably familiar to Wharton—William Hogarth's *A Rake's Progress* (1733–34), Edouard Manet's *Olympia* (1865), and Hugo von Hofmannsthal's *Der Rosenkavalier* (1911)—use black servants to mark the illicit sexuality of main characters who are white (206–9). "It is this iconography," according to Anne DuCille in *The Coupling Convention,* "that helped make a bare-breasted Josephine Baker the rage in Paris in the twenties" (73)—just after Wharton completed *The Age of Innocence.*

15. Lauren Berlant, "The Queen of America Goes to Washington City: Harriet Jacobs, Frances Harper, Anita Hill," *American Literature* 65, no. 3 (September 1993): 554.

16. Ibid., 555.

17. Ibid.

18. See Ruth Frankenberg, *White Women, Race Matters: The Social Construction of Whiteness* (Minneapolis: University of Minnesota Press, 1993): "Jewish Americans, Italian Americans, and Latinos have, at different times and from varying political standpoints, been viewed as both 'white' and 'nonwhite.' And as the history of 'interracial' marriage and sexual relationships also demonstrates, 'white' is as much as anything else an economic and political category maintained over time by a changing set of exclusionary practices, both legislative and customary" (11–12).

19. Ibid., 1. Here, I combine three of Frankenberg's definitions of "whiteness": "First, whiteness is a location of structural advantage, of race privilege. Second, it is a 'standpoint,' a place from which white people look at ourselves, at others, and at society. Third, 'whiteness' refers to a set of cultural practices that are usually unmarked and unnamed" (1).

20. Nancy Bentley in *The Ethnography of Manners* observes: "Wharton's portrait of a class that in fact retained and strengthened its claim to power and wealth through the tumultuous social changes of fin-de-siècle America is demographically correct. In spite of a pervasive sense of WASP decline—indeed, in part through that very sense—the northeastern elite expanded its social influence and helped to acculturate the American polity to a new society of consumption and corporate capital" (113).

21. Ralph Ellison, *Invisible Man* (New York: Random House, 1972), 192, 195–97.

22. Frankenberg, *White Women, Race Matters,* 13.

23. Ibid., 14, 13.

24. Shari Benstock in *No Gifts from Chance* reports that Wharton "based Beaufort on financier August Belmont (rumored to be Jewish), who kept a mistress . . . and provided her with a canary-yellow carriage" (358). Annette Zilversmit informed me at the Edith Wharton at Yale Conference (in honor of R. W. B. Lewis, April 1995) that Belmont was a Schoenberg and the only Jew

in Old New York during the 1870s. Susan Meyer interpreted Beaufort's Jewish identity in quite interesting ways in "Jews, Sex, and Edith Wharton" (session on Edith Wharton and Taboo, annual meeting of the Modern Language Association, Washington, D.C., December 28, 1996).

25. For an opposing view of Fanny's marriage, assimilation, and the changes in thinking about race of the 1920s, see Walter Benn Michaels, *Our America: Nativism, Modernism, and Pluralism* (Durham, N.C.: Duke University Press, 1995), 110–12. Nancy Bentley's interpretation of this marriage in *The Ethnography of Manners*, on the other hand, supports my sense of it as one of the events in which Old New York absorbs the vitality of outsiders without taking on their "color." Although in Bentley's words "the taboos against exogamous marriage . . . have been lifted, . . . the disorder is an energy harnessed by Archer's children" (113).

26. Edith Wharton, *The House of Mirth,* ed. Elizabeth Ammons, Norton Critical Edition (New York: Norton, 1990), 40.

Edith Wharton's Italian Tale: Language Exercise and Social Discourse

GIANFRANCA BALESTRA

> ... & nello stesso momento un signore giovane ed elegante
> coi baffi arricciati & gli abiti all'ultima moda uscì dal bureau
> per andare incontro alla gentile signora sulla soglia dell'Hotel.
> "La Marchesa di Fabiano?" le chiese ossequiosamente.
> "Sono la cameriera della Marchesa," rispose l'altra a bassa
> voce, quasi intimidita. "La mia signora viene dopo pranzo,
> coll'automobile."
> "Ah? Va bene," disse il direttore, voltandosi bruscamente.

"O GIFTED POLYGLOT! WHAT FUN TO BE ABLE TO SWIM & SPLASH about like that in a foreign tongue. The most I have accomplished is to forget my own."[1] Expressing her admiration to Bernard Berenson on his having written an article in beautiful Italian, Edith Wharton complimented him and lamented her own inadequacy. Years of expatriation and negative comments on the part of some critics made her wonder at times about her command of English.[2] However, she was herself a "gifted polyglot," fluent, to different degrees, in French, German, and Italian. Her competence in the first two languages has been examined by other scholars.[3] I would like to address the question of her knowledge of Italian, drawing on her autobiography, published and unpublished correspondence, as well as other manuscripts.[4] In particular, among the wealth of unpublished material held at the Beinecke Library, I discovered an Italian manuscript that documents Wharton's relative proficiency in the language: an unfinished short story about a young maid traveling with a haughty Marquise. Apart from its linguistic significance, this text has intrinsic value in terms of subject matter, technical mastery, and psychological analysis. Moreover, it is of interest to the Wharton scholar because it touches upon her concern with maids and housekeepers throughout her life and in her fiction. In fact, it represents one of her best attempts at depicting the life of a servant, whose plight in a class-ridden

Italian society is portrayed with sensitivity and acute attention to detail. For these reasons, this unfinished short story will be examined both as a language exercise and as a fictional endeavour.

"Discovering Italian ... was to be the source of such joys," Edith Wharton wrote in *A Backward Glance*. She also recalled the happy hours spent in Florence as a child with a charming young woman who taught her Italian: "My lessons amused me, and the new language came to me as naturally as breathing, as French and German had already." She considered it fortunate to learn modern languages at an early age because "the speech acquired is never afterward lost, however deep below the surface it may be embedded."[5] Later on, she had the opportunity to improve and practice her Italian through extensive reading and traveling in the country. In her study of Wharton's reading in European languages, Helen Killoran provides a useful sample of representative titles in Italian compiled from "booksellers' lists, private papers, from published and unpublished letters, and from direct literary allusions in Edith Wharton's writing."[6] Although incomplete, the list is impressive and suggests the range of Wharton's exploration in Italian language and culture. The "Italian period," which saw the publication of *The Valley of Decision* (1902), *Italian Villas and Their Gardens* (1904), and *Italian Backgrounds* (1905), was marked by an enormous amount of reading, including many Italian texts.[7]

Wharton in fact read Italian throughout her life. In 1930, she would read *Gli indifferenti,* Alberto Moravia's first novel, commending it to Berenson for its artistic mastery but also as a way of "limbering up her tongue" before going to Italy.[8] Later she would express her doubts about this rising star of Italian letters, while she would consider *Le sorelle Materassi* (1934) by Aldo Palazzeschi "the best Italian novel since the *Promessi Sposi.*"[9] She appreciated some of D'Annunzio's poetry, especially the third volume of his *Laudi,* under whose enchantment she wrote to Sara Norton.[10] She read and attended his plays, and commented on them with less enthusiasm, but with astute perception of his typical lavishness of detail and lack of dramatic movement.[11] Her divided response to this flamboyant figure of Italian aestheticism is best expressed in a letter to Brownell: "I hate to admit it, for I hate D'Annunzio, but his Francesca is very fine."[12] In spite of her reluctance, when in 1927 the Nobel prize was awarded to Grazia Deledda, "she felt strongly that if it was indeed Italy's turn to be honored, the prize should have gone to

Gabriele D'Annunzio."[13] These few examples of Wharton's complex relationship with contemporary Italian literature confirm her constant interest: she kept herself up to date, reading what was coming out at the time, and reading it in Italian.

However, it was in the past that she found the source of her greatest joys, and particularly in Dante, whom Killoran rightly identifies as her most significant Italian influence.[14] In *Hudson River Bracketed*, Vance Weston wants to learn Italian "so as to be able to read Dante,"[15] a necessary step in the education of a writer. Wharton herself read *La Divina Commedia* in the original, as documented by numerous references in her correspondence and diaries. Quotations testify to the pervasiveness of Dante's influence, especially when they appear as personal idiomatic phrases. One case in point is Wharton's recurring use of the expression "Non ragioniam" to mean "Let us not speak of it." This rather cryptic usage would not be immediately understood without reference to Virgil's warning to Dante in *Inferno* III 51: "non ragioniam di lor, ma guarda e passa" (Let us not talk of them; look and pass on). But, as the editors of her letters point out, Dante "supplied her not so much with quotations as with ways of focusing herself at key moments."[16] For example, in her diary she chose the famous love scene of Paolo and Francesca to mark the progression of her own affair with Morton Fullerton.[17] Although R. W. B. Lewis discusses Wharton's readings and quotations from Dante, a comprehensive study of her relationship to Italian literature and culture in general has yet to be done.[18]

Italian references appear in her diaries and in her correspondence with people who could recognize them, such as Bernard Berenson, who lived in Florence, admired Italian culture, and spoke the language. Her letters to Berenson are interspersed with learned quotations as well as with everyday Italian expressions. In response to Berenson's challenge to show him some Petrarch that was worthwhile, she lists a number of sonnets and some "sudden cries of grief" from other poems that seem to her to "have a great accent."[19] This correspondence demonstrates the breadth of Wharton's reading in Italian literature as well as her ability to manipulate the language, mixing English and Italian to coin new words in a personal lexicon. For instance, she would call Berenson "friendissimo,"[20] adding the Italian suffix for the superlative to the English word, or she would take the Italian expression "piove dirottamente"—which she also used, meaning "raining in torrents," "pouring down"—and turn it into the amusing "it has been raining di-rottenly."[21]

One little known episode in Wharton's career, mentioned by Lewis,[22] is her professional translation into English of three stories by Italian writers—"A Great Day" and "College Friends" by Edmondo De Amicis, and "It Snows" by Enrico Castelnuovo—for a collection of *Stories by Foreign Authors* published by Scribner's in 1898.[23] Her ironic question to Edward L. Burlingame, the editor at Scribner's, indicates a certain uneasiness in her unaccustomed role as translator: "How do you think my rendering of Signor Castelnuovo's poetry compares with Jack Chapman's Inferno?"[24] Indeed, she agrees to have the translations attributed to her only when Burlingame proclaims them satisfactory. In another letter, she explains that she had "once or twice paraphrased the Italian rather freely where a more literal version would have been too puerile."[25] This actually happens more than "once or twice" and is usually done very effectively, with a writer's flair for English as well as a basic understanding of the Italian meaning. If at times subtle nuances of the language escape Wharton, her translations are generally accurate and highly readable, further demonstrating her fluency in Italian.[26]

Her extensive readings in Italian, her translations from Italian into English, her quotation of Italian words and authors, her playful coinage of Italianate words, all attest to Wharton's knowledge and love of the language. Only a few months before her death, she wrote Alfredo Zanchino, who was doing an Italian translation and theater adaptation of "The Old Maid": "If you prefer to write to me in Italian, please do not hesitate to do so as I have known the language since I was a child; I write in English because I am out of the habit of speaking and writing Italian."[27] However, it is likely that Wharton's reading abilities in Italian were always superior to her speaking and writing abilities, as she herself admitted in her correspondence. At different times in her life she tried to improve her spoken and written Italian by taking private lessons. For instance, in a letter to Brownell, she talked of comparing his "Lingua Berlitziana" to her own "hap-hazard Italian," and explained: "I chartered a Professor at San Remo to polish my diction a little, but he insisted on doing all the talking, so I am no better off."[28]

Writing, especially creative writing in a foreign language, is a formidable task. We know that she wrote in French "Les Metteurs en scène" for the *Revue des Deux Mondes,* an experiment that did not meet with the approval of Henry James, who insisted that *"she must never do it again."*[29] Further, she began

Ethan Frome as an exercise to polish and enlarge her French vocabulary when she moved to Paris, and resumed it a few years later to create her masterpiece.[30] But it is not widely known that she had done something similar in Italian: Apparently her Italian exercise didn't have such a successful follow-up; it remained incomplete and was never rewritten into English. The text of this untitled, undated, unpublished short story in Italian is contained in a "Composition Exercise in Italian" held at the Beinecke Library among Wharton's personal papers.[31] The folder includes as well some handwritten pages of Italian verb conjugations and polite expressions for letters and everyday situations. Since there is no date or specific reference, the genesis of this work must remain a matter of conjecture.

In a 1908 letter from Paris to Sara Norton,[32] Wharton mentions that she is taking French and Italian lessons. Further, at this time she wrote her "French Ethan Frome." I surmise that she did the same to improve her Italian at roughly this time because for her, writing a story was the most natural language exercise. Moreover, a linguistic analysis of the Italian manuscript shows an evident French influence, both in terms of vocabulary and syntax. In some cases, Wharton starts from a French word or sentence and then translates it into Italian,[33] which suggests either that she had a teacher who could speak French but not English, or that she was at this point in her life more comfortable with French than Italian and it was easier for her to work between these two romance languages. All these clues support my tentative placing of the story in the period around 1908 when she was studying both French and Italian in Paris.

The manuscript consists of nineteen pages and contains numerous corrections, persistent mistakes, and awkward constructions. The corrections appear to be in Wharton's own hand, but it is impossible to determine if they are due to personal revision or to outside supervision. The fact that in some cases the mistakes remain untouched questions the very existence of a teacher, or at least introduces a further element in the mystery of the identity of the possible teacher, who might not have been a native speaker of Italian. In any case, the corrections might indeed be self-corrections, afterthoughts on the part of a writer who is trying to remember a language "embedded deep below the surface" by helping herself with a dictionary and a grammar book. To stress the mistakes, however, risks giving a distorted impression of Wharton's language ability: they are mostly small mistakes, sometimes these are mere questions of nuance, at

Si precipitavano anche i chasseurs *valletti* che stavano ~~nel~~ *aggruppati* nell'atrio per ~~descendere~~ già innumerevoli sacchi, e i facchini per levare i bauli dal tetto; e nello stesso momento un ~~g~~ signore giovane ed elegante, coi baffi arricciati~~ss~~ e gli ~~abb~~ abiti all'ultima *moda* ~~uscira~~ dal bureau per ~~riccorre la~~ *andare incontro alla* gentile signora sulla soglia dell'hôtel.

"La Marchesa di Tabiano?" le chiese ossequiosamente.

"Sono la cameriera della Marchesa," rispose l'altra a bassa voce, quasi intimidita. "La mia signora viene dopo pranzo, coll'automobile."

"Ah? Va bene," disse il direttore rivoltandosi bruscamente. ~~Fate vedere~~ Tornerò senz'altro al bureau, e la giovane cameriera stava sola nell'immensa sala d'un... tutta rivestita di marmo giallo ...na di bagnanti, di servi, di... ...ciulli che correvano qua e...

Facsimilie of "Composition Exercise in Italian," page 2. Reprinted by permission of the Beinecke Library, Yale University.

others they are obvious errors that might have been immediately corrected by the writer herself. The choice of words is generally appropriate, and ranges from refined and precise descriptions to idiomatically phrased dialogues. Wharton masters the complexities of Italian verb forms and syntax, and through multiple corrections and trials successfully overcomes the most arduous obstacles.[34] Her competence often implies a trained ear more than a mastery of Italian grammar. In a letter to Berenson, Wharton refers to having started oil painting and being blocked after having bought a book on the technique. She makes the following analogy: "I felt as faint as I did on first encountering an Italian grammar after having read, and even spoken, the language from the cradle."[35] These two modes of learning the language, the earlier direct method and the later theoretical one, probably explain the apparent contradictions of this Italian manuscript, where impeccable idiomatic forms and difficult syntactical structures coexist with strange lapses in competence associated with easier expressions. The various corrections eliminate most of the mistakes, so that the language exercise proves successful and the revised text is finally a remarkable linguistic feat.

At this point, I would like to offer a close reading of Wharton's Italian story, focusing on its thematic aspects, as well as its biographical reverberations. Of special significance here is Wharton's ability to show the world from the perspective of the maid. Technically this is done through third-person narration which focuses on this figure, following the Jamesian method that Wharton adopts in much of her work. The first scene introduces the protagonist, a young woman described as thin, dark, and dressed in black. She is the only passenger in a bus loaded with trunks and suitcases that stops in front of the "Hotel des Bains," an elegant resort surrounded by oleanders. Although the exact location is not mentioned, the few details suggest the Italian Riviera, in spite of the French appellation that was common at the time. As numerous porters start unloading her luggage, this woman is met by the hotel manager, who with obvious deference addresses her as the "Marchesa di Fabiano." Her answer creates embarrassment and a drastic change in manners: She is the Marchesa's maid, and her lady will arrive later in her automobile. Immediately she is abandoned in the hall and viewed with scorn, her questions are rudely dismissed, and she has to walk up three flights of stairs carrying her lady's most precious, and heavy, belongings. The use of the elevator is forbidden to servants, and the separate route through dark and dirty corridors and stairways shows the other side of the shining marble facade of this residence for the rich and elegant. This thematic use of place, a Wharton trademark, underscores the complete reversal of perspective which is at the center of this tale, from the front of the stage to behind the scenes, from the world of the wealthy to that of the poor who work for them.

The apartment assigned to the Marchesa, composed of a large sitting room with a balcony, a bedroom, and a bathroom, is soon filled with trunks and suitcases brought up by the porters, who sweat and swear at their job, and can't believe that all the luggage is for one person only. The maid will have to unpack before the Marchesa's arrival and make certain that everything is in order. Having had only a cup of coffee at six in the morning before going to the train station, she does not even have time for lunch. Tired and hungry, she panics initially when she cannot find the keys to the luggage, but she finally gets to her work in a frantic way.

After these first scenes, a flashback allows the reader to situate the young maid. Maria has been working for the Marchesa for four months, having taken the position of her aunt, who retired to marry the coachman. Her aunt, who is described as a lively woman with the health of a peasant and the mind of a business-man, has imagined that she has made her niece's fortune by recommending her to the Marchesa. This detail realistically re-flects Italian society and its endemic crisis of unemployment, where handing down jobs among members of the same family has long been a widespread practice. At first Maria is so nervous that her hands shake when she is serving the lady, but with the help of her aunt, who trains her, she becomes an expert maid. In fact Maria takes pride in working for such an elegant and distinguished lady. She admires the Marchesa's beautiful house with painted ceilings and precious carpets, and even likes wear-ing the lace-trimmed apron. But when the two travel, the maid's fears and sense of inadequacy return. Maria feels she will never answer all the Marchesa's demands: to pack her clothes in such a way that they will not be crumpled; to remember where she packed each small object; to buy the tickets and send the lug-gage; to keep an eye on her fur coat, jewels, and keys; and to have everything ready when the Marchesa arrives. It is more the job for a general or chief of police than for a maid. After a month of traveling through France, Switzerland, and Italy from one fashionable hotel to another, Maria has lost so much sleep and weight that she fears being fired for reasons of health. Moreover, she dislikes hotel life, especially having to deal with the hotel staff and the other guests' servants. She cannot get used to their bad manners, coarse jokes, and fights.

Following this flashback, the narrator describes the maid's present situation, when she feels particularly disheartened. She is tired and dizzy, afraid of forgetting some detail that will provoke her lady's anger. She unpacks the huge trunks, giving way to an expanded description of their contents: the objects, dresses, and linens constitute a sort of catalog of the elegant possessions of an aristocratic lady, in a linguistic *tour de force* with ironic and possibly erotic undertones.[36] Among this excess of lace, silk, gold, and enamel, one indispensable object is missing, a little notebook the Marchesa uses for marking her points at bridge.

While Maria searches for it, the lady arrives in her motoring outfit, overcoat, and hat with a large veil. Wharton's story depicts her as beautiful, but with a constant expression of discontent that makes her cold and regular face look tired and almost old. Her first words are ones of reproach because the maid has not closed the shutters, even though she knows that the sunshine gives the Marchesa a headache. Maria turns red and hastens to remedy her negligence, but in her hurry she bumps into the little table where she has put the clock, which falls on the floor and breaks into pieces. The maid screams in terror, while the Marchesa only turns more pallid and moves into her bedroom without a word. There she complains about the flowers and orders the maid to take them out: She should know that she cannot stand even a rosebud in her bedroom. Maria obeys, then comes back still shaking in fear and apologizes for having broken the clock. The Marchesa doesn't care about that, since she intended to buy a new one anyway, but she wants to take a bath immediately. Maria prepares the water, helps the lady disrobe, and, after the bath, combs her hair and helps her into her dressing gown. The Marchesa wants to rest; Maria can go down to the dining room hoping to find some food, but at this hour the staff will not give her even a piece of bread and cup of tea. She has to pay a kitchen boy to obtain some unappetizing dried-out cheese and sausage, which she eats out of pure hunger. When she gets back to the apartment, an irritated Marchesa complains about her absence and demands to get ready for her bridge game. With her maid's assistance, the Marchesa dresses for the occasion until she is faced with the difficult choice of a hat. Maria brings all the hats out one at a time, but the lady cannot make a decision. She doesn't like any of them and bursts out crying. Her sobs leave the poor maid dumbfounded, incapable of offering consolation or some kind of solution, and she once again feels inadequate. The manuscript ends at this point, leaving pending the seemingly irresolvable issue of the hat and the question of the missing notebook.

More relevantly, one wonders what direction Wharton's story could take. Nothing "happens"; a possible plot has not yet taken shape. This idea that description is subordinate to narration can be traced back to the classical concept of "descriptio ancilla narrationis." However, this precept overlooks the deeper implications of Wharton's description itself. Behind the apparent lack of diegesis, the descriptive sequences delineate not a plot of action, but rather a plot of thought and social class. Wharton foregrounds the discourse of class from the very beginning, when the maid is mistaken for the Marchesa: an ironic misunderstanding that highlights the inherent equality of human beings and the arbitrariness of the class system. The maid's physical description is rather sketchy, devoid of the details of dress and manner that would probably reveal her status. At first glance she can be taken for an aristocratic lady, especially since she arrives loaded with expensive luggage marked by a coat of arms: Class is determined by possessions and inherited privilege. Once established, the issue of class is aptly developed: The maid becomes almost invisible to the hotel personnel, she receives no help, she cannot partake of the comfort reserved for the clients. Class conflict is signalled by a series of oppositions: excess is opposed to scarcity, wealth to poverty, ennui to work, and appearance to reality. Spatial opposition is particularly significant: A complete separation divides the space of the servants and the space of the rich; their lives mingle only insofar as it is necessary for the former to serve the latter. However, no solidarity or complicity develops among the servants, who have accepted their role and internalized the value system of the society in which they live. Maria, whose sensibilities are superior, hates the vulgarity and coarseness of the other servants; in contrast, she admires her lady and appreciates her elegant surroundings.

In many ways, the manuscript realistically depicts the class structure at the beginning of the century, in particular in Italy, but Wharton's class bias and preferences can also be detected: She is no revolutionary who would advocate the unity of workers to subvert an unjust social system, but rather an upper-class woman with sympathy for the less privileged. References to the maid are occasionally condescending: "la piccola cameriera," "la povera ragazza" ("the little maid," "the poor girl"). What is stigmatized in the story is the Marchesa's excessive wealth, her egotistical concern with futile aspects of life, as well as her indifference to her maid's plight. Although the Marchesa is portrayed as an arrogant Italian aristocrat, precisely as a way to avoid identification with Wharton herself, structurally the Marchesa takes on the role of the elite author, who was familiar with the experience of traveling comfortably by motorcar while her servants were dispatched by train with the luggage. In a number of works, Wharton describes her "happy wanderings"[37] in the motorcar, which "has restored the romance of travel."[38] In this text, she looks at the other side of the story, the more uncomfortable one of the servant, with a sympathetic eye.

In her study of Wharton's short fiction, Barbara White points out that in the early stories, with the important exception of "The Lady's Maid's Bell," "servants remain in the background as part of the furniture." Regarding "Autres Temps," White finds it difficult to sympathize with the plight of the rich protagonist precisely because of the constant presence of the maid, who takes care of her luggage and facilitates her life. White finds herself "perversely wondering about [the maid] and her story, which has not been told."[39] This Italian manuscript anticipates White's complaint and suggests Wharton's own interest in telling the maid's tale. Moreover, if my 1908 dating of the story is correct, this unpublished story offers an early and significant counterpoint to White's argument that in the late stories "there is a greater lower-class presence with the perspectives of lower-class characters, especially servants, being presented more strongly and sympathetically."[40] Although she identifies this as the most significant development in her short fiction, I would argue that Wharton shows a constant, if marginal, concern for servants and lower-class characters throughout her work. Memorable lower-class characters are present in an early text such as *Bunner Sisters,* as well as in a late novel like *The Buccaneers.* Domestic workers and other servants are especially relevant in the ghost stories, including "The Lady's Maid's Bell," "The Triumph of Night," "Mr. Jones," "A Bottle of Perrier," "After Holbein," and "All Souls." It would be impossible to evaluate here the function of servants in these stories, but their act of loyalty, mistreatment, revenge, and desertion often suggest Wharton's fears and anxieties, not only at the psychological and sexual level, but also at the social and economic level.[41] The manuscript I have examined represents a small but significant addition for a critical revision of the point of view of Wharton who, beginning with Vernon Parrington, was condemned for her social class and the limitation of her social perspectives.

In conclusion, we know that Wharton established close relationships with a number of her personal employees. In particular, we know of Wharton's intimate attachment to some devoted domestics who played a central role in her life, from her beloved childhood nurse Hannah Doyle (Doyley) to her respected housekeeper Catharine Gross to her personal maid Elise Duvlenck. The "rich all-permeating presence" of Doyley is exalted in Wharton's autobiography,[42] while the warmest personal acknowledgment of the other two women can be found in her correspondence. Soon after Elise's death, she wrote to Elizabeth Cameron:

> so many kind people seem not to know how dear a friend a devoted maid may become, & sympathyze chiefly on the ground of the inconvenience caused! The fact that my dear old Gross's mind failed completely at the very moment when Elise was taken ill added a deep distress to my other anxiety, & I emerged from it all considerably shattered. . . . The mere idea of packing & unpacking, & getting a move on, without Elise's guiding hand, is still very frightening.[43]

Wharton's fiction contains memorable portraits of servants, perhaps not completely exempt from class bias, but generally sensitive and considerate. The neglected Italian manuscript I have examined furthers this view of a writer who tries to transcend her social limitations and represent another side of reality: It is an exploration of foreign territories as well as a language experiment. In the general context of her "Italian connection," it adds an unknown and important element: Not only did Wharton know and love the Italian language, she even tried her hand at writing a short story in Italian.

Notes

1. Edith Wharton to Bernard Berenson, December 19, 1921, Berenson Archives, Villa I Tatti.

2. R. W. B. Lewis, *Edith Wharton: A Biography* (1975; rpt. New York: Fromm, 1985), 446.

3. See Roger Asselineau, "Edith Wharton: She Thought in French and Wrote in English," in *Wretched Exotic: Essays on Edith Wharton in Europe,* ed. Katherine Joslin and Alan Price (New York: Lang, 1993), 355–63; and

Richard H. Lawson, *Edith Wharton and German Literature* (Bonn: Grund-mann, 1974).

4. I am grateful to the Yale Collection of American Literature, Beinecke Rare Book and Manuscript Library, Yale University, for permission to quote from the manuscript and letters in the Edith Wharton Collection. I am also grateful to the following institutions for permission to quote from Wharton's manuscript letters and diaries: Manuscript Division, Department of Rare Books and Special Collections, Princeton University Libraries; Houghton Library, Harvard University; The Library of Congress, Washington, D.C.; Lilly Library, Indiana University; and the Villa I Tatti, Settignano, Italy.

5. Edith Wharton, *A Backward Glance, Novellas and Other Writings*, ed. Cynthia Griffin Wolff (New York: Library of America, 1990), 815.

6. Helen Killoran, "Edith Wharton's Reading in European Languages and Its Influence on Her Work," in Joslin and Price, *Wretched Exotic*, 374.

7. Lewis refers to the "prodigious amount of authentic scholarly research" Wharton did in preparation for *The Valley of Decision,* and to the "learning taken from books in four languages dating back to the seventeenth century" for *Italian Villas and Their Gardens (Edith Wharton,* 103). See also Gianfranca Balestra, "Il Settecento italiano di Edith Wharton," in *Il passaggiere italiano: Saggi sulle letterature di lingua inglese in onore di Sergio Rossi*, ed. Renzo Crivelli and Luigi Sampietro (Roma: Bulzoni, 1994), 471–87.

8. *The Letters of Edith Wharton,* ed. R. W. B. Lewis and Nancy Lewis (New York: Scribner's, 1988), 529.

9. Letter to Berenson of August 4, 1935, Villa I Tatti. In another letter to Berenson of August 14, 1935, she talks of "hearing dear Morra read aloud Moravia, as to whom I remain unconverted & incorrigible—because Faulkner & Céline did it *first,* & did it *nastier" (The Letters of Edith Wharton,* 589).

10. Edith Wharton to Sara Norton, May 21, 1911, bMS Am 1088.1 (1007), Houghton Library.

11. See her comments on D'Annunzio's *Francesca da Rimini* which end on this note: "It would have been impossible to do justice to Signor d'Annun-zio's drama without dwelling at some length on the exquisite incidental touches which create its peculiar charm; yet it must be owned that these touches impede the action, and that the drama, when stripped of them, shows a complete arrest of movement in the third act" ("The Three Francescas," *North American Review* 175 [July 1902]: 25). See also Alberta Fabris Grube, "La fortuna americana di D'Annunzio" in *Gabriele D'Annunzio e la cultura inglese e americana,* ed. Patrizia Nerozzi Bellman (Chieti: Solfanelli, 1990), 35–42.

12. Edith Wharton to William Crary Brownell, May 23, 1912, Box 167, Folder 2, Scribner's Archives, Princeton Library.

13. Lewis, *Edith Wharton,* 482.

14. Killoran, "Edith Wharton's Reading," 368.

15. Edith Wharton, *Hudson River Bracketed* (London: Virago, 1986), 213.

16. 16. Lewis and Lewis, "Introduction," *The Letters of Edith Wharton,* 19.

17. 1908 Diary, Lilly Library, Indiana University. Lewis explains this and other allusions to the *Commedia* and the *Vita Nuova (Edith Wharton,* 205, 209–10). See also Eleanor Dwight, *Edith Wharton: An Extraordinary Life* (New York: Abrams, 1994), 146–47.

18. I am presently writing a book-length study of the Italian connection which includes such a chapter.

19. Edith Wharton to Bernard Berenson, August 7, 1917, Villa I Tatti.

20. Edith Wharton to Bernard Berenson, July 16, 1915, Villa I Tatti.

21. Edith Wharton to Bernard Berenson, October 6, 1911, Villa I Tatti.

22. Lewis, *Edith Wharton*, 81.

23. Enrico Castelnuovo, "Nevica," *Alla finestra* (Milano: Treves, 1878); and Edmondo De Amicis, "Un gran giorno" and "Gli amici di collegio," *Novelle* (Milano: Treves, 1878). English translation by Edith Wharton, "It Snows," "A Great Day," and "College Friends," *Stories by Foreign Authors* (New York: Scribner's, 1898).

24. Edith Wharton to Edward L. Burlingame, Undated, Box 168, Folder 16, Princeton Library.

25. Edith Wharton to Edward L. Burlingame, Undated, Box 168, Folder 16, Princeton Library.

26. Without going into a detailed analysis of these translations, I would like to point out some curiosities. In "College Friends," there is a rather vulgar and common expression "Fossi minchione!" which derives from a word meaning "penis" and is used as an epithet for a simpleton, a fool. Wharton translates, "What do you take me for?" (*Stories by Foreign Authors*, 141), which renders the general meaning, avoiding the specific vulgar term that would be impossible in English. Another epithet, "Testone," which refers to the fact that the protagonist has a big head, but also means figuratively "blockhead," is aptly paraphrased as "What are you going to do with a head like that?" (144), because in English the pun would not work. A less successful solution is Wharton's rendering of "dove si fanno pettegolezzi da donnicciuole e si covano segrete ambizioni virili" with "a life teeming with feminine meannesses and virile ambitions" (143), where "pettegolezzi" could have been literally translated with "gossip," a term less strong than "meannesses."

27. Edith Wharton to Alfredo Zanchino, October 13, 1935, Box 39, Folder 1206, Beinecke Library.

28. Edith Wharton to William Crary Brownell, April 29, 1903, Box 167, Folder 3, Princeton Library.

29. Wharton, *A Backward Glance*, 921.

30. Ibid., 1003–4.

31. Box 50, Folder 1505.

32. Edith Wharton to Sara Norton, February 6, 1908, Box 29, Folder 902, Beinecke Library. She also notes it down in her 1908 Diary.

33. For instance, the French "lauriers roses" is translated into the Italian "oleandri" (1), "chasseurs" into "valletti" (2); the sentence "Elle jeta un coup d'oeil autour de la chambre" becomes "Girò lo sguardo tutt'intorno nella camera." "Subito che si fu fermata la vettura" (1) is a typical French structure literally translated into a very awkward Italian phrase and subsequently corrected into "Appena la vettura si fu fermata."

34. Compound tenses cause the most problems both in the choice of the auxiliary verb and the tense itself. With the verb "bastare," meaning "to be enough," she employs the auxiliary "to have" instead of "to be," following the French usage with "suffire": the present conditional "basterebbe" is changed into the past conditional "avrebbe bastato" instead of "sarebbe bastata" (12). The final clause "so that they wouldn't be creased" is rendered in two different ways before reaching the correct solution: The first version is with the past perfect "non erano spiegazzate," the second with the past conditional "non

sarebbero spiegazzate," the third one with the past perfect subjunctive "non fossero spiegazzate" (11).

35. Edith Wharton to Bernard Berenson, April 5, 1920, Villa I Tatti.

36. Unpacking the trunks is a recurrent image in Wharton's work, often used metaphorically. In her letters to Morton Fullerton, she "unpacks her trunks" to him, revealing her deepest feelings and desires. See Clare Colquitt, "Unpacking Her Treasures: Edith Wharton's 'Mysterious Correspondence' with Morton Fullerton," *Library Chronicle of the University of Texas* ns 31 (1985): 73–107. I wish to thank Clare Colquitt for bringing this to my attention, as well as for many helpful comments and suggestions.

37. Wharton, *A Backward Glance,* 857.

38. Edith Wharton, *A Motor-Flight Through France,* ed. Mary Suzanne Schriber (1908; DeKalb: Northern Illinois University Press, 1991), 1.

39. Barbara A. White, *Edith Wharton: A Study of the Short Fiction,* Twayne's Studies in Short Fiction 30 (New York: Twayne, 1991), 92.

40. Ibid., 98.

41. For an analysis of these aspects, I refer to my own *I fantasmi di Edith Wharton* (Roma: Bulzoni, 1993).

42. Wharton, *A Backward Glance,* 804.

43. Edith Wharton to Elizabeth Cameron, July 3, 1933, Box 5, The Papers of the Nelson A. Miles Family, The Library of Congress. On Wharton's household as well as the presence of servants in her fiction, see also Dwight, *Edith Wharton,* 230–33.

The Children: Wharton's Creative Ambivalence to Self, Society, and the "New World"

ELLEN PIFER

EDITH WHARTON DID NOT LAUNCH HER CAREER AS A NOVELIST UNTIL she was in her forties. By all accounts, however, she was a born writer given, from an early age, to casting herself as a character. In the midst of daily life and its vicissitudes, Wharton liked to adopt an outside perspective, to observe herself in various situations in order to glean their dramatic possibilities.[1] As a practicing novelist, she quite obviously made use of her talent for self-dramatization. But as Wharton's long and distinguished career was nearing its end, the novelist's tendency to observe herself from outside—to see herself as another or the *other*—took a remarkable turn. In *The Children,* published in 1928, Wharton both dramatized and critiqued herself as a character, recasting her relationship to the society that shaped her.[2] At the same time, she answered what was, in her view, the major challenge confronting the American novelist in the postwar era. As she said in an essay published a year before *The Children:*

> It is useless, at least for the story-teller, to deplore what the new order of things has wiped out, vain to shudder at what it is creating; there it is, whether for better or worse, and the American novelist, whose compatriots have helped above all others, to bring it into being, can best use his opportunity by plunging both hands into the motley welter.[3]

Seizing on this artistic "opportunity," Wharton launches *The Children* by imagining herself as an outsider named Martin Boyne, a man who has lived for "years in the wilderness" (21). Through the eyes of this male *other,* Wharton proceeds to explore the character of Rose Sellars and her female opposite, Judith Wheater. As several critics have observed, the character of

Rose Sellars closely reflects Wharton's own distinct habits, tastes, and cultivation—so closely, in fact, that Louis Auchincloss has called her the novelist's "spokesman."[4] The epithet hardly seems warranted, however, by the degree of *critical* scrutiny Rose Sellars receives in the novel. Adhering to Boyne's outside vantage, Wharton is able, as Janet Goodwyn says, "to stand back from her subject and look at the other side of the sexual equation."[5] More important, Wharton stands back from herself, from the very values, standards, and beliefs that threatened to cut her off from the novelist's domain: the "new world" in all its "motley" disorder. Secure in her identity, defined by her history, Rose Sellars is a woman whose traditional tastes and temperament alienate her from the conditions of postwar life—conditions that Wharton vowed, as a novelist, to plumb.

Admittedly, it is Rose Sellars who, like her author, has endured a protracted and loveless marriage with patience and dignity. Released, at long last, from years of dull routine by the death of her husband, Rose would appear highly deserving, in Wharton's eyes, of some personal happiness. Yet in her depiction of Rose Sellars, Wharton exploits her noted ability to treat female characters in an "ambiguous" manner, and she takes that process a step further. By relegating Rose Sellars to "object, rather than subject, status," Wharton distances herself, as godlike author, from the very creature she molds in her image.[6] Through the eyes of Martin Boyne, she reveals the flaw in Rose's refinement. "Her exquisite aloofness," Boyne observes, "had kept her in genuine ignorance of the compromises and promiscuities of modern life, and left on her hands the picture of a vanished world" (141). Here Wharton betrays an awareness, subliminal if not self-conscious, that such uncompromising standards pose a threat to the novelist's vocation. In developing Boyne's ambivalent view of Rose Sellars, Wharton evinces a bracing capacity, so necessary to her survival as a writer, for radical (one might almost say surgical) self-criticism.[7]

As for Martin Boyne, whatever his inhibitions and shortcomings (and critics have not failed to point them out), he evinces some of the novelist's most vital characteristics.[8] Like Newland Archer in *The Age of Innocence,* Boyne has a taste for adventure, spontaneity, and freedom. Unlike Archer, he has succeeded in putting psychological as well as physical distance between himself and the strictured New York society in which he was raised. To gain a modicum of personal freedom, Boyne has crossed even more continents than Wharton managed, in her own life, to explore. Then, after spending "years and years in the wilderness," Boyne returns to the civilized gardens of Europe. He quickly learns, however, the truth of what Miss Scope, the Wheater children's governess, has told him: "[T]he real wilderness is the world *we* live in" (21).

In the *terra incognita* of the postwar era, Wharton suggests, Newtonian laws of gravity have all but given way to Einsteinian relativity. In quest of novelty and change, men and women live lives as fluid and insubstantial as those that flicker on the silver screen. With dazzling rapidity, social and sexual relationships dissolve and reconjoin in a kaleidoscope of changing patterns of attachment sanctioned by the sudden popularity of divorce. Born of these chaotic conditions are the novel's eponymous children. A motley assortment of siblings, half-siblings, and step-siblings, the Wheater children are grounded in nothing more stable than the shifting sands of temporary marital alliances. At the center of this tenuous skein of relationships stands Judith Wheater, whose enchanting image, I shall argue, embodies for Wharton—specifically Wharton the "story-teller" or novelist—the ambiguous allure of the modern wilderness in all its "fitful beauty" and "perilous" charm (281).

In composing *The Children,* Wharton's gifts as a writer, her talent for casting herself in the role of another or the *other,* clearly took precedence over her most cherished social standards and critical views. Here one is reminded of Tolstoy, who, in the process of bringing *Anna Karenina* to life, overcame as an artist his patriarchal intolerance and moral didacticism. In dramatic contrast to his stated intentions, Tolstoy transformed a frail and fallible adulteress into one of Western literature's most sympathetic heroines. With similar unpredictability, I would suggest, Wharton in *The Children* artistically undermines her intense personal antipathy to the modern era and its avatars. In bold opposition to her cherished vision of the past, its civilization and values, Wharton evokes—through the eyes of her protagonist and male *other,* Martin Boyne—the sylvan figure of Judith Wheater, whose untamed image captures all the spellbinding appeal of the wilderness. Fascinated, and ultimately besotted, by Judith's mercurial image, Boyne conjures a romantic vision of the "new world" in all its shimmering freedom and possibility. Imaginatively participating in Boyne's rapture, Wharton's readers share in that optimistic vision.

At the opening of *The Children,* even before the steamship liner that he boards in Algiers has left the dock, Martin Boyne

is already (and deliciously) at sea in the "new world." So disori-
ented is the middle-aged engineer that he cannot decide whether
little Judith Wheater is a child or a mother, a "young woman"
or "a slip of a girl" (5). And the more he sees of Judith, "the
more she perplexed him, the more difficult he found it to situate
her in time and space" (31). Judith's elusive, indefinable nature
and the thrill of uncertainty Boyne experiences in her presence
weave a spell of enchantment that gains increasing power over
his heart and imagination. Half-child, half-woman, Judith is as
yet unfinished, incomplete—the mercurial image of promise.

In contrast to Judith Wheater, Boyne's fiancée, Rose Sellars,
is a mature woman in every sense; Rose's tastes and habits,
identity and comportment are fully formed and defined. Although the history Rose shares with Boyne—their common
background, upbringing, and culture—offers safe "haven" to a
man who has spent years in the hinterlands, it also threatens
to entrap him, much as Wharton's own habits of cultivation
threatened to close her off from the modern wilderness she was
determined, as a novelist, to explore (78). Similarly, what Boyne
fears in an alliance with Rose is that it will cut him off from
that world of "adventure" he has long sought, although "adventure worthy of the name [has] perpetually eluded him." Unlikely
as it may seem in this "critical cautious man of forty-six," as the
novel puts it, Martin Boyne still yearns, in Keatsian fashion, to
"burst all the grapes against his palate" (4). The "restlessness
and impulsiveness" that initially drove Boyne, as a young man,
to abandon the staid society of New York for the wilds of Argen-
tina, Australia, and Egypt still fuel his quest for "the romantic or
the unexpected." In his unexpected encounter with the Wheater
children, that promise begins, tantalizingly, to take shape. To
the children, steeped in nothing so much as "mutability," the
future clearly belongs. To that future, Martin Boyne, like his
"critical cautious" author, is imaginatively drawn (67).

Dedicated to action, change, and heedless "forgetting," the
postwar era, as Wharton renders it, ushered in a new age of
"bloodless savagery" (141–42). Yet in the Wheater children, who
are both product and emblem of this new world, the "savagery"
of a society losing its memory (and perhaps its mind) proves
strangely liberating. To enter the children's charmed circle is,
Boyne says, "like getting back from a constrained bodily position
into a natural one." In this world of childish or "savage" spontaneity, the burden of memory, history, and tradition miraculously
dissolves, restoring Boyne to his "natural" self. Like an acolyte

of Rousseau, Boyne discovers the benignity of the wilderness, the nobleness of the savage, and wakes to a new sense of himself as "being simply and utterly at ease" (199). Here Wharton evokes Boyne's delight in the children's spontaneous games with such intensity that her readers are also caught up in that thrilling sense of release. Exercising the freedoms of creative imagination, Wharton the novelist cuts loose from the weight of history and culture, undermining the traditional standards and values to which she cleaved in her daily life.

Crucial to Boyne's awakening, and to the reader's participation in that revelation, is the novelist's startling evocation of Judith Wheater's youthful image—an image that stirs the adult's romantic yearning for what cannot be fixed "in time and space." Judith, Wharton's protagonist observes, is "like a thought, a vision, an aspiration": "[Y]ou grope for her identity and find an instrument the wind plays on, a looking-glass that reflects the clouds, a . . . sensitive plate" (32). Oscillating between grown-up anxiety and childish spontaneity, "shrewdness" and "simplicity," Judith is as mercurial, Boyne reflects, as the wind that "changes every hour." Like the wind, she has no fixed presence and is here "only intermittently" (214, 32). Existing in an atmosphere of impermanence and change, Judith, like the wind, inspires Wharton's male *other* with new life—quickening thought, feeling, and desire. Soon after he meets her, Boyne is struck by the fact that "most of Judy's feelings were beginning to reverberate in him" (48). That sympathetic vibration originates, of course, in the novelist's own sensibility and imagination.

When, in a game the children play, Judith avows her ambition to become an "explorer," she strikes yet another responsive chord in her adult observer. As soon as he registers the word "explorer," "something darted through Boyne like a whirr of wings" (239). This evocative phrase, "whirr of wings," has already occurred in the narrative on several earlier occasions; the phrase initially appears in a lyrical passage celebrating the beauties of an Alpine wood. As he walks through the undergrowth, Boyne's senses come "alive" to "the uncurling of perfumed fronds, the whirr of wings in the path, and that continual pulsation of water and wind and grasses which is the heart-beat of the forest" (70). The lyrical force of this passage suggests, to this reader at least, that Judith's stated desire to become an "explorer" evokes in Boyne the magic of unexplored places—whether remote mountain forests or the hidden depths of the heart. Alive to the "whirr" of insect wings and to the "heart-beat of the forest,"

Boyne is also stirred by Judith's nature and presence, a presence which quickens his own "heart-beat" and the "pulsation" of his blood.[9] In a later scene, Boyne, having returned from Venice, invites Judith to explore these regions with him. As they climb the Alpine path together, what quickens his senses is no longer the reverberation of insect wings or the "pulsation of water and wind." It is the sylph like presence of the young girl herself: "the nearness of her light young body was like wings to him" (146).

Judith Wheater's "elusive," mercurial being, Wharton makes vividly clear, awakens middle-aged Martin Boyne to passionate life. In a crucial scene that takes place at a picnic in the Dolomites, Boyne acknowledges, for the first time, the desire (and the jealousy) he feels for Judith. It is at this point, tellingly, that Judith's image becomes even *more* elusive in Boyne's eyes. As Martin reclines on a mossy slope, gazing at Judith's lithe body stretched out beside him, he raptly takes in the girl's mercurial rather than physical attributes: "Directly in the line of his vision, Judith's sandalled feet lay in a bed of bracken, crossed like a resting Mercury's. He could almost see the little tufted wings at the heels" (170–71). Judith's identification with Mercury, divine messenger of the gods, operates on several levels in the novel. Most obviously, the "tufted wings" Boyne envisions on her "sandalled feet" register, in another key, that sylvan world of freedom he associates with her image. In Judith's presence, Boyne feels so utterly changed—so charged with light, energy, and youth— that he becomes, momentarily, as mercurial as she. Thus, as he retraces, one summer night, the path of his earlier walk with Judith, Martin recalls how his own feet "had seemed winged" like the god's: "[H]e remembered that other night . . . when he had climbed the same path and his feet had seemed winged, and the air elixir, because a girl's shoulder brushed his own" (204–5).[10]

Judith's association with Mercury, or Hermes, as the Greeks called him, becomes still more telling when viewed in the light of Wharton's "lifelong obsession" with the myth of Persephone.[11] As Virgil reports in the *Aeneid,* the god Mercury was in charge of conducting souls from the upper to the lower world, that same region to which Persephone was carried off by Hades. According to ancient myth, Persephone, when still a young maiden, was forced to abandon the cultivated daylight world of her mother, the corn-goddess Demeter, or Ceres. After her abduction by Hades, she dwelled for part of every year in the underworld. In Wharton's artistic vision, this shadowy region or mythic realm signifies the ultimate *terra incognita* of the human heart. In the unseen depths lurking beneath the visible world of appearances, the novelist discovers, in the words of one Wharton critic, the "underworld of experience."[12]

Discussing the significance of the Demeter-Persephone myth in Wharton's short verse-play, "Pomegranate Seed" (1912)—a reworking of her earlier story, "The Bunner Sisters" (1900)—Susan Goodman observes that, as Wharton well knew, Demeter and her daughter were "considered a dual goddess" and "worshipped as one" by the ancients. In "Pomegranate Seed," therefore, the mother and daughter represent "halves of a whole, forming the entirety of nature." And yet from another perspective, Goodman goes on to point out, the play reveals how Persephone's "experience of the other side" also "separates her from" and "makes her superior to her parent." Her "initiation" makes her conscious "of a grief that her mother is incapable of knowing. The two are separated as surely as the Victorians were from their postwar young."[13] Similarly, I have been suggesting, Rose Sellars can be seen to embody that aspect or element of Wharton's nature, her traditional "feminine" self, which held her aloof from the postwar era and its disturbing reality. As a novelist, on the other hand, Wharton's task was to bridge the gulf yawning between the two generations, to span the old world and the new. The key, as in all bridge building, was to find the necessary structural balance. In *The Children,* Wharton achieves this balance by narrating her novel through the eyes of Martin Boyne. By establishing her authorial distance from Rose Sellars, she cultivates imaginative sympathy for the symbolic "daughter," Judith Wheater, and the plight of the "postwar young."

Expelled like Persephone from "the world of the mother," Judith Wheater (whose surname suggestively links her to Ceres's daughter) is exposed very early in life to its harsh reality.[14] "So bared to the blast" are the Wheater children, Boyne observes, that they have plumbed depths beyond their years (37). In Judith he discovers "a precocity of experience so far beyond" Rose Sellars's that at times the young girl even "frightened him." At times he would like "to believe either that [Judith] was five years older ... , or else that she did not know the meaning of the words she used" (34, 51). Still, what frightens Boyne also attracts him. To Rose's orderly "conception of life," he contrasts Judith's profound "experience of it" (100); to Rose's "tact," Judith's candor (88, 93, 140, 159). In contrast to Judith's youthful spontaneity, Rose's "special art" of "preparation" hints at both her talent for "disguising things" and her tendency to deny the untidy depths of experience (77). "No one," he thinks, "could arrange a room half so well; and [Rose] had arranged herself and her life just as skilfully" (33).

Just as Judith Wheater's name links her with Persephone and the "underworld of experience," so Rose's "pretty" name suggests her more conventional identity (187). In this sense, Rose Sellars plays the role of a subtler, more enlightened Lily Bart, the protagonist of Wharton's prewar novel, *The House of Mirth* (1905). Lily's association, in her author's mind, with a rose as well as a lily is suggested by the titles Wharton lent to several previous, unpublished versions of that novel—"The Year of the Rose" and "A Moment's Ornament." Like Lily, Rose has "been brought up," as Wharton's narrator comments in *The House of Mirth,* "to be ornamental." Like Lily, she is a "highly specialized," carefully cultivated "product" fashioned, "like some rare flower," to "adorn and delight."[15] The floral or "ornamental" aspects of Rose's identity not only link her to Lily Bart but to her author. As a girl, Wharton confesses in "Life and I," she had a profound "love of pretty things—pretty clothes, pretty pictures, pretty sights." Governing her earliest aesthetic responses to appearances was the "wish *to make the picture[s] prettier.*" As an adult and particularly as a writer, Wharton had to overcome her "feminine instinct of pleasing" in order to master, in Candace Waid's phrase, "the masculine and adult province of knowledge and power."[16]

The ornamental qualities implied by Rose's name are not lost upon Martin Boyne. Seated in the parlor of her rented châlet, Boyne notes how every detail of "the little low-ceilinged room" creates an "atmosphere" imbued with her feminine presence— from the charming arrangement of "books and flowers" to "the bit of needle-work" gracing an armchair (137). As Martin soon realizes, even the "bowl of cunningly-disposed wild flowers" on Rose's dining table hints at her artful ability to "arrange" and repress the untamed elements of existence (193); and, when Martin "follow[s] his betrothed" to the table for "a late dinner," the "bowl of wild roses [standing] between them" serves as a concrete metaphor for the emotional barrier that will ultimately estrange them (172–73). Later, in fact, when Boyne goes to Paris to break off his engagement to Rose, her "ornamental" and flowery presence strikes him as having overtaken her aunt's apartment: "The room [overlooking the Tuileries] was large, airy, full of flowers. A fire burned on the hearth; Rose Sellars's touch was everywhere" (257).

Long before their estrangement, however, Boyne—in reaction to the subtle constraints Rose's presence imposes on him—takes increasing pleasure in the free play of impulse and appetite. Dining alone at his hotel one evening, he is struck by the contrast between the crude meal the waiter brings him and the refinements of Rose's table, with its inevitable supply of candlelight and "amusing food." As he attacks his "coarse roll" and "savourless soup" Boyne experiences "an appetite he was almost ashamed of." With a thrill of defiance, Martin declares to himself, "Decidedly, I'm a savage" (193).

Viewed in the light of Rose's traditional "feminine" identity, Judith Wheater's mercurial image becomes charged with historical significance, hinting at the promise as well as disorder inherent in the postwar era. Only a child born of this "savage" new world, Wharton suggests, can hope to escape the social forces that have shaped and strictured Rose Sellars. In Judith Wheater's still unformed and unformulated identity, hidden sources of the self may be ready to spring forth and flourish. Out of the chaos of the modern "wilderness," a new generation of women (and of men) may well emerge—one that is destined, as Wharton says elsewhere, to "breathe a freer air."[17]

From this new generation, Martin Boyne is quite obviously excluded. At the end of *The Children,* Boyne appears cut off from Judith's world, literally and figuratively. Although three years have passed since the last time he saw her, Boyne refrains from greeting Judith when he spies her in a crowded hotel ballroom. Standing outside on the terrace, separated from her by a pane of glass, Boyne gazes with "passionate attentiveness" at the sylphlike being who still moves him. Three years older but essentially unchanged, Judith looks, even in her formal pink gown, less like a proper young lady than a wood nymph or goddess: "as she stood motionless, her hands seemed to float like birds on little sunlit waves. Her hair was moulded to her head in close curves like the ripples of a brown stream" (281). The evocation of Judith's sylvan beauty recalls a well-known scene in *The House of Mirth,* in which Lily Bart exposes "the long dryad-like curves" of her body against "a background of foliage"—stunning the audience of the *tableaux vivants* staged at the Wellington Brys' party (129). Here, and not for the first time, Lawrence Selden, like Martin Boyne, is awed by the "wild-wood grace" and "sylvan freedom" of the lovely nymph who eludes him. Early on in the novel, Selden already thinks of Lily as "a captured dryad subdued to the conventions of the drawing-room" (11). One has only to change the word "drawing-room" to "ballroom," and Selden's simile eloquently captures Boyne's ultimate vision of Judith Wheater.

In contrast, however, both to Lily Bart and Rose Sellars—each of whom is named after "some rare flower grown for exhibition, a flower from which every bud had been nipped"—Judith Wheater does not appear fated to dwell in social captivity (*The House of Mirth*, 305). Everything about Judith's sylvan beauty, even the "diamond arrow" thrust in her hair, points to a new world of "fitful beauty" and "perilous" freedom. Through this shimmering wilderness, Judith, like an elusive Diana with her quiver of arrows, seems destined to roam. True to her role as Boyne's muse—the muse, one might say, of modernity—Judith's image still works its magic on her middle-aged acolyte. Even now that she is nearly nineteen, Boyne cannot tell whether she is "still a child" or a young woman on the threshold of marriage. All he knows is that "he would never know" (281–82). The crystal windowpane through which he gazes is like time itself: a transparent barrier separating him, irrevocably, from the boundless future to which Judith Wheater belongs.

Like Martin Boyne, Edith Wharton gazed with rapt attention at the modern world and its children. Like Boyne, too, she was awed and a little frightened by the "queer quarrelling elements" she read in their countenance (281). In her published autobiography, *A Backward Glance,* Wharton speaks of her lifelong tendency to turn away from the noisy world, to withdraw to the inner sanctum of poetry and art. Even as a small child, she confesses, "there was in me a secret retreat where I wished no one to intrude." Later, as a practicing writer, Wharton learned to cultivate that "secret garden" in which, as she says, her youthful imagination first took root.[18] Still, as a novelist, Wharton was compelled to witness the world in all its "motley" disorder and confusion. "The welter is always there," she announced at the end of *A Backward Glance,* "and the present generation hears close underfoot the growling of the volcano on which ours danced so long" (379).

In *The Children,* Wharton sounds that volcano and warns of its blast; but she pays tribute, all the while, to the new world's "perilous" beauty and freedom. Through the eyes of her male *other,* Martin Boyne, Wharton conveys a sympathetic, if ambivalent, vision of the modern wilderness she personally dreaded.

As novelist and "story-teller," she triumphantly announces her freedom from the strictures of the society that shaped her. By exposing herself to the wilderness, Wharton heralded the future in which we, her present readers, now exist and to which we can amply testify. Who among us would deny her vision of the new century in all its noise, vigor, and forgetfulness, all its "savage" beauty and power? We are, after all, its children—and we know, in our bones, what it is to live in that wilderness.

Notes

1. According to Robert Norton, Wharton cast herself as a character to improve upon actual experience: "An experience that in the living of it had been a series of *contretemps* she would reset as she would have wished it and was thereafter convinced that it had happened so," "Memoir" (Percy Lubbock Papers, Beinecke Library, Yale University) 49; cited in Susan Goodman, *Edith Wharton's Inner Circle* (Austin: University of Texas Press, 1994), 75. As *The Children* demonstrates, however, Wharton was too fine a writer to indulge in mere wish fulfillment.

2. Edith Wharton, *The Children* (1928; rpt. New York: Macmillan, 1992). Subsequent references to this edition will be cited in parentheses in the text.

3. "The Great American Novel," *Yale Review* 16 (July 1927): 655.

4. Louis Auchincloss, *Edith Wharton: A Woman in Her Time* (New York: Viking, 1971), 174.

5. Janet Goodwyn, *Edith Wharton: Traveller in the Land of Letters* (London: Macmillan, 1990), 99.

6. Susan Goodman, *Edith Wharton's Women: Friends and Rivals* (Hanover, N.H.: University Press of New England, 1990), 16–17.

7. In *Edith Wharton: A Critical Interpretation* (Rutherford, N.J.: Fairleigh Dickinson University Press, 1970; rev. 1982), 165, Geoffrey Walton observes that in Wharton's depiction of Rose Sellars, "there is an element of self-criticism." The novelist "created a character rather like herself"—a "fastidious woman who has lived a sheltered life."

8. My interpretation obviously differs from Judith Sensibar's analysis in "Edith Wharton Reads the Bachelor Type: Her Critique of Modernism's Representative Man," *American Literature* 60 (1988): 575–90. In Sensibar's view, Boyne frantically "attempts to deny his fear of the absence of desire [for a woman]" to mask his "fantasy of homosexual desire" (576, 586). In her reading, Boyne's motives and desires are radically distorted by his fear and denial, projections and fantasies. She finds, for example, that Boyne is "no more in love with the actual Judith than he ever was with the actual Rose. But he doesn't know this" (589). Sensibar suggests, furthermore, that Wharton is consciously engaged in "mask[ing] her true subject." Admitting that the novel's "title centers attention on . . . children whose plight is its stated subject," she finds its "deeper concern" lies "with "boys (Boynes?) who compulsively masquerade heterosexual desire" (576).

9. Ignoring these evocative associations, David Holbrook reduces Boyne's complex response to the word "explorer" to a psychosexual cliché: "[H]e is excited by the possibility of her exploring his body; the dangers are consider-

able" *Edith Wharton and the Unsatisfactory Man* (London: St. Martin's, 1991), 179.

10. In keeping with her theme of latent homosexuality, Sensibar maintains that by envisioning Judith as Mercury, Boyne "fantasizes that [Judith] is a boy" (587). In my reading, the god's magical attributes are more telling than his gender.

11. R. W. B. Lewis, *Edith Wharton: A Biography* (New York: Harper, 1975), 495.

12. Candace Waid, *Edith Wharton's Letters from the Underworld* (Chapel Hill: University of North Carolina Press, 1991), 13.

13. Goodman, *Friends and Rivals* 147.

14. Waid, *Edith Wharton's Letters,* 3.

15. Edith Wharton, *The House of Mirth* (1905; New York: Bantam, 1984), 286, 305, 289. Subsequent references to this edition will be cited in parentheses in the text.

16. Edith Wharton, "Life and I," *Novellas and Other Writings,* ed. Cynthia Griffin Wolff (New York: Library of America, 1990), 1071–74; Waid, *Edith Wharton Letters,* 11.

17. Edith Wharton, *French Ways and Their Meaning* (New York: D. Appleton, 1919), 102.

18. Edith Wharton, *A Backward Glance* (New York: Scribner's, 1934), 70, 198. Subsequent references to this edition will appear in parentheses in the text.

Contributors

GIANFRANCA BALESTRA is an Associate Professor of American literature at the University of Siena, Italy. A specialist in the literature of the fantastic, she is the author of a book on Edith Wharton's ghost stories (*I fantasmi di Edith Wharton* [1993] and one on Poe (*Geometrie visionarie. Composizione e decomposizione in Edgar Allan Poe* [1990]). She has published extensively on Wharton in the United States and Italy, and has edited, with introductions, the Italian translations of *The Reef* and *The Touchstone.* Co-editor of *Benjamin Franklin: An American Genius* (1993), she has also written on contemporary American, Canadian, and Caribbean literature.

STEPHANIE BATCOS is a doctoral student at the University of Delaware, where she is completing her dissertation on Edith Wharton's non-fiction. Her reviews of recent criticism on Wharton have appeared in *Studies in American Fiction.*

CLARE COLQUITT teaches American literature at San Diego State University and is the bibliographic editor of the *Edith Wharton Review.*

SUSAN GOODMAND is a professor of English at the University of Delaware and the author of *Ellen Glasgow: A Biography* (1998), *Edith Wharton's Inner Circle* (1994), and *Edith Wharton's Women: Friends and Rivals* (1990).

MAUREEN HONEY is a professor of English and women's studies at the University of Nebraska-Lincoln where she teaches courses on American women writers and popular culture. She has published books on wartime propaganda, women's poetry of the Harlem Renaissance, and on New Woman popular fiction. She is currently writing a book on art and women writers at the turn of the century.

KATHERINE JOSLIN is the author of *Edith Wharton* in the Women Writers Series and co-editor of *Wretched Exotic: Essays on Edith Wharton in Europe*. Her other publications include essays on Willa Cather, Kate Chopin, and Theodore Dreiser. She is currently working on a book about Jane Addams as a literary figure. Joslin, a professor at Western Michigan University, directs the Graduate Studies Program in English and has received the Alumni Teaching Excellence Award.

JEROME LOVING is the author of a number of books on American literature, including *Emerson, Whitman, and the American Muse* (1982); *Emily Dickinson: The Poet on the Second Story* (1986); *Lost in the Customhouse: Authoship in the American Renaissance* (1993); and *Walt Whitman: The Song of Himself* (1999).

ANNE MACMASTER teaches English, women's studies, and American Studies at Millsaps College in Jackson, Mississippi. She is currently at work on a book that explores intertextualities among the works of Edith Wharton, Nella Larsen, and Jessie Fauset.

MIA MANZULLI received her PhD in 1997 from New York University and is now an Assistant Professor of English at the United States Military Academy at West Point. She is currently revising her dissertation, "Writing, Sexuality, and the Garden: The Project of Edith Wharton," for publication as a book.

ELLEN PIFER is Professor of English and Comparative Literature at the University of Delaware. Her published works include over three dozen essays on modern and contemporary fiction, as well as three books: *Nabokov and the Novel*, *Saul Bellow Against the Grain*, and *Critical Essays on John Fowles*. She has just completed a new study of twentieth-century fiction entitled *Demon of Doll: Changing Images of the Child in Contemporary Writing and Culture*.

MARY SUZANNE SCHRIBER, Distinguished Professor of English at Northern Illinois University, has published essays on Edith Wharton's fiction and travel writing, an edition of Wharton's *A Motor-Flight Through France,* and most recently, *Writing Home: American Women Abroad, 1830–1920*.

Currently a Fellow at the Virginia Foundation for the Humanities and Public Policy, Judith L. Sensibar teaches American literature and culture as well as modernism at Arizona State University. Her books include *The Origins of Faulkner's Art* (1984), *Faulkner's Poetry* (1988), and, most recently, a monograph, "Writing for Faulkner, Writing for Herself; Estelle Oldham's Anti-Colonial Romance" and "'Star Spangled Banner Stuff'" in *Prospects: An Annual of American Cultural Studies* (1997). Her essays on Edith Wharton have appeared in *American Literature, The Journal of American Studies*, and several collections.

CANDACE WAID is the author of *Edith Wharton's Letters from the Underworld: Fictions of Women and Writing*, as well as numerous essays on Wharton, including introductions for her editions of *The Custom of the Country, Summer, A Backward Glance*, and *The Buccaneers*, and her selection of Wharton's short fiction, *The Muse's Tragedy and Other Stories*. Currently editing the Norton Critical Edition of *The Age of Innocence*, Waid teaches at the University of California in Santa Barbara.

FREDERICK WEGENER is an assistant professor of English at California State University, Long Beach, and the editor of *Edith Wharton: The Uncollected Critical Writings*. His essays have appeared in such journals as *Modern Language Studies, New England Quarterly*, and *Texas Studies in Literature and Language*. He is currently a member of the executive board of the Edith Wharton Society.

DENISE WITZIG is the Coordinator of the Women's Studies Program and a Lecturer in English at Saint Mary's College, California. Her previous essays on Wharton include "'The Muse's Tragedy' and the Muse's Text: Language and Desire in Wharton," in *Edith Wharton: New Critical Essays*, and "Letters from an Unknown Woman: Edith Wharton's Correspondence with Authority," in the journal *Women's Studies*.

Index